Index to the
Bonds of Guardians
of
Sonoma County, California

1852–1907

Steven M. Lovejoy

HERITAGE BOOKS
2020

HERITAGE BOOKS
AN IMPRINT OF HERITAGE BOOKS, INC.

Books, CDs, and more—Worldwide

For our listing of thousands of titles see our website
at
www.HeritageBooks.com

Published 2020 by
HERITAGE BOOKS, INC.
Publishing Division
5810 Ruatan Street
Berwyn Heights, Md. 20740

Cover image: First page of John Roan's Sonoma County
bond of guardian (1852) housed in the
Sonoma County Archives.

Heritage Books by the author:
Guide to the Court of Sessions Records of Sonoma County, California, 1850–1863
Index to the Bonds of Guardians of Sonoma County, California, 1852–1907
Index to the Probate Court Records of Sonoma County, California, 1847–1879
Index to the Public Official Bonds of Sonoma County, California, 1850–1892

International Standard Book Number
Paperbound: 978-0-7884-0188-6

Contents

Introduction

During the summer of 1987, members of the Sonoma County Genealogical Society (SCGS) completed organizing a collection of original Sonoma County bonds of guardians then housed in the Archives section of the Sonoma County Library.[1] Information from each bond was extracted and placed on index cards, which were then alphabetized by ward's name and used in the Sonoma County Room of the Sonoma County Library as a finding aid. At some time after this the information on these index cards was typed into a 198-page manuscript which included a 14-page index. The Sonoma County Historical Records Commission published this work, one of the first compiled by members of the SCGS, as *Bonds of Guardianship*.[2]

During 2019–2020, the collection of original Sonoma County bonds of guardians used to produce *Bonds of Guardianship* stored in the Sonoma County Archives in two banker's boxes was reexamined and reorganized. Further information from each bond was extracted, and missing or erroneous information from the previous project was added or corrected. In addition, eight bound volumes of recorded Sonoma County bonds were utilized to provide information from bonds of guardians not found among the surviving originals. Bonds from each probate case were grouped together and placed in acid-free folders labeled with the appropriate probate case numbers. These numbered folders were then placed in five acid-free, flip-top archival boxes which are now stored in the Sonoma County Archives.

This publication comprises two parts. The first part is an all-name index containing over 4,000 entries of every bond principal, bond surety, and ward named in each Sonoma County bond of guardian listed in the second part. The second part is a tabulation of the 1,700 Sonoma County bonds of guardians dated 1852 through 1907 (original, recorded, or both) housed in the Sonoma County Archives. The information given for each of the bonds of guardians includes: the probate case number, the name of the bond principal, the names of the bond sureties, the name of the person or entity to which the bond principal and sureties are bound, the type of probate case (minor, incompetent, or insane person), the amount of the bond, the date of the bond, and the book and page(s) on which the bond is recorded.

---

[1] "Guardianship—Sonoma County," *The Sonoma Searcher* 15 (September 1987): 12.

[2] Sonoma County Genealogical Society compiler, *Bonds of Guardianship* ([Santa Rosa, California]: Sonoma County Historical Records Commission, no date). This work is available for purchase from the Sonoma County Clerk-Recorder's Office (https://sonomacounty.ca.gov/Historical-Records-Commission/Publications-for-Sale/).

How to Use this Index

When searching for a specific individual among the Sonoma County bonds of guardians, 1852–1907, the researcher should begin by consulting the first part of this publication, **Name Index**, a four-column table alphabetically listing the names of every bond principal, bond surety, and ward given in each Sonoma County bond of guardian listed in the second part. As spelling in the 19th century was not standardized, names, especially surnames, could be spelled a variety of ways even within the same bond. Researchers are advised to look for all possible variations of a name.

The first column of the Name Index, **Name**, gives the names of every bond principal, bond surety, and ward found in every Sonoma County bond of guardian, 1852–1907. The names are listed alphabetically.

For each line in the **Name Index**, the second, third, and fourth columns — **Principal**, **Surety**, and **Ward** — give the probate case number of the bond for the name listed in the first column, **Name**. Thus, Alfred Abbey's name appears in a bond of guardian as a bond principal in probate case number 3868 and as a bond surety in probate case number 3839. Similarly, Alfred B. Abbey's name appears in a bond of guardian as a ward in probate case number 3868. The researcher should turn to the appropriate probate case number in the second part of this publication to find the details of the bond. Note that there may be several bonds of guardians for some probate case numbers. Each of these bonds should be examined by the researcher to find the name desired.

The second part of this publication, **Bonds of Guardians**, is a 9-column table listing the 1,700 Sonoma County bonds of guardians dated 1852 through 1907 (original, recorded, or both) housed in the Sonoma County Archives. The bonds are arranged in the table in order of increasing probate case number. Information within brackets, such as [Minor] or [4 Jan 1886], indicates that that information is not included in the bond itself, but has been added by the author from other sources. A question mark within brackets, [?], indicates that that information is not given in the bond and could not be determined by the author. For example, [?] Nov 1857 indicates that the exact date in November of 1857 is not given in the bond.

The first column of the Bonds of Guardians table, **Case #**, gives the probate case number under which each bond was filed. There may be multiple bonds for any given probate case number. Several wards in the same probate case, usually siblings, are at times named together in the same bond, and at other times they are named in separate bonds but with the same probate case number. A bond principal may have had to file a number of bonds for the same ward but with different penal sums as the probate case progressed in the court. An asterisked probate case number, such as 62*, indicates that that bond is not among the original Sonoma County bonds of guardians, 1852–1907, stored at the Sonoma County Archives. The information extracted from these asterisked bonds comes from the recorded copies of the bonds.

The second column, **Principals**, gives the name of the bond principal. There is usually only one bond principal, but in a small number of cases there are two or more. Where no one surname spelling predominates, variations are indicated by a slash (/) between variations. For example, Rosenberg/Rosenburg indicates both forms of the surname, Rosenberg and Rosenburg, are found in the bond.

The third column, **Sureties**, lists the sureties of the bond. In most cases there are two sureties per bond, but there can be any number, and in some cases bond surety companies have been used.

The fourth column, **Bound to**, lists the name or names of the person or persons to whom the bond principals and sureties are bound. Generally the name of the ward is given here, but the State of California can be also. When this is the case further information about the appointing of the guardian which names the ward has been extracted. In some bonds the wards are identified as heirs or children of deceased persons. For example, in probate case number 34, William W. Cameron is identified as the heir of T. P. Cameron, dec'd. These identifications appear in parentheses after the ward's name when given in the bond. The notation, dec'd, after a person's name is a contraction of the word "deceased."

The fifth column, **Amount ($)**, gives the amount of the bond in US dollars. Larger amounts in this column indicate larger ward estates.

The sixth column, **Type**, lists the type of ward, either minor, insane, or incompetent person.

The seventh column, **Date**, gives the date of the bond. This is the date, given at the end of the first part of the bond, on which the bond principal and sureties indicated that the bond was sealed with their seals and dated.

The eighth and ninth columns, **Book** and **Page(s)**, give the book and page(s) on which the bond was recorded. Table 1 below serves as a key to the various bound volumes utilized in this publication. Further descriptions of these volumes are given below in the "Records Utilized" section.

Book	Description
A	Letters of Administration and Bonds, Probate Court, Book A
C	Bonds, volume C
D	Probate Bonds, Superior Court, volume D
1	Bond of Guardian Upon Qualifying, Superior Court, No. 1
2	Bond of Guardian Upon Qualifying, Superior Court, No. 2
QUAL	Bond on Qualifying, Superior Court, No. 1
MISC	Miscellaneous Bonds
AD 2	Bond of Administrator, Superior Court, No. 2

Table 1. Key to the bound volumes utilized in this publication.

History of the Statutes Concerning Bonds of Guardians

Near the end of its first session in 1850 the California legislature passed an act composed of 49 sections entitled "An Act to provide for the appointment and prescribe the duties of Guardians."[3] Section eight of this act directed judges, before appointing a person as a guardian of a minor, to require such persons to give a bond to the minor with sufficient sureties conditioned as follows:

> 1.) to make a true inventory of all the estate, real and personal, of his ward, that shall come to his possession or knowledge; and to return the same within such time as the judge shall order,
>
> 2.) to dispose of and manage all such estate according to law, and for the best interest of the ward, and faithfully to discharge his trust in relation thereto; and also in relation to the care, custody, and education of the ward,
>
> 3.) to render an account on oath of the property, estate, and moneys of the ward in his hands; and all proceeds or interest derived therefrom, and of the management and disposition of the same within one year after his appointment, and at such other times as the Court shall direct, and,
>
> 4.) at the expiration of his trust to settle his accounts with the Probate Judge, or with the ward if he be of full age, or his legal representatives; and to pay over and deliver all the estate, moneys, and effects remaining in his hands, or due from him on such settlement, to the person or persons who shall be lawfully entitled thereto.

Section fourteen of the act required bonds of guardians of insane or incompetent persons with like conditions. Every bond given by a guardian was to be filed and preserved in the office of the Clerk of the Probate Court.

In 1861, the guardianship act of 1850 was amended.[4] Changes affecting the bonds of guardians included: 1.) when the penal sum of the bond exceeded two thousand dollars, each of the sureties could become liable for portions of the penal sum, making in the aggregate the whole penal sum, 2.) the guardian was to render an account within three months of his appointment rather than within one year, 3.) the bonds of guardians were to be conditioned that the guardians

---

[3] *The Statutes of California, Passed at the First Session of the Legislature, Begun the 15th Day of Dec. 1849, and Ended the 22nd Day of April, 1850, at the City of Pueblo de San José* (San José: J. Winchester, State Printer, 1850), pp. 268–273, Chap. 115, "An Act to provide for the appointment and prescribe the duties of Guardians" (hereinafter cited as *The Statutes of California, First Session*).

[4] *The Statutes of California, Passed at the Twelfth Session of the Legislature, 1861: Begun Monday the Seventh Day of January, and Ended on Monday, the Twentieth Day of May* (Sacramento: Charles T. Botts, State Printer, 1861), pp. 603–607, Chap. DXXXI, "An Act to amend an Act entitled An Act to provide for the appointment and prescribe the duties of Guardians, passed April nineteenth, eighteen hundred and fifty" (hereinafter cited as *The Statutes of California, Twelfth Session*).

would faithfully execute the duties of their trust according to law, 4.) the conditions of the bond were to be deemed to form part of the bond without being expressed in the bond, and 5.) all bonds of guardians were to be recorded by the Clerk of the Probate Court in a book kept by him in his office.

When the laws of California were codified in 1872 those concerning bonds of guardians and the recording thereof as discussed above were included in the Code of Civil Procedure in sections 1754, 1756, and 1765 and remained in effect at least through 1905.[5] Bonds today are still required of guardians in California.[6]

---

[5] James H. Deering, Walter S. Brann, and R. M. Sims, eds., *The Code of Civil Procedure of the State of California, Adopted March 11, 1872, and Amended up to and Including 1905. With Statutory History and Citation Digest up to and Including Volume 147 of California Reports* (San Francisco: Bancroft-Whitney Company, 1906), pp. 657–678, Part III (Special Proceedings), Title XI (Proceedings in Probate Courts), Chap. XIV, "Of Guardian and Ward," §§ 1747–1810.

[6] "California Law," database, State of California, *California Legislative Information* (https://leginfo.legislature.ca.gov/faces/home.xhtml : accessed 12 March 2020), Probate Code, Division 4 (Guardianship, Conservatorship, and Other Protective Proceedings), Part 4 (Provisions Common to Guardianship and Conservatorship), Chapter 4 (Oath, Letters, and Bond), Article 3, "Bonds of Guardians and Conservators," § 2320.

Format of the Bonds of Guardians

Bonds of guardians of the 1850s were entirely handwritten, but by the 1860s pre-printed forms were starting to be used, and by the 1880s and 1890s almost all bonds of guardians were fill-in-the-blank, pre-printed forms. No matter whether handwritten or pre-printed form, bonds of guardians generally followed the same format. In the first section of the bond, the bond principal and his sureties were named along with his ward, the bond amount, and the date of the bond. The next section gave the conditions of the bond, generally restating the appropriate statute. This was followed by the signatures and seals of the bond principal, bond sureties, and witness. In the final section of the bond the bond sureties swore that they were residents and householders or freeholders in the State.

An example of the first page of an early (1852), entirely hand-written bond of guardian is given in Figure 1 below. In this bond, John Roan, who had applied to be appointed guardian of the minor children of Sergeant Travers, along with his sureties, Matthias Purcell and Peter Campbell, bind themselves to the State of California in the sum of $1,000. The conditions of the bond come directly from the 1850 act concerning the appointment and duties of guardians.[7]

Belknap gives an example of a fill-in-the-blank, pre-printed form that could be used for bonds of guardians in the appendix to the 1873 third edition of his *Probate Law and Practice in California*.[8] This is reproduced below in Figure 2. The words in italics would be filled in by the preparer of the bond. Note that because of the 1861 amendments to the 1850 guardianship act the bond is conditioned that the guardian shall faithfully execute the duties of his/her trust according to law, and the conditions set out in that 1850 act, such as making a true inventory of all the ward's estate, real and personal, and disposing of and managing the ward's estate according to law, are now deemed to form a part of the bond without being expressed in the bond.[9]

---

[7] *The Statutes of California, First Session*, pp. 268–273, Chap. 115, "An Act to provide for the appointment and prescribe the duties of Guardians," specifically p. 269, § 8.

[8] D. P. Belknap, *The Probate Law and Practice of California Containing All the Provisions of the Codes, of 1871–2, and Other Statutes Relating Thereto, with Judicial Decisions of this and Other States, and an Appendix of Forms*, 3d ed. (San Francisco: A. L. Bancroft and Company, 1873), ccxiv–ccxv. Belknap notes that this form is "Bancroft's Printed Blank, No. 932."

[9] *The Statutes of California, Twelfth Session*, pp. 603–607, Chap. DXXXI, "An Act to amend an Act entitled An Act to provide for the appointment and prescribe the duties of Guardians, passed April nineteenth, eighteen hundred and fifty," specifically p. 604, section 2.

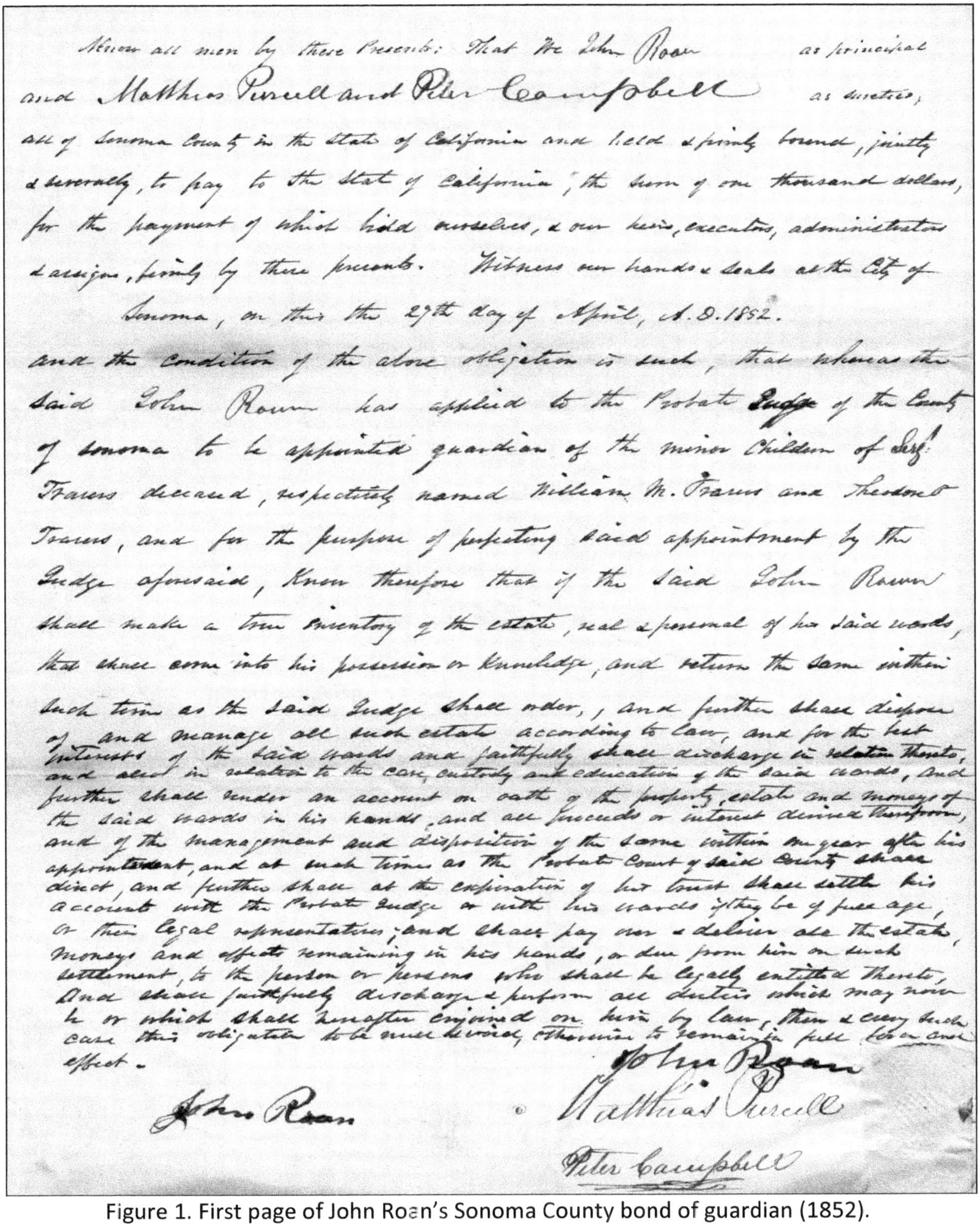

Know all men by these Presents: That We John Roan as principal and Matthias Purcell and Peter Campbell as sureties, all of Sonoma County in the State of California and held & firmly bound, jointly & severally, to pay to the State of California; the sum of one thousand dollars, for the payment of which hold ourselves, & our heirs, executors, administrators & assigns, firmly by these presents. Witness our hands & seals at the City of Sonoma, on this the 27th day of April, A.D. 1852.

And the condition of the above obligation is such, that whereas the said John Roan has applied to the Probate Judge of the County of Sonoma to be appointed guardian of the minor children of Serg! Travers deceased, respectively named William M. Travers and Theodore Travers, and for the purpose of perfecting said appointment by the Judge aforesaid, Know therefore that if the said John Roan shall make a true inventory of the estate, real & personal of his said wards, that shall come into his possession or knowledge, and return the same within such time as the said Judge shall order, and further shall dispose of and manage all such estate according to law, and for the best interests of the said wards and faithfully shall discharge in relation thereto, and also in relation to the care, custody and education of the said wards, and further shall render an account on oath of the property, estate and moneys of the said wards in his hands, and all proceeds or interest derived therefrom, and of the management and disposition of the same within one year after his appointment, and at such time as the Probate Court of said County shall direct, and further shall at the expiration of his trust shall settle his accounts with the Probate Judge or with his wards if they be of free age, or their legal representatives, and shall pay over & deliver all the estate, moneys and effects remaining in his hands, or due from him on such settlement, to the person or persons who shall be legally entitled thereto, And shall faithfully discharge & perform all duties which may now be or which shall hereafter enjoined on him by law, then & every such case this obligation to be null & void, otherwise to remain in full force and effect.

John Roan

John Roan   Matthias Purcell
                   Peter Campbell

Figure 1. First page of John Roan's Sonoma County bond of guardian (1852).

Bond of Guardian

Know all men by these presents:

That we, *Mary Jones as principal, and John Doe and Richard Roe as sureties*, are held and firmly bound unto *William Jones*, a minor, in the sum of *one thousand* dollars, lawful money of the United States of America, to be paid to the said *William Jones*, minor, for which payment well and truly to be made, we bind ourselves, our heirs, executors and administrators, jointly and severally, firmly by these presents:

Sealed with our seals and dated this *twelfth* day of *December*, A. D. 1872.

The condition of the above obligation is such, that whereas, an order was made by the Probate Judge of the *city and* county of *San Francisco*, State of California, on the *tenth* day of *December*, A. D. 1872, appointing the above bounden *Mary Jones* the guardian of the *person and estate* of said minor, and directing that letters of guardianship be issued to *her* upon *her* giving a bond to said minor, with sufficient sureties, to be approved by said Probate Judge, in the penal sum of *one thousan*d dollars, conditioned that said guardian shall faithfully execute the duties of *her* trust, according to law:

Now, therefore, if the said *Mary Jones* shall faithfully execute the duties of *her* trust, according to law,

Then this obligation shall be void and of no effect, else to remain in full force and virtue.

Mary Jones, [L. S.]
John Doe, [L. S.]
Richard Roe, [L. S.]

Signed, sealed and delivered in the presence of *C. Bartlett*.

State of *California, City and* County of *San Francisco*, ss.

John Doe and Richard Roe, being duly sworn, each for himself, says that he is one of the sureties named in the above bond, that he is a resident and *house* [or *free, as the case may be*] holder within said State, and is worth the said sum of *one thousand* dollars over and above all his just debts and liabilities, exclusive of property exempt from execution.

John Doe,
Richard Roe.

Subscribed and sworn to, before me, this *twelfth* day of *December*, A. D. 1872.

F. J. Thibault,
Notary Public.
[Notarial Seal.]

Figure 2. Bancroft's Printed Blank, No. 932, Bond of Guardian, as given in Belknap's *Probate Law and Practice in California* (1873).

Records Utilized

1. Original Sonoma County bonds of guardians, 1852–1907, as found among the collection entitled "Bonds of Guardians, 1852–1911" in the 1982 Inventory of Records of the Sonoma County Clerk's Office stored at the Sonoma County Archives.[10] These original bonds have been microfilmed, and the images are contained on microfilm reels 21–23 of the collection entitled "Old Miscellaneous Sonoma County Records, 1850-1958" in the 1982 Inventory of Records.[11] These microfilms are housed in the Sonoma County Clerk-Recorder's Office in Santa Rosa, California and can be viewed there.

2. Letters of Administration and Bonds, Probate Court, Book A. This bound volume, Sonoma County Archives accession number 1376 and inventory number 289 in the 1982 Inventory of Records of the Sonoma County Clerk's Office, is stored at the Sonoma County Archives.[12] It contains 388 pages of a variety of recorded documents, such as appointments, oaths, appraisements, bonds on sale of real estate, and bonds of administrators, executors, guardians, and appraisers, dated 7 August 1861 through 29 March 1871. Pages 278–388 are blank.

3. Bonds, volume C. This bound volume, Sonoma County Archives accession number 1625 and inventory number 21 (also listed as number 299) in the 1982 Inventory of Records of the Sonoma County Clerk's Office, is stored at the Sonoma County Archives.[13] It contains 620 pages. Recorded on page numbers 1–169 are Sonoma County public official bonds and a few other miscellaneous bonds dated from 1869 to 1872. Recorded on page numbers 170–620 are Sonoma County probate bonds (administrator, executor, and guardian) dated from 1874 to 1881. There is a surname index of the bond principals in the front of the volume. Page numbers 254–255 are blank and glued together.

4. Probate Bonds, Superior Court, volume D. This bound volume, Sonoma County Archives accession number 1324 and inventory number 302 in the 1982 Inventory of Records of the Sonoma County Clerk's Office, is stored at the Sonoma County Archives.[14] It contains 640 pages of a variety of hand-written, recorded Sonoma County probate bonds (administrator, executor, guardian, agent, and on sale of real estate) dated 9 May 1881 through 29 April 1901. Pages 632–640 are blank.

5. Bond of Guardian Upon Qualifying, Superior Court, No. 1. This bound volume, Sonoma County Archives accession number 1571 and inventory number 300 in the 1982 Inventory of Records of the Sonoma County Clerk's Office, is stored at the Sonoma County Archives.[15] It contains 398

---

[10] Sonoma County Records Inventory Project, *Inventory of Records, 1847-1980, Office of the Clerk, Sonoma County, California* ([Santa Rosa, California]: Sonoma County Historical Records Commission, 1982), 76. These documents are inventory number 187.

[11] Ibid., 68. These microfilms are inventory number 180.

[12] Ibid., 111–112.

[13] Ibid., 8 and 115–116.

[14] Ibid., 117.

[15] Ibid., 116.

pages. On each page are two pre-printed, fill-in-the blank guardian bond forms. The recorded documents are dated 26 December 1883 through 20 August 1901. Pages 301–398 are blank. A few administrator and executor bonds are included on pages 60–65 and 67–69.

6. Bond of Guardian Upon Qualifying, Superior Court, No. 2. This bound volume, Sonoma County Archives accession number 1570 and inventory number 300 in the 1982 Inventory of Records of the Sonoma County Clerk's Office, is stored at the Sonoma County Archives.[16] It contains 396 pages. On each page are two pre-printed, fill-in-the blank guardian bond forms. The recorded documents are dated 19 August 1899 through 22 March 1916. Pages 393–396 are blank. A name index of bond principals appears in the front of the volume.

7. Bond on Qualifying, Superior Court, No. 1. This bound volume, Sonoma County Archives accession number 1631 and inventory number 301 in the 1982 Inventory of Records of the Sonoma County Clerk's Office, is stored at the Sonoma County Archives.[17] It contains 398 pages. On each page are two pre-printed, fill-in-the-blank bond forms, which have been used mainly for recording administrator and executor bonds, but also for a few guardian bonds. The documents are dated 3 March 1884 through 7 June 1897. Pages 363–398 are blank.

8. Miscellaneous Bonds. This bound volume, Sonoma County Archives accession number 1628 and inventory number 305 in the 1982 Inventory of Records of the Sonoma County Clerk's Office, is stored at the Sonoma County Archives.[18] It contains 640 pages of a variety of hand-written, recorded Sonoma County bonds dated 8 May 1901 through 15 August 1919. Pages 95–640 are blank.

9. Bond of Administrator, Superior Court, No. 2. This bound volume, Sonoma County Archives accession number 1325 and inventory number 304 in the 1982 Inventory of Records of the Sonoma County Clerk's Office, is stored at the Sonoma County Archives.[19] It contains 398 pages. On each page are two pre-printed, fill-in-the-blank bond forms, which have been used mainly for recording administrator and executor bonds, but also for a few guardian bonds. The documents are dated 16 June 1897 through 12 October 1906. An index of bond principals is included in the front of the volume.

---

[16] Ibid., 116.
[17] Ibid., 116.
[18] Ibid., 117.
[19] Ibid., 117.

Further Reading

Belknap, D. P. *California Probate Law and Practice. Being a Compilation of All the Statutes of this State, Relating to Probate Courts, the Organization and Jurisdiction Thereof, and Proceedings Therein, the Estates of Deceased Persons, Executors, Administrators, Guardians and Wills. With Notes of Judicial Decisions, and an Appendix of Forms.* San Francisco: Sterett and Butler, 1858.

Belknap, D. P. *The Probate Law and Practice of California Containing All the Provisions of the Codes, of 1871–2, and Other Statutes Relating Thereto, with Judicial Decisions of this and Other States, and an Appendix of Forms.* Third edition. San Francisco: A. L. Bancroft and Company, 1873.

Black, Henry Campbell. *A Dictionary of Law Containing Definitions of the Terms and Phrases of American and English Jurisprudence, Ancient and Modern.* 1st edition. St. Paul, Minnesota: West Publishing Co., 1891.

Blume, William Wirt. "California Courts in Historical Perspective." *Hastings Law Journal* 22 (No. 1, November, 1970): 121–195.

Coy, Owen C. *Guide to the County Archives of California.* Sacramento, California: California Historical Survey Commission, 1919.

Davis, W. N., Jr. "Research Uses of County Court Records, 1850–1879, and Incidental Intimate Glimpses of California Life and Society, parts I and II." *California Historical Quarterly* 52 (No. 3, Fall, 1973): 241–266 and (No. 4, Winter, 1973): 338–365.

Lovejoy, Steven M. *Index to the Probate Court Records of Sonoma County, California, 1847–1879.* Berwyn Heights, Maryland: Heritage Books, Inc., 2020.

Rose, Christine. *Courthouse Research for Family Historians: Your Guide to Genealogical Treasures.* San Jose, California: CR Publications, 2004.

Sonoma County Genealogical Society. *Bonds of Guardianship.* [Santa Rosa, California]: Sonoma County Historical Records Commission, no date.

Sonoma County Genealogical Society. *Index and Abstracts of Wills, Sonoma County, California, 1850–1900.* Westminster, Maryland: Heritage Books, Inc., 2007.

Sonoma County Genealogical Society. *Probate Records, Sonoma County, California, Index for 1847 to 1959, Volume 1: A–K.* Berwyn Heights, Maryland: Heritage Books, Inc., 2014.

Sonoma County Genealogical Society. *Probate Records, Sonoma County, California, Index for 1847 to 1959, Volume 2: L–Z.* Berwyn Heights, Maryland: Heritage Books, Inc., 2014.

Acknowledgments

The author thanks the staff of the Sonoma County History and Genealogy Library for access to the original Sonoma County bonds of guardians and the various bound volumes containing the recorded copies held at the Sonoma County Archives.

About the Author

Steven M. Lovejoy, PhD, is a retired chemist living in Sebastopol, Sonoma County, California. He is currently (2020) the president of the Sonoma County Genealogical Society and a Sonoma County Historical Records Commissioner. He holds a Certificate in Genealogical Research from Boston University and can be contacted at stevelov@comcast.net.

Name Index

Name	Principal	Surety	Ward
Abbey, Alfred	3868	3839	
Abbey, Alfred B.			3868
Abbey, Richard		444	
Abelbeck, F. D.		485	
Abendroth, F.	2327		
Abraham, Caspar		1308	
Abshier, J. H.		1189	
Abshire, Dorlesca	3531		
Abshire, James H.			3531
Acker, R. W.		675	
Ackerman, Harriet Bell			884
Ackerman, Mary Bell			884
Ackerman, Nannie	884		
Ackerman, Rebecca Jane			884
Ackermann, B. Henry	494		
Ackermann, Louis Dan			494
Adams, Bertha Porthenia			2233
Adams, John		549	
Adams, Mary Edith			2233
Adams, Mary M.	2233		
Adams, R. S.		2258	
Adamson, Bertha			2002
Adamson, Edward F.		2923	
Adamson, Jacob	186		
Adamson, James T.			2002
Adamson, Mary E.	2002		186
Adler, Lewis		620, 621	
Agnew, Clairisse Adele			1930
Agnew, Richard Arthur			1930
Agnew, S. J.		1175, 1233	
Agnew, Samuel J.		1874	
Aguillon, C.		1344	
Aiken, Della			1747
Akers, Stephen		85, 198	
Alexander, Caroline		1598	
Alexander, Carrie	1440		
Alexander, Charles		1178, 1398	
Alexander, George Cyrus			1598
Alexander, Henry		1598	
Alexander, Joseph	1598		

Name	Principal	Surety	Ward
Alexander, Thomas		1598	
Alleman, Arzola Lee			3881
Allen, Harriet A.	2997		
Allen, Mary		2601	
Allen, Mary C.			2997
Allen, O. S.		623	
Allen, Samuel I.		1397, 1512	
Allen, Samuel J.		980	
Allen, W. T.		1178	
Alley, Charles W.			336
Allingham, Adda	4248		
Allison, George		272, 293, 354	
American Bonding Company of Baltimore, Maryland		4246, 4248, 4321	
American Home Finding Association	3564		
American Surety Company of New York		2953	
Ames, C. G.		1018, 1507	
Amesbury, Carl			3767
Amesbury, Herbert			3767
Amesbury, Mary	3767		
Anderson, Catharine V.	1951		
Anderson, Emma J.			1951
Anderson, J. A.		4001	
Anderson, James W.		1670	
Anderson, Jennie P.			1951
Anderson, John	2657		
Anderson, John A.			1951
Anderson, Paul J.			1951
Andrews, J. F. W.		1780	
Andrews, John	148	188	
Andrews, W. E.	1780		
Andrews, Walter J.	4142		
Annis, William O.	329		
Appleton, Caroline Spring			2029
Appleton, Eliza G.			1640
Appleton, Horatio	1640, 2029		
Appleton, W.		3333	
Appleton, William G.			1640
Archer, John		546	
Armstrong, Albert			3298
Armstrong, E. J.	3298		

Name	Principal	Surety	Ward
Armstrong, Earl N.			3298
Armstrong, Frank L.			3298
Armstrong, Hazel			3298
Armstrong, J. B.		1292	
Armstrong, James		1160	
Armstrong, Lewis A.			3298
Armstrong, Rosanna			578
Armstrong, Roy V.			3298
Armstrong, Ruby A.			3298
Arnold, A. W.		3245, 4062	
Arnold, G. W.		62	
Arnold, George W.			152, 1499
Arnold, W. J.		1492	
Ashley, Martha E.			1983
Asti, Joseph		3032	
Atherton, Albert W.			794
Atherton, Dwight C.			794
Atherton, Isaac W.	794		
Atherton, Joseph N.	2507		
Atkinson, J.		3315	
Atkinson, Louis		159	
Atkinson, Minnie J.	3315		
Atkinson, P. H.		4223	
Atkinson, Percy Herbert	2267		
Atterbury, William B.		299, 348	
Atwater, F. H.		2346	
Atwater, H. H.		557, 808, 1181	
Augustine, Albert		122	
Aull, A. B.	227	196	
Aull, George			436
Aull, Laura			436
Auser, Elijah W.		175	
Austin, Charles A.			2537
Austin, Emile W.			2537
Austin, Herbert W.	1397		
Austin, James		1397	
Austin, James Howard			1397
Austin, Rosa	2537		
Avilla, Anton	4015		
Avilla, Anton, Jr.			4015

Name	Principal	Surety	Ward
Avilla, Frank			4015
Ayers, W. D.	3535		
Ayers, William		587	
Baber, B. F.		931	
Baccala, Della			4143
Baccala, Henry			4143
Baccala, Joseph K.	4143		
Baccala, Peter, Jr.			4143
Bacigalupi, N.		2850, 3686, 4128	
Badger, Joseph	489		
Baer, George		4032	
Baer, George B.	2796		
Baer, R. E.		3240	
Baer, Reuben E.		2395	
Bagley, H. F.	3375		
Bagley, J. W.		677	
Bahr, Albert F.			1344
Bailey, B. H.	1824		
Bailey, James B.		641	
Bailhache, John N.		814	
Baird, Mary E.	597		
Baker, A. M.		1097	
Baker, Bloomer		1095	
Baker, Henry		1126	
Ballard, Carrie H.	1507		
Ballou, Eunice			3821
Baptista, Lena			3469
Baptista, Mary			3469
Baptista, Rosie			3469
Baralli, Joseph		504	
Barbarin, Augustina			2461, 2941
Barbarin, G.		1844	
Barbarin, Gratien			2165
Barbarin, Jean Baptiste	2461		
Barbarin, Louissa	2941		
Barham, H. W.		2712	
Barnes, A. N.		304	
Barnes, Arthur			3668
Barnes, Dora Harlan			2901

Name	Principal	Surety	Ward
Barnes, E. H.	926, 1006, 2290	778, 1079, 1276, 1376, 1473, 1517, 2176, 2537, 2897, 3516, 3633, 3643, 3852, 3962	
Barnes, Etta Ellen			2901
Barnes, Henry		2921	
Barnes, Ivan Aaron			3682
Barnes, Jehu		316	
Barnes, Jennett			1625
Barnett, J. D.		2202, 2358	
Barney, Anna E.	3052		
Barney, M. W.		887	
Barry, Ellen Agnes			641
Barry, Julia	641		641, 4324
Barry, Mary Elizabeth			641
Barry, Susan Ann			641
Barry, Thomas			641
Barry, Thomas F.		1670	
Barry, William			641
Barry, William R.	4324		
Bartlett, Clara Theresa			2626
Bartlett, Ella			2626
Bartlett, George R.			2626
Bartlett, Harris		1114	
Bartlett, John			1095
Bartlett, Lydia A.			1114
Bartlett, Mary Jane	1114		
Barton, Archa			3014
Bassett, W. D.		4179	
Bates, George E.		1626	
Bates, H. F.	620	621	
Bates, Laura			911
Bates, Neely			911
Baxter, George P.		2267, 2901	
Baxter, T. P.		1640	
Bayer, Herman		3281	
Baylis, Theo. H. T.	1533		
Baylis, Theodore			608

Name	Principal	Surety	Ward
Beal, Kirk S.			2473
Beall, Mary F.			2020
Beall, Susan E.	2020		
Bean, Joseph M.			1381
Bean, Mary F.			1381
Beasley, Jesse		85	
Beasly, Jesse		137	
Beattie, Anthony		2903	
Beattie, Susan C.	2903		
Beatty, Mary		863	
Beatty, William	863		
Beaver, Henry		117, 129	2689
Beaver, William J.	2689		
Beck, Robert		87	
Bedwell, Franklin	252		
Bedwell, Ira	93	93	
Bedwell, James			93
Beedle, Louis S.	3032		
Beeson, William S.		950	
Behmer, Daniel		3673	
Behrens, Albert			2817
Behrens, Carl			2817
Behrens, Dora			2817
Behrens, Henry	2817		
Belden, C. C.		3790	
Bell, Albert K.		789	132
Bell, Amelia Ann	2897		
Bell, G. S.		2897	
Bell, George K.		132	
Bell, Henry		1027, 2923	
Bell, Henry H.			132
Bell, James S.		132	
Bell, John W.			132
Bell, Louisa F.			132
Bell, Margaret		132	
Bell, R. W.	2827		
Bell, Rosa E.			2827
Bell, W. M.		2797	
Bell, W. S.	3104	3528	
Bell, William T.	132		

Name	Principal	Surety	Ward
Bendit, Samuel		1626	
Benson, Henry			530
Benson, Josiah			530
Benson, Josiah H.	530		
Benson, Laura			530
Benson, Louis E.			530
Benson, Martha			530
Benson, Nathaniel			530
Benson, William			530
Bentley, A.		3630	
Bentley, Harriet A.	2450		
Benton, L. J.	2619		
Berger, M.		416	
Berggren, John Fr.	98		
Bernhard, Isaac		684	
Berri, V.		3066	
Berri, Vittore		1837	
Berry, James		354	
Berry, Joseph			3375
Bertolani, P. A.		3526	
Berton, Flavien Mars			3742
Berton, Germain Mais Just			3742
Bice, Frank S.		3288	2073
Bicknell, Anna			652
Bicknell, Charles			652
Bicknell, Elizabeth	652		
Bicknell, Ida			652
Bidwell, Ira	93		
Bidwell, Nancy			93
Bidwell, Thomas J.	93, 166	93	
Bishop, T. C.		85, 1772	
Bishop, Tennessee C.	85	1666	
Black, Houston		365	
Blackburn, Charles	924	122	
Blackburn, Frank L.	4340		
Blackburn, J. S.		2914, 3188, 3228	
Blackburn, John S.	3104	2619, 3180, 3372	
Blair, Frank P.			1422
Blair, Samuel		1896	

Name	Principal	Surety	Ward
Blair, Thomas N.	1422		
Blakeley, Eugene			912
Blakeley, Martin L.			912
Blakeley, Unity			912
Blakeney, J. C.		85, 137	
Blaney, Andrew J.	2044	2129	
Bledsoe, A. C.	843½		
Bledsoe, Linn		2295	
Blish, Bessie			3409
Bliss, William D.		243	
Bloch, George		2537	
Bloom, D.		233, 296	
Bloom, Jonas	1054	919	
Bloom, Joseph		107, 571	
Blucher, Lillie			1217
Blume, Julius	1693		
Blyth, James		175	
Bolla, Elvezio			2665
Bolla, Ida			2665
Bolla, Oliva			2665
Bolla, Olympio			2665
Bond, J. W.		3127	
Bonetti, Joseph		4196	
Bonham, B. N.		34	
Booth, Jesse		1611	
Bostwick, Guadalupe Ignacio Carroll			3342
Bostwick, N. W.		262	
Boswell, J. H.		1611	
Bosworth, Albert H.			1009
Bosworth, C. M.	1009		
Bosworth, Climena D.			1009
Bosworth, Fannie L.			1009
Bosworth, James O., Jr.			1009
Bosworth, John H.		130	
Bosworth, Lorinda W.			1009
Bosworth, Viola			1009
Bottini, Julia	3877		
Bottini, Louis			3877
Bower, Louis		1523	
Bower, M. J.		2987	

Name	Principal	Surety	Ward
Bowers, H. A.		4138	
Bowles, Joseph M.	103		
Bowman, F. J.	1349		
Bowman, F. Josephine	1349		
Bowman, Hattie P.		1349	1349
Bowman, Henry		1344	
Bowman, John P.			1349
Bowman, John Percy		1349	
Bowman, Robert B.			1349
Boyce, Annie V.	3526		
Boyce, J. F.		623, 721	
Boyce, J. F. (Dr.)		873	
Boyce, John E.			3526
Boyce, John F.	422	62	
Boyce, Ruth A.			3526
Boyd, George W.		582	
Boyd, James		4138	
Boyd, R. S.		3562	
Boyson, C. C.		1951	
Brackett, J. H.		3858	
Brackett, J. S.	616		
Brackett, Johanna		3858	
Bradshaw, Arthur			1676
Bradshaw, Emma (Mrs.)	1676		
Brainard, L. E.		2360	
Brainerd, H. P.		1520, 2377, 2435, 3003, 3784, 3805	
Braly, M. A.		159	
Brandon, Elvus	2601		
Brandon, James Emmet			2601
Brandon, Joseph R.	368		
Brandon, Kate		2601	
Brannan, Anthony			1996
Brannan, Gertrude			1996
Brannan, James			1996
Brannan, Joseph			1996
Brannan, Margaret			1996
Brannan, Peter			1996
Branscom, B. F.		866	

Name	Principal	Surety	Ward
Breckwoldt, Joe		2740	
Breitenbach, Louis		1625	
Bremer, Elmira			4149
Bremer, Jeanette			4149
Brewer, Harry		2763	
Brewster, John A.		85	
Brians, William		490	
Bridges, I. N.		3630	
Brockman, Israel	85	5, 25, 85, 98, 137	
Brooke, T. J.	1807	2198	
Brooks, Earnest K.			1411
Brooks, Elmont		1782	
Brooks, Emma S.	1411		
Brooks, Frederick A.			1411
Brooks, Thomas			93
Brooks, William	607		
Brown, A. M.		272, 535	
Brown, Ada E.			1751
Brown, Alice J.		1751	
Brown, Arthur	889	889	
Brown, Calvin H.			435
Brown, Carrie			2176
Brown, Carrie P.	3642		
Brown, Catherine	1751		
Brown, Charlotte	3385		
Brown, Charlotte M.	3385		
Brown, Daniel	3189	475	780
Brown, Edith			1751
Brown, Edward S.			2642
Brown, Edwin M.			3385
Brown, Elizabeth J.	435		
Brown, Genevieve			1751
Brown, H. K.		778, 986, 1878	
Brown, Harry C.		1567	
Brown, Harry O.			3675
Brown, Henry W.	2642		
Brown, James W.			780
Brown, John	351	485, 526, 729	
Brown, John McA.		1751	
Brown, John McAllen, Jr.			1751

Name	Principal	Surety	Ward
Brown, Martha E.			780
Brown, Mary		1751	
Brown, Mary R.			435
Brown, Oliver			435
Brown, Orrin			435
Brown, Robert S.		1751, 2954	
Brown, Sarah E.	3675		
Brown, Thomas A.	34		
Brown, Thomas L.			435
Brown, Viola			2613
Brown, Walter T.			2982
Brown, Warren		34	
Bruner, C. M.		3202	
Bruner, Edith T.	3202		
Bruning, Caroline			1240
Bruning, Henry W.	1240		
Brunner, Christian		5	
Bruns, Harmann		85	
Brush, D. C.	488		
Brush, Frank A.	2613		
Brush, Fred W.		3992	
Brush, J. H.		2613, 3482½, 3584	
Brush, William T.		2014, 2217, 3240	
Bryan, Annie			1238
Bryan, Elizabeth	1238		
Bryan, Fred J.			1238
Bryan, John Leo			1238
Bryan, Joseph			1238
Bryan, Katy			1238
Bryan, Mary			1238
Bryan, Rosa			1238
Bryan, William			1238
Bryan, William J.		2638	
Bryant, Allen		1930, 3614	
Bryant, Ann Augusta			1169
Bryant, Arthur S.		3614	
Bryant, C. G.		1283, 1603	
Bryant, Charles G.		1186	
Bryant, John E.			1169

Name	Principal	Surety	Ward
Bryant, Thomas H.	1169		
Bryant, Thomas P.			1169
Buck, Carl	3694		
Buckins, William L.		1603	
Buckle, Thomas		1242	
Bumpus, C. H.		672	
Bundesen, Charles		3326	
Bundesen, Martin		3326	
Bunnell, Viola			2613
Burbank, Caleb			616
Burbank, Samuel F.	616		
Burdell, Galen		3488	
Burdell, James B.	3488		
Burdell, James B., Jr.			3488
Burg, Ferdinand			2358
Burger, Elmer Ross			3408
Burger, Lillian			3408
Burk, Margaret			459
Burke, J. H.		3733	
Burnett, A. G.		1360	
Burnett, Albert G.		2232	
Burnham, John H.		655	
Burns, Annie J.		4247	
Burns, Edward	3441		
Burns, Elizabeth Frances			4247
Burns, Ellen		3237	
Burns, J. F.	3237		
Burns, John		270	
Burns, Joseph			3441
Burns, Mary Gertrude			4247
Burns, Sadie R.	4247		
Burns, William			87
Burns, William K.			87
Burr, Frank		2626	
Burris, David	698, 897		
Burris, Jesse		2165	
Burris, L. W.		1807, 2849, 3756	
Burrough, James		2217	
Burrus, G. W.	461		
Burrus, James A.			461

Name	Principal	Surety	Ward
Burrus, Mary C.			461
Bush, Eli		2488, 2829, 3643, 3675	
Bush, G. H.		4291	
Bushnell, Amasa		1523	
Butcher, Charles Walter			3147
Butcher, Squire	3147		
Button, I. V.		807	
Butts, Florence	3651		
Butts, Nellie			3651
Byington, Charles T.		2626	
Byrn, George M.			2295
Byrns, James W.			843½
Cabel, E. H.		2925	
Cabral, John		4338	
Cadwell, Jacob A.	1540		
Cady, M. K.		1640	
Caldwell, F. M.		725	
Caldwell, Hugh		250	
Caldwell, John G.			250
Caldwell, Samuel T.			250
Caldwell, William	2217	344	
Callaway, David	2282		
Caltoft, John		2817, 3007	
Cameron, G.		1532	
Cameron, Gordon		2395	
Cameron, Jennie	2395		
Cameron, Mary E.			34
Cameron, Russell L.			2395
Cameron, William W.			34
Campbell, George O.		3999	
Campbell, George Samuel			358
Campbell, George W.		270	
Campbell, Harry			281
Campbell, James A.		358, 482	
Campbell, Joseph	2377	1035	
Campbell, Margaret Jane	358		
Campbell, Peter		17	
Campion, Tom		2982	
Camron, Alva O.			34

Name	Principal	Surety	Ward
Camron, David E.			34
Camron, John M.	34	81	
Camron, Oliver P.			34
Canan, William S.		499	
Canevascini, S. J.		3684	
Canfield, William D.	1095	540	
Cannon, J. P.	940		
Cannon, L. L.		940, 2892	
Cannon, R. B.		980	
Cardoza, Anton		4015	
Carico, J. W.			3456
Carithers, D. N.	1465	1058, 1499, 1676, 1870	
Carlton, Austin		238	
Carmichael, Emily	3684		
Carmichael, Leona			3684
Carmody, James		1198	
Carmody, Patrick		1198	
Carpenter, L. F.		652	
Carr, Charles F.		2689	
Carr, James	490		
Carr, Nelson		135	
Carr, W. M.		3375	
Carr, William		4047	
Carriger, Nicholas		25, 1083, 1175, 1365	
Carriger, Solomon			25
Carrillo de Fitch, Josepha	41		
Carrillo, Amelia C.			704
Carrillo, Catherine A.			704
Carrillo, Elizabeth		704	
Carrillo, Fannie B.			704
Carrillo, Frank J.			704
Carrillo, Fred A.			704
Carrillo, Frederick A.			704
Carrillo, Henry G.	704		
Carrillo, J. Frank			704
Carrillo, Joaquin	704	704	
Carrillo, Julio		41, 85, 87, 100, 117, 159, 182	

Name	Principal	Surety	Ward
Carrillo, Lizzie		704	
Carrillo, Louisa A.			704
Carrillo, Mary F.			704
Carroll, James	106		
Carroll, P.		2354	
Carroll, Patrick		106, 1065	
Carroll, Thomas		1602	
Carson, Jennie Blanche			3584
Carson, Mabel Alma			3584
Carson, R. W.		264	
Carter, Andrew J.			482, 1027
Carter, Andrew Jackson			482
Carter, Dan P.		2010	
Carter, E. D.		1983	
Carter, J. W.		704	
Carter, Margaret L.			482
Carter, Mary E.	482		
Carter, Nancy V.			482
Carver, Dora C.			1824
Carver, Rolla E.			1824
Carvey, James	2354		
Carvey, Kate			2354
Case, A. B.		475, 651	
Case, Sarah J.	4292		
Case, W. E.		4292	
Casey, David Earl			2450
Casey, Elbert Hiram			2450
Casey, Julia L.		2450	
Cashdollar, Algia Beatrice			668
Cassebohm, William		85	
Cassiday, J. W.		1169	
Cassidy, J. W.		651	
Cassin, J. M.	2427, 3757		
Castens, Henrey	627		
Castens, Sophia			627
Cathey, George			344
Cathey, James			344
Cathey, John			344
Cathey, Paralee			344

Name	Principal	Surety	Ward
Cavanagh, John	808	122, 368, 1247, 1641	
Cereghino, A.	2383	1693, 1990, 2258, 2954	
Cereghino, Antonio		1135, 3372	
Cereghino, Antonio D.			2258
Cereghino, Attillio			2258
Cereghino, Francis			2258
Cereghino, Frederick			2258
Cereghino, Joseph			2258
Cereghino, Mary	2258		
Cereghino, Verna M.			2258
Chalfant, J. E.		1349	
Chamberlain, A. F.		3214	
Chamberlain, David		142	
Chambers, T. K.		85	
Champlain, E.		488	
Champlin, Charles C.		1874	
Chandler, George W.	2257		
Chandler, Lafayette		2257	
Chandler, Noah			2257
Chapman, Charles L.			2044
Chapman, Edwin A.		1419	
Chapman, Elliott C.			1419
Chapman, Harry E.		1419	
Chapman, L.		544	
Chapman, Maria			2044
Chapman, Mary C.	1419		
Chapman, Mary L.			1419
Chapman, Phoebe M.			1419
Chapman, T. M.		530	
Charles, Leon Lester			1729
Charles, Nellie Gertrude			1729
Charles, Vernetta	1729		
Chauvet, Joshua	2165	2461	
Cheeseman, F. S.		475	
Cheney, D.		935	
Cheney, R. J.		935	
Cheney, T. H.		843, 888	
Chenoweth, Miles H.		586	

Name	Principal	Surety	Ward
Chinn, Lewis F.	665		
Christie, Alfred		1420	
Christie, Frances A.	1420		
Christie, Georgie			1420
Christie, John			1420
Christie, Nellie			1420
Church, A. M.		571	
Church, Carrie	3365		
Church, Edith			3365
Church, Herman H.		3365	
Churchill, H. H.	1853		
Churchman, John			721
Churchman, Maggie			722
Churchman, William			720
Ciucci, S.		2971	
Clack, J. W.		2488, 2631, 2897	
Clanton, D. C.	1567		
Clanton, Samuel T.			1567
Clark, Benjamin		607, 1027, 2421	
Clark, Charles P.			422
Clark, D.		1058, 1096	
Clark, David		1676	
Clark, David S. F.			2925
Clark, Edgar B.			4242
Clark, Estella			735
Clark, Estelle		1555	1555
Clark, F. W.		1555	
Clark, Fannie E.	1630		
Clark, Florence B.			422
Clark, Frederick W.			735, 1555
Clark, George W.	1365	620	
Clark, Gertrude			735
Clark, Gertrude L.			1555
Clark, Howard			1365
Clark, J. P.		1126	
Clark, James M.			735
Clark, James P.	735	62, 358	
Clark, James W.	3836	3834	
Clark, Jarena	89		

Name	Principal	Surety	Ward
Clark, Lettie Ann			2925
Clark, Margaret E.	1555		735
Clark, Mary Alice			422
Clark, Maud E.			1630
Clark, Minnie L.	2925		
Clark, Samuel B.		2925	
Clark, Sarah J.	3834	3836	
Clark, William T.			89
Clark, Zoe		1630	
Clarke, Charlotte F.	1647		
Clarke, Jeremiah			1647
Clary Abigail E.			3259
Clary, Agnes	3259		
Clary, Agnes E.	3532		
Clary, Dennis G.			3532
Clary, Ida M.			3259
Clary, Mary K.			3259
Clary, Paul D.			3259
Clary, Thomas P.			3259
Claussen, August A.		1976	
Clawson, Charles	655		
Cleaveland, Harry James			3694
Cleaveland, Robert Fuller			3694
Clement, L. G.	3014		
Cline, J. W.		3173	
Clough, M. E.		3965	
Clyman, Alice C.			457
Clyman, Frances M.			457
Clyman, James I.			457
Clyman, Lancaster	457	131, 179	
Cnopius, J., Jr.		2480	
Cnopius, Johan		2480	
Cobb, O. O.		4047	
Coburn, George			3079
Coburn, James	3733		
Coburn, Joseph			3733
Coburn, Mabel			3733
Coburn, Walter			3079
Cochron, A. E.	1376		
Cocke, W. E.		1082	

Name	Principal	Surety	Ward
Codoni, G. A.		3660	
Coffey, Ellen A.	2434		
Coffey, H.		2434	
Coffey, J. H.		2434	
Coffman, Henry W.			2957
Coffman, J. T.		2681	
Coffman, Mary Gertrude			2957
Coffman, N. B.	2957	1745	
Cohen, Nettie			1054
Cohen, Rosa			1054
Cohn, Isaac H.		174	
Cohn, S.		1535, 1666	
Cohn, Samuel		919, 1054	
Collier, Ira		142	
Collier, Shedrick F.			549
Collier, Susan	549		
Collins, C. N.		1978	
Collins, F. M.	3276, 3277	1713, 2914, 2954, 3886, 4340	
Colton, F. D.	122		
Coltrin, H. C.		4253	
Coltrin, Laura L.	4253		
Commary, P.		60	
Comstock, William		475	
Congrove, Lucy A.	1492		
Conniff, Bridget			2398
Conniff, Sadie F.	2398		
Connolly, Adele G.		3188	
Connolly, Arthur H.			3188
Connolly, Arthur Henry			1533
Connolly, B. F.	1151		
Connolly, Clarence			3188
Connolly, Frank			1151
Connolly, Frank B.		3188	
Connolly, Leo V.			3188
Connolly, Louisa A.	3339		
Connolly, Minnie A.	3188		
Connolly, Paul A.			3188
Connolly, Theodore			1151
Connolly, Thomas			1151

Name	Principal	Surety	Ward
Constoll, F.		233	
Cook, Charles		344	
Cook, E. D.		3147, 3835, 4140	
Cook, F. W.		3776	
Cook, Finess Lee			125
Cook, Israel			3516
Cook, J.		1178	
Cook, J. W.		107	
Cook, James G.		135	
Cook, James W.			125
Cook, Jesse G.			125
Cook, John		1375	
Cook, John B.	125		
Cook, John H.			125
Cook, Lucinda E.			125
Cook, Mary Ann			125
Cook, Valentine B.		135	
Cook, William Y.			125
Cooke, Martin E.	5	87	
Cooley, Charles H.		1349	
Cooley, John B.		2232, 2450	
Coolidge, Jane	1329		
Coolidge, Nellie			1329
Coon, Hannah A.	3060		
Coon, Hugh			396
Coon, James M.	396		
Coon, John		3060	
Coon, Robert W.		396	
Cooper, F. M.		3531, 3873	
Cooper, James		87	
Cooper, Richard		863	
Cooper, William M.		186	
Cootes, Mary L.	3876		
Cootes, William F.			3876
Copeland, Alexander		136	
Corban, Margaret Ann Kelly			316
Corbin, George Benjamin			3173
Corbin, George H.		3173	
Corbin, Ruth G.	3173		
Cornelius, George H. H.		1083	

Name	Principal	Surety	Ward
Corria, A. F.	4291		
Corrick, Louisa			2231
Coston, Addie			506
Coughran, W.		1479	
Coulter, S. T.		62	
Covey, George			546
Covey, Mary			546
Cowan, William		1146	
Cowen, Philip		1283, 1501	
Cox, A. E. (Mrs.)	3373		
Cox, B. F.		1661	
Cox, George W.			710
Cox, Henrietta A.			3373
Cox, Henry F.			147
Cox, Jessie I.			3373
Cox, John W.			147
Cox, W. E.		1172, 1278	
Coy, W. B.		3917	
Crabtree, Mary J.			148
Craig, D. N.		2892	
Craig, James			4232
Craig, O. W.		1175, 1365	
Craig, Oliver W.		2029	
Craig, Sophia T.			3861
Craig, William		1647	
Cramer, D. R.	1782		
Crane, G. L.		166	
Crane, Joel	143	140, 142	
Crane, R.		1141, 1736	
Crane, R. H.		316	
Crane, Richard H.	140, 182	141, 142, 143, 182	
Crawford, R. F.		1853	
Creghino, Antonio		1135	
Crigler, W. E.		3456	
Crigler, William E.		710, 1308	
Crilly, Nicholas	270		
Crisp, John B.			252
Crisp, Sarah Judith			252
Crisp, William H.			175

Name	Principal	Surety	Ward
Crist, A. B.		2982	
Crist, Katie M.	2982		
Cronin, P.		1533	
Crook, J. J.			174
Cross, Cynthia J.			525
Cross, John L.	525		
Crow, John L.		76	
Crow, William W.			1492
Crowell, A.	4239		
Crowell, Albert	1028		
Crowell, Roy Victor			4239
Culbertson, Maria	3873		
Cumming, John		1966	
Cummings, Frank		2775	
Cummings, Harry W.	2775		
Cunningham, John F.	2715		
Cunningham, Joseph H.		2715	
Cunningham, Samuel	2385		
Curtis, Tyler	159		
Curtiss, J. H.		978, 1315, 1398	
Cutter, J. S.		494	
Dabner, Anton		1296	
Dabner, Frank			1296
Dabner, Manuel			1296
Dabner, Mary	1296		
Dabner, William		1296	
Dahlman, Frederick S.			1135
Dahlman, Henry			1135
Dahlman, Martha			1135
Dahlmann, Alba F.			4041
Dahlmann, Augusta	1135		
Dahlmann, Eugene C.			4041
Dahlmann, Eunice F.			4041
Dahlmann, Gladys M.			4041
Dahlmann, Henry	4041	1135	
Dahlmann, Martha		1135	
Dahlmann, Merriam K.			4041
Dahlmann, Wadsworth H.			4041
Dahlmann, Wilma G.			4041
Dalton, William H.		738	

Name	Principal	Surety	Ward
Daly, John		1824, 3127, 3519	
Daly, Mary	3519		
Dana, Alfred H.			2198, 2334
Dana, Alfred W.	2198		
Dana, Charles B.			2198, 2334
Dana, E. Mabel			2198, 2334
Dana, Frank			2198, 2334
Dana, Harold B.			2198, 2334
Dana, John A.			2198, 2334
Dana, Mary B.	2334		
Dana, Ruth			2198, 2334
Dana, W. S. B.			2198
Dana, William S.			2334
Daniel, H. H.		1146	
Darby, Floyd Donald			3452
Darby, Jasper	3452		
Darby, Jasper Basil			3452
Darr, Flora E.	3827		
Darrow, J. O.	293		
Davidson, Adam		3315	
Davidson, James		1186	
Davidson, John	1186		
Davidson, Smith E.			4001
Davies, Jonathan		85	
Davis C. E.		182	
Davis, Alys Marie			4062
Davis, B. J.		2484	
Davis, Calvin P.			2788
Davis, Charles M.	677		
Davis, Edwin			677
Davis, Ella			677
Davis, G. V.		1782, 1867, 2121	
Davis, H. S.		3822	
Davis, Henry			677
Davis, Henry Clay	2788		
Davis, Ira	578	596	
Davis, J. M.	4248		
Davis, L. T.		482	
Davis, Levi		755	

Name	Principal	Surety	Ward
Davis, M. S.		1286	
Davis, Mary E.			4248
Davis, Preston		634	
Davis, W. S.		3012	
Davis, Walter S.	4062		
Davis, William Boyd			3641
Dawson, Rebecca		2927	
Dayton, Carrie F.	4164		
Dayton, John J.			4164
Dayton, W. A.		4164	
DeBernardi, Giovanni	2971		
DeBernardi, Pietro			2971
Decker, Peter		1730	
Decoe, T. C.	2892	2921	
Deems, Carrie Mabel			1978
Delafield, Robert H.	1663		
Delahanty, May			2385
Demetz, Anna			1808
Demetz, Edward			1808
DeMetz, Edward			2543
Demetz, Louisa			1808
Denman, E.		1437, 1520	
Denman, Frank H.		2954, 3131, 3671, 3899	
Dennett, Edward P.		2827	
Derby, A. B.		475	
Derrick, J. C.	81		
Deveraux, E. W.		1820	
Dibble, N. P.		3619	
Dibble, P. K.	1052		
Dickenson, William N.		482	
Dickey, S. R.		147	
Dickinson, Charles		770½	
Dickson, D. S.	525		
Dickson, Joshua Bates			1369
Dietrich, Albertine	1451		
Dietrich, Gottlieb		1451	
Dillingham, John J. L.			107
Dillingham, Mary E.			107
Dillingham, Sarah E.			107

Name	Principal	Surety	Ward
Dillingham, Susan M.			107
Dillingham, William K.			107
Dinwiddie, J. L.	1520, 2435, 2470	475, 967, 1369	
Dittemore, J. Wallace		746	
Dittemore, Theodore		330	
Dittmann, Adolph		2903	
Dixon, C. H.		3584	
Dixon, Charles H.			3935
Dixon, George Harold			3584
Dixon, Jennie (Mrs.)	3584		
Dixon, Leona			3584
Dixon, Walter Church			3584
Dixon, William H.	3935		
Dixon, Winona			3584
Doane, L. W.		3014	
Dodge, L. C.	131		
Doggett, W. J.		3448	
Doggett, William J.		2712	
Dolan, Annie			1324
Dolan, Charles			1324
Dolan, Katie			1324
Dolan, Maggie Alice			1324
Dolan, Martha Rose			1324
Dolan, Peter	1324		
Domingan, Isabel			351
Donahue, John		652	
Donahue, T. P.		2588	
Doran, W. M.		2385, 2732	
Dorman, William	621		
Dortmund, H.		1378	
Doss, John W.		3535	
Doty, A.		843, 888	
Dougherty, John		552, 704, 866	
Dougherty, S. K.		1540	
Dowd, F. E.		3165	
Dowd, Frank E.		3442, 3757	
Dowdall, R. J.		3514	
Downs, Vernon	721, 722	1808	
Doyle, F. P.		2931, 3245, 3610	

Name	Principal	Surety	Ward
Doyle, Frank P.	2504	2931	
Doyle, John Charles			3198
Doyle, M.		283, 918, 1381, 2121, 2504	
Doyle, Winifred			3198
Dozier, E. C.		726	
Dozier, L. F.		726	
Dozier, Melville	726		
Dozier, Roland			726
Drago, Nelson, Sr.		3032	
Drahms, A.	1405		
Drake, Ben F.			4047
Drake, Emma	4047		
Drake, Harry D.			4047
Drake, Louis G.			4047
Drees, C. P. A.			2013
Drees, Carson F.			2013
Drees, E. E.		1871	
Drees, Ernest Emil			1348
Drees, Grace E.			4355
Drees, Gustave A.	1871		
Drees, H. A.			1871
Drees, Herman Adolph			1348
Drees, J. E.		1871	
Drees, Johanna Elizabeth			1348
Drees, Johanne H. L.	1348		
Drees, John R. A.			2013
Drees, L. H.		1871	
Drees, Marie A. C.	2013		
Drees, Matilda A.	4355		
Drees, Sybil V.			4355
Drees, W. E.			1871
Drees, William Elimar			1348
Driscol, John	459		
Drummond, Donald		770½, 935	
Drummond, I. H.		1797	
Duck, Ah			1455
Ducker, Andrew	2964		
Ducker, Sarah			2964
Dudley, Annie	2616		

Name	Principal	Surety	Ward
Dudley, W. S.		2473, 2616	
Duffy, Thomas		459	
Duhring, Frederick T.		2684, 3364, 3441, 3881	
Dunbar, John		1836, 1978	
Duncan, A.		1105	
Duncan, Daniel		730	
Duncan, James P.		730	
Dunn, Philip H.	2308		
Dunning, E. B.		724	
Durst, Fridolin			3351
Eardley, W. J.		2987, 3373, 4273	
Easley, Amanda M.			414
Easley, Sarah F.			414
Easley, William P.			414
Edgeworth, W. J.		4340	
Edmunson, Emily			142
Edmunson, Emma			142
Edmunson, Hugh R.			142
Edmunson, John C.	142		143
Edmunson, Richard P.			140
Edmunson, Thomas J.	142		
Edmunson, Thomas Jefferson			141
Edmunson, William F.			142
Edsall, Juana B.			1780
Edwards, Benjamin			2610
Edwards, Bessie H.			2610
Edwards, Frank G.			2610
Edwards, George			544
Edwards, Hannah	544		
Edwards, James R.		3283	
Edwards, Joseph			544
Edwards, Joseph L.			2610
Edwards, Leland S.			2610
Edwards, Lulu A.			2610
Edwards, Mary			544, 2610
Eikenbery, John S.	789		
Einhorn, J. H.		2071, 2327	
Einhorn, Joseph H.		3396	
Einhorn, Mary A.	3396		

Name	Principal	Surety	Ward
Elder, Charles G.			755
Elder, Hellena M.			755
Elder, J. W.	755		
Elder, Jessie M.			755
Elder, John M.			755
Elder, Madison L.			755
Elder, Monroe C.			755
Eliason, W. A.		391	
Ellis, John J.		283	
Ellis, William		22, 85, 137	
Ellsworth, Clara	1894		
Ellsworth, Leonard F.			1894
Ellsworth, Percy L.			2741
Emerson, Henry		168, 864	
Emery, F. A.		3838	
English, John M.	159		
Ensign, J. C.		790	
Epperley, Levi Oliver			864
Epperly, Levi O.			2106
Esmond, Cornwell		238	
Espey, John H.		1294	
Espy, G. T.		196	
Espy, John		196	
Evans, Charles William			811
Evans, John Wirt			811
Evans, Lucy Jane			811
Evans, Mary Ellen	811		
Ewell, E. C.	1759		
Ewell, Fred F.	1759		
Ewell, Mary M.			1759
Ewell, P. D. F.		1405	
Ewing, Ida B.			1052
Fader, Anna H.			651
Fader, Annie K.			651
Fader, Helen M.			651
Fader, Kate A.			651
Fader, Katie A.			651
Fader, Katie H.			651
Fader, Victor V.			651
Fahrion, Harold C.			2655

Name	Principal	Surety	Ward
Fahrion, Wallace G.			2655
Faio, Amelia			3596
Faio, Frances B.	3596		
Faio, Ida			3596
Faio, Maria			3596
Faio, Mariana			3596
Fairbanks, D. B.	2231, 2256, 2741	3104, 3528	.
Fairbanks, H. T.	1520	616, 1135, 1834, 2231, 2256, 2741	
Fairbanks, J. F.		2231, 2741, 3237	
Falkner, M. H.		1492	
Farmer, C. C.	2180	958, 1082	
Farmer, E. T.	1082	252, 281, 365, 597, 897, 1006, 1294	
Farmer, Elijah T.		897	
Farmer, George	2636		
Farmer, J. A.	958		
Farmer, William		125, 143	
Farquhar, Mary A.	444		
Farquhar, Nora		.	444
Farquhar, Winnifred			444
Farrar, M. C.	1242		
Faudre, Stewart W.	1983		
Fay, J. P.	1996		
Feehan, Edward M.			2498
Feehan, John P.	2498		
Feehan, Mary G.			2498
Feehan, Ursula E.			2498
Fehrmann, Johann		1739	
Feltz, Louise			1827
Ferguson, H. O.		1068½, 2290, 2989	
Ferguson, John J.		1151	
Ferguson, John N.		950, 2989	
Ferguson, Russel	931		
Ferguson, W. W.		3846	
Fernald, J.		475	
Fernald, Orlando Johnson			2377

Name	Principal	Surety	Ward
Ferrari, Angelica			2383
Ferrari, Carlo			2383
Ferrin, Cornelia L.		2909	
Fick, Henry William			1794
Fick, Hermine Dorethe			1794
Fick, John Frederick			1794
Fick, Margarette F.	1794		
Fidelity and Deposit Company of Maryland		2788, 2901, 2989, 3081, 3425, 3686	
Field, Effa			908
Field, Erma			908
Field, J. C.	651		
Field, James		506	
Fike, N.		194, 293	
Fike, Nathan	213, 272	499	
Fike, Stephen Spencer			535
Filippini, Achille	2665		
Filippini, Charles		2192, 2941	
Filippini, Leonard R.		2665	
Fillebrown, Almira B.		711	
Findley, David			584
Findley, Elizabeth		584	584
Findley, Harvey			584
Findley, Katharine			584
Findley, Samuel			584
Fine, Abraham			327
Fine, Emiline/Emeline			327
Fine, Emsly			327
Fine, I. Holt		103	
Fine, W.		2270	
Finley, H.		2804	
Finley, Harrison		3873	
Finley, John	584		
Fiori, Attilio		4139	
Fiori, Henry E.	4139		
Fiori, Orazio		4139	
Fiscus, George W.			906
Fisher, A. L.		1079, 1759, 1867, 2732	

Name	Principal	Surety	Ward
Fisher, Augustus L.			3245
Fisher, B. O.		2360	
Fisher, Clare V.			2360
Fisher, Mary L. V.	2360		
Fisher, Rebecca A.	3245		
Fisk, Clara S.	711		
Fisk, Frank			711
Fisk, J. C.		711	
Fisk, John C.		711	
Fitch, Anna			41
Fitch, Charles			41
Fitch, Clara			986
Fitch, Frederick		41	
Fitch, Henry Edward		41	
Fitch, Herman			986
Fitch, Isabel			41
Fitch, John			41
Fitch, Joseph	986		41, 1141
Fitch, Joseph, Jr.			1141
Fitch, Joseph, Sr.	1141		
Fitch, Josephine			41
Fitch, Natalia			986
Fitch, William	216		
Fitch, William C.			986
Fix, J. K.	1782		
Fix, Jesse K.		457	
Flege, Henry			348
Flier, Tille			3796
Flood, Michael		608	
Flynn, Patrick			406
Focha, Anna M.	3597		
Focha, C. J.		3597	
Fochetti, Julius		1759, 2941	
Foerstler, Mary	2712		
Fopiano, John		3877	
Ford, John W.		3442	
Ford, Lydia E.			2855
Fordyce, Emma	1763		
Fordyce, Grace			1763
Fordyce, Mabel			1763

Name	Principal	Surety	Ward
Foreman, William R.		475	
Forsyth, B.		2844	
Forsyth, Benjamin	1058		
Forsyth, H. M.		3822	
Forsyth, Henry Mizer			1058
Forsyth, Robert		564, 1217	
Forsyth, Robert A.	2106	2844, 3641	
Forsythe, Charles		1354	
Forsythe, Robert A.		1294	
Fowler, Edgar J.			675
Fowler, James E.	391, 675		
Fowler, John H.		3641	
Fowler, Robert B.	1175		
Fowler, Robert F.			1175
Fowler, William Warren			675
Fox, Henry		1824	
Frain, Alice	3857		
Frain, Maria			3857
Frain, Marie			3857
Frain, Thomas		2507	
Frampton, Hannah	1535		
France, Frank D.			2290
France, Mabel A.			2290
France, Waldo E.			2290
Francisco, Joseph		2087	
Frasier, D. S.	300		
Fredericks, M. H.		2740	
Fredricks, Francisca		3668, 3682	
Fredricks, J. W.	3668, 3682		
Freeland, Albert Clark			117
Freeland, Nancy M.	117		
Freeman, C. J.		3684	
Freeman, E. R.		1167	
Freeman, John M.	668		
Freeman, Mary E.	2901		
Freeman, W. D.	1167		
Frei, A.		3044	
French, Milton		4138	
Frick, George W.		352	
Fricke, John F.		1976	

Name	Principal	Surety	Ward
Frideger, Daniel S.	4243		
Frideger, Mary			4243
Fried, Henry		1004	
Fritch, J. Homer	3099		
Fritsch, John	1278	100, 475, 1400, 1749, 2377	
Fritsch, Mabel Isabel			3984
Fritsch, W. S.	3984		
Fritsch, Walter Mecham			3984
Frohlking, William		3180	
Frost, C. W.		1479, 1829	
Fruits, Jacob	376		
Fruits, John S.			376
Fruits, Robert F.			376
Fulkerson, Richard		897	1828
Fulkerson, S. T.	1828		
Fullagar, Alfred		576	
Fullagar, Elizabeth			576
Fullagar, William	576		
Fulton, David	377		
Fulton, James		376, 377, 1052	
Gaines, Crockett		937	
Gaines, W. C.		1276	
Galaway, A. J., Jr.			746
Galaway, Allen R.			746
Galaway, Amanda A.			746
Galaway, Nancy E.			746
Gale, Demus	1744		
Gale, M. C.		2959	
Gale, Otis		1744	
Gallagher, John		270	3339
Gallagher, John P.	3339		
Gallaway, A. J.	746	928	
Galusha, D. A.		186	
Gannon, James	1586		
Gardner, D. P.		2020	
Garnett, W. H.		2459	
Garrow, Edward	278		
Garzoli, William		1837	
Gaston, Dora E.			1092

Name	Principal	Surety	Ward
Gaston, Hamilton		1092	
Gaston, Hugh	1092		
Gauldin, Benjamin F.			179
Gauldin, John V.			179
Gauldin, Martha Anne			179
Gauldin, Willis Wilson			179
Gaver, A. P.		1092	
Gaver, Andrew P.		675	
Geick, F.		1827	
Geick, Leo		1739	
Geiger, Anna	2543		
Genazzi, John		3660	4051
Genazzi, Mary N.	4051		
Gentry, J. C.		755, 1052	
George, Daniel W.	3992		
George, Lilla E.			3992
Gerkhardt, H. F.	829	488, 794	
Giacomini, M.	2954		
Giannini, Henry G.		278	
Gibbens, A. S.		4366	
Gibbens, Margaret M.	3957		
Gibbens, Rose Elliot			3957
Gibbens, Rose Elliott			3957
Gibbs, Elizabeth A.	1292		
Gibbs, Henry		884	
Gibbs, Sophronia			3886
Gibson, J. A.		4239	
Gibson, L. B. (Mrs.)		1630	
Gibson, Silas W.	1878		
Gieske, Henry C.		2543	
Gilbert, Jacob		34	
Gilbride, R.		908	
Gill, Ann	504		
Gill, Antonette			504
Gill, Charles			2484, 3666
Gill, George Q.		504	
Gill, George W.	4373		
Gill, H.		790	
Gill, Leon			4373
Gill, Warren S.			4373

Name	Principal	Surety	Ward
Gillam, Mitchel		866	
Gilliam, Emily		3293	
Gilliam, Mitchel		176	
Gilman, P. E.		3919	
Gird, H. S.	778	2989	
Gird, Henry S.	778	93	166
Gird, Richard		166	
Gist, John L.		3409	
Givens, Ada			1644
Givens, Anna J.			1644
Givens, David G.			1644
Givens, Elisha	126		
Givens, Grace M.			1644
Givens, R. R.	1644		
Glenn, Robert		1264	
Glover, Albert B.			1198
Glover, Delia	1198		
Glover, Josephine M.			1198
Goddard, Albert D.			795
Goddard, Frank W.			795
Goddard, Jane M.	795		
Goddard, Jesse P.			795
Goddard, W. H.	908		
Goddard, Wellman			795
Godwin, Frederick Oscar			770½
Godwin, Henry Talmond			770½
Godwin, Hiram Ladd			770½
Godwin, Phebe A.	770½		
Goeppert, George	2903		
Golden, James			3519
Goncalves, Antonio F.	3469		
Good, W. C.		2198, 2334	
Goodman, David			2400
Goodman, L. S.	2400	584	
Goodman, S. F.			2400
Goodspeed, Anson	1068½		
Goodspeed, Charles A.			1068½
Goodspeed, Willerton T.			1068½
Gordon, Joseph		106	
Gordon, Rhoda			3564

Name	Principal	Surety	Ward
Gossage, Harry S.			1697
Gossage, Jerome B.			1697
Gossage, Joseph		1697	
Gossage, Rachel A.	1697		
Gossage, Winfield S.			1697
Gossage, Z.		748	
Gould, W. H.		1344	
Grace, F. P.		2295	
Grace, Frank P.		2427, 2504, 3165, 3409, 3686	
Grace, J. T.		2850	
Graeter, Ida S.	2054		
Graham, A. D.		3514	
Graham, Arthur W.			1119
Graham, Ida J.			1119
Graham, Mary E.	2901		
Graham, W. F.		3060	
Grainger, W. C.		2002	
Grandi, S.		3660	
Granice, H. H.		1759, 2103, 2941	
Grant, Anita F.	2402		
Grant, C. N.	3989		
Grant, Frederick T.			2402
Grant, Henry D. F.			296
Grant, John D.	296	1141	
Grass, Peter		3339	
Grater, J. F.		571, 1976, 2290	
Graves, Georgie			2081
Graves, Hill B.			2081
Graves, J. Q.		1354	
Graves, Luella B.	2081		
Gray, J. W.	1096	1465, 1499, 1877	
Gray, James		377, 3535	
Greely, Justus		1349	
Green, C. C.		148, 152	
Green, Emily			4138
Green, G. D.		530	
Green, I. L.		4138	

Name	Principal	Surety	Ward
Green, Lyman	3276, 3277		
Green, P. H.	4138		
Green, Stella M.	4138		
Green, W. S.		3012, 3942	
Greene, Shadrack	416		
Greening, William	76		
Gregg, Isaac		722	
Gregory, Annie E. (Mrs.)	1796		
Gregory, Lulu			1796
Gregory, Mattie M.	1796		
Gregson, James		457, 1782	
Grewell, Howard Marshall			3293
Grewell, Lottie B.	3293		
Griess, George		4222	
Griess, George J.		4222	
Grieves, Samuel H.			1877
Grieves, William	1877		
Griffin, Catherine			3815
Griggs, J. H.		436	
Griggs, Joseph H.		89	
Griggs, W. B.	2844	3250	
Groff, Caroline			1321
Groff, Louis W.			1321
Groff, Maria	1321		
Groff, Sarah E.			1321
Groff, William S.			1321
Gropp, Charles			829
Groshong, Uriah		135	
Grosse, Guy E.		1292	
Grosse, Joseph E.			1292
Grothaus, F.		2471	
Grove, C. C.	1480		
Grove, David	281	190, 238, 819	
Grove, William H.	3229		
Grover, James M.			127
Grover, Thomas J.	127		
Gryff, John A.		2792	
Guay, John B.		1157	
Guerne, George E.		1264	
Guidotti, C.			3686

Name	Principal	Surety	Ward
Guidotti, Celestine			3686
Guidotti, G.	3686		
Guldager, Louis		1157	
Gum, Clara	2488		
Gum, Isaac		1532	
Gum, Nellie Hazel			2488
Gum, Schuyler Colfax	2488		
Hadrich, C. F. Hugo		3018	
Hadrich, Charles F. H.		3562	
Haehl, Amy Mary			2011
Haehl, Harry L.			2011
Haehl, Henry		1490	
Haehl, Jacob		2011	
Hagedohm, Herman		2337	
Hagedohm, Johanna		2337	
Hagedohm, William			2337
Hager, George D.	748½		
Haggard, Ida Mabel			1360
Hagmayer, Gottlob		1490	
Hahman, F. G.		62, 572, 1031, 1083, 1275	
Hahman, Henrietta A.		3440	
Haigh, Edwin		2283, 2999	
Haigh, John		213	
Haight, Robert		1654	
Hale, O. A.		4085	
Hale, William	1626		
Hall, A. S.		2779	
Hall, Annie W.	3840		
Hall, D. W.		213	
Hall, E. G.		1184	
Hall, Gil P.		2504	
Hall, H. L.		3840	
Hall, J. E.	1217	1455	
Hall, J. W.		3840	
Hall, L. B.		748½	
Hall, L. J.	778, 976	778, 1666	
Hall, Robert		3999	
Hamill, John			3666
Hamilton, Alethia Blanche			3081

Name	Principal	Surety	Ward
Hamilton, G. W.		2732	
Hamilton, Georgia H.	3081		
Hamm, Ellen E.			1157
Hamm, Mary A.	1157		
Hand, Ella N.			3340
Haney, Frank		1314, 1641	
Hansen, Emma	4149		
Hansen, Peter	4149		
Harbine, L.	1477		
Hardcastle, Job			698
Hardin, George M.			283
Hardin, George W.			1479
Hardin, Henry			1479
Hardin, James A.	1479	283, 564, 1507, 3373	
Hardin, James T.	426		
Hardin, Lucinda	283		
Hardin, Stonewall J.			283
Hardin, W. J.	1119		
Harmes, Catherine D.	3326		
Harmes, Charles M.			3326
Harmes, Clarence			3326
Harmes, Frederick K.			3326
Harmes, Leland			3326
Harmon, F. V.	1375		
Harmon, H. H.		305	
Harmon, Owen			1375
Harmon, Samuel H.		940	
Harper, Maggie Ann			3165
Harper, Sarah			3442
Harrington, Alfred B.			3616
Harrington, Florence E.			3616
Harrington, Huldah N.	3616		
Harrington, John F.	608		
Harrington, John O.			3616
Harrington, Mabel E.			3616
Harrington, Ralph I.			3616
Harrington, William B.			3616
Harris, A. L.	2849		
Harris, B. F.		1242	

Name	Principal	Surety	Ward
Harris, G. S.		2471	
Harris, Granville S.		2941, 3441	
Harris, Jacob		1016, 1355, 1561, 1717, 1747, 1807, 1815	
Harris, R. J.		2642	
Harris, W. F.		1725	
Harrison, George		3385	
Hart, B. F.	2797		
Hart, Charles E.			2797
Hart, V. E.		3827	
Hartman, J. W.		83, 494	
Hartsock, Bonnie			2390
Hartsock, Florence A.	2390		
Hartsock, Freedom			2390
Harvey, Calvin A.			2132
Harvey, Charles A.			1096
Harvey, Ella			748½
Harvey, Elmer R.			2132
Harvey, Sarah V.			1096
Harvey, Thomas J.		142	
Hasbrouck, H. B.		475	
Haskell, Euna G.			1749
Haskell, W. B.		604	
Haskell, William B.	1749	1474, 1697, 1933, 2398, 2470, 2610	
Haskins, M. D.		821	
Haskins, Robert	2102		
Haskins, T. J.		1267	
Haskins, Thomas J.		1167	
Hassett, A.		724½, 778, 976	
Hassett, Aaron	780	746, 819, 1666, 1782, 1878	
Hassett, Carrie Josephine			2283
Hassett, J. D.		296, 724½, 976	
Hassett, James H.		490	
Hassett, John D.	819	461	
Hassett, Ora T.	2283		
Hassett, Sarah E.	2631		

Name	Principal	Surety	Ward
Hatch, Chester P.			2256
Hatcher, George J.		4273	
Hatfield, Francis A.			596
Hatfield, Francis J.			1146
Hatfield, Joseph A.			596, 1146
Hatfield, Rebecca			596, 1146
Hatfield, William P.			596, 1146
Haub, Conrad		3872	
Haubrick, Peter			3229
Haupt, Charles W.		3625	
Hausch, Anna Bell			635
Hausch, Charles H. J.			635
Hausch, Christian	635	435	
Hausch, Ellsey			635
Hausch, Flora			635
Hausch, Hannah May			635
Hausch, Henery Etta			635
Hauto, Anna			4344
Hauto, Anna F.	4344		
Hauto, Dora			4344
Hauto, Edward			4344
Hauto, Elsa			4344
Hauto, Ernest			4344
Hauto, Marie			4344
Hauto, Olga			4344
Haven, C. E.		4128	
Haven, Celina	3858		
Haven, Elsie			3858
Haven, Joshua P.	130		
Hawkins, Mamie			1717
Hawkins, Mark			1717
Hawkins, Maud			1717
Hayden, Birdie			3626
Hayden, Richard			3626
Hayden, Rodney			3626
Hayden, S. R.	3626	3625	
Hayes, Emma	1815		
Hayes, Rosa			1815
Hazen, Frank		2957	
Heald, George William			196

Name	Principal	Surety	Ward
Heald, Jacob G.	599		
Heald, John Edson			599
Heald, Thomas T.		196, 672	
Healey, D. J.		3188, 3945, 4007	
Healey, Maggie		4007	
Healey, W. E.		2010, 2071, 2651	
Hearn, James		142	
Heavey, B. J.		995	
Hegeler, Gerhard			627
Hehir, T. L.		3790	
Heinrich, John A.		3295	
Heisel, Caroline			1966
Heisel, Ellen		1966	
Heisel, John			1966
Heisel, Nellie			1966
Heisel, Paul	929		1966
Heitmann, Frederick	3397		
Heitmann, William			3397
Held, Henrietta Georgina			750
Hembree, Andrew T.		482	
Hemenway, Alice T.	3228		
Hemenway, D. D.		3228	
Hendley, Frank P.			1465
Hendley, John		62, 85, 252, 579	
Hendley, William G.			1465
Hendrick, E. W.	506		
Hendricks, George L.	3643		
Hendricks, J. M.		2390, 3779	
Hendricks, Leon			3643
Hendrix, E. U.	1284		
Hendrix, Lewis		1284	
Henley, Barclay		770, 1018	
Henrichsen, Henry			2740
Henrichsen, Henry Richard	2740		
Henrichsen, Nicolaus			2740
Herges, Mary Elizabeth			2721
Herron, Amy			790
Herron, Belle			790

Name	Principal	Surety	Ward
Hershberger, Charles			947
Hershberger, Frank			947
Hershberger, Jeremiah		142	
Hertel, R.		222, 950	
Hess, Fred		1348	
Hess, Frederick		1135	
Hiatt, E. M.		2233	
Hicklin, George T.	2459		
Hicklin, Georgia			2459
Hicklin, Mabel E.			2459
Hickman, B. F.		906	
Hickman, John E.	906		
Hickson, Clarence			2804
Hickson, Mabel			2804
Hickson, Willie			2804
Higgins, Percy Clarence			3315
Hiland, O. A.		5	
Hilby, Agatha M.			488
Hilby, Francis M.			488
Hill, A. B.		3104, 3276, 3277, 3397, 4223	
Hill, Amos			821
Hill, Emily			2569
Hill, John H.	87		
Hill, William	1381	651, 1437, 1729, 2132, 2435	
Hill, William McPherson		87	
Hillis, John A.		1780	
Hinkston, Annie	2914		
Hinkston, Nancy			918
Hinrichs, Carl			1693
Hinshaw, E. C.		1076, 2354, 2790	
Hinshaw, William Pettis	2989		
Hirth, Albrecht			3018
Hirth, Fred	3018		
Hitchcock, Hollis		584	
Hoadley, George H.			2121
Hoadley, Harriet	2121		
Hoag, O. H.	1016	720, 1561	

Name	Principal	Surety	Ward
Hoar, B. F.		2619	
Hockin, William		2516, 2868	
Hockman, Jacob	568		
Hodge, Robert		3440	
Hodgson, W. H.		1867	
Hoen, Berthold		87	
Hoffer, C. A.	2712	2589	
Hoffstetter, Albertine	1451		
Hoffstetter, B. (Dr.)		1451	
Hoffstetter, Eleanora			1451
Hoffstetter, Jeanne			1451
Holland, Annie F.			3131
Holland, Maggie M.			3131
Holland, Michael H.			3131
Holloway, George W.			129
Holloway, Henrietta			129
Holloway, J. C.		1349	
Holloway, Lyscomb [Lipscomb] C.	129		
Holloway, Mary E.			129
Holm, Jacob F.		2435	
Holman, E. Josephine	2627		
Holman, J. H.		2627	
Holman, John H.	120, 152	634	
Holmes, Carrie Edna			3458
Holmes, Emma M.	3458		
Holmes, H. P.		1422	
Holmes, Henderson P.	62		
Hood, Albert			843
Hood, George		704	
Hood, John		2613, 2902	
Hood, Mary			843
Hood, Sarah			843
Hood, Stella Blanche			888
Hood, T. B.		281, 341, 1360	
Hood, Thomas B.		168, 665	
Hood, William			3440
Hopes, E.		641	
Hopkins, Hiram			2779
Hopkins, Lottie			2779
Hopkins, M. D.	2779		

Name	Principal	Surety	Ward
Hopkins, S. J.		3104, 3886, 4287	
Hopkins, Willott			2779
Hopper, Climama			863
Hopper, Edward			863
Hopper, Emma Belle			863
Hopper, Eugene			863
Hopper, J. W.	2804	1657, 1663	
Hopper, Thomas	1664	1294, 2180, 2804	
Hosking, Mary Jane Elizabeth			2715
Hoskins, T. D.	1561		
Hoskins, William		2469	
Hotchkiss, B.		928	
Hotchkiss, W. J.		1567	
Houche, C. H., Sr.		3253	
Houx, W. D.		3671, 3784, 3805	
Howard, George		2537	
Howard, John F.		515	
Howard, John James			3032
Howard, Mary Ellen	596		
Howe, Edwin A.		383	
Howe, Robert	3165, 3442		
Howell, O.		1780	
Howell, Orrin		2011	
Howell, Stephen T.	586		
Hoyle, G. W.	3456		
Hubbard, Henry		3333	
Hubbard, William		57	
Hubbell, Orton		3530	
Hubbell, Orton B.		3530	
Hubbell, Phoebe	3530		
Hudson, Elizabeth	529		
Hudson, Henry W.			529
Hudson, T. W.		196, 227, 461, 908	
Hudspeth, J. M.		1402	
Huff, John G.		81	
Hughes, John	947	135, 949	
Hughes, Josephine			489

Name	Principal	Surety	Ward
Huhn, Fritz	2485		
Huie, George W.		352	
Humphries, Charles		578	
Huni, Otto			3044
Hunt, Benjamin W.	564		
Hunt, Charles	348		
Hunt, Charles W.			564
Hunt, Francis W.			564
Hunt, Hazel Berna			4253
Hunt, James B.			564
Hunt, Jane Doe			1293
Hunt, Katie			1265
Hunt, Lottie E.			564
Hunt, Sarah C.			564
Hunt, W. J.		4253	
Hunter, John	582		
Hunter, Nathaniel	1455		
Hunter, Olin M.			525
Hunter, Wilbur L.			525
Huntley, John Stanley			1745
Huntley, Will	1745		
Hurd, Charlotte Psyche			738
Hurd, G. W.	738		
Hurd, George Henry			738
Hurd, Lizzie J. T.			738
Hurd, Washington		475	
Hurn, John			278
Hurn, Seth			278
Hurn, Sibbie			278
Hurn, Solomon			278
Hurn, William			278
Husler, E. A.		3984	
Hutchinson, F. A.		1411	
Hutchinson, Richard		576	
Hutchinson, T. J.		2931	
Hutton, Charles E.	194		
Hyde, F. A.		3340	
Hyde, M. D.	3340		
Hyde, Patrick		1543	
Hynes, Alma R.	1283		

Name	Principal	Surety	Ward
Hynes, James		641	
Hynes, John P.			1247
Hynes, Laura			1283
Hynes, Laura A.			1283
Hynes, Wildric			1283
Hynes, Wildric F.			1283
Ingalls, Chester A.			2666, 2999
Ingalls, J. C.	2999	2473, 3588	
Ingalls, Timothy A.	2666		
Ingmansen, John			2657
Ingram, John		85	
Ink, W. P.		2233	
Irwin, S. P.		3564	
Irwin, Thomas N.		911, 912	
Isaacs, Esther	919		
Isaacs, Louis			919
Isaacs, Marks			919
Isola, A.		4291	
Isom, H.		147	
Isom, Hugh		142	
Jackson, Abraham Joseph			587
Jackson, Beatrice Anna			2457
Jackson, Fanny Victoria			587
Jackson, Gideon			587
Jackson, Jane	587		
Jackson, L. W.		2457	
Jackson, Margaret			587
Jackson, Mary Jane			587
Jackson, Maye D.	2457		
Jackson, Ward Sutliff			2457
Jacobs, G. H.		330	
Jacobs, George H.	250	568	
Jacobsen, C. A.		2721	
Jacobson, J. H.		3229	
Jacobson, Jacob		98	
Jamison, James M.			3836
Jamison, Rachel			3834
Jamison, Sarah J.		3834	
Jamison, Sarah Jane		3836	
Jewell, D. H.		720	

Name	Principal	Surety	Ward
Jewell, George W.			1772
Jewell, Grace A.	1772		
Jewell, I. R.		399	
Jewell, Ida M.			1772
Jewell, Jesse		300	
Jewell, Ruby Grace			1772
Jewett, John H.		1730	
Jewett, L. L.	3079		
Johnson, Bertha			1126
Johnson, C. A.		85	
Johnson, Charles			122
Johnson, David Q.	3821		
Johnson, Elizabeth (Mrs.)	1126		
Johnson, George A.		843½, 926	
Johnson, Henry	1369		
Johnson, J. J.	264		
Johnson, Margaret J.		3821	
Johnson, Mary			1870
Johnson, Melville	532		
Johnson, Peter		929	
Johnson, Rachel	864, 866	866	
Johnson, William A.			122
Jones, Charles		1097	
Jones, Elizabeth A.	623		
Jones, Fred			623
Jones, Frederick S.	355		
Jones, H. M.		2507	
Jones, John H.	1611		
Jones, Martha	1611		
Jones, Mary J.	3372		
Jones, Minnie			623
Jones, Patrick Carroll	3342		
Jones, Reuben A.		677	
Jones, Robert R.			3372
Jones, Walter		1894	
Jones, William		675, 1894	
Jones, William J.		3342	
Joost, Anna			3251
Joost, Carl			3251
Joost, Harry			3251

Name	Principal	Surety	Ward
Joost, Jacob	2469	3251, 3281	
Joost, Martin	3251		
Joost, Nettie			3251
Joost, Rudolph			3251
Jorg, Crescenz			3502
Jose, Emanuel	1739, 1827		
Jose, Louisa			1739
Jose, Paul Henry			1739
Jose, Sophia			1739
Joy, Benjamin		675	
Jud, Christian		1836, 3044	
Judkins, L. M.			100
Judson, Egbert		444	
Juilliard, C. F.	1264		
Juilliard, L. W.	4128	2767	
Justice, S. A.		770	
Kaen, Thomas L.		1602	
Kahn, A.		3351, 3717	
Kahn, Achille		668	
Kahn, M.		3984	
Kahn, Moise		1661	
Kaler, George		2116	
Kamp, Harold Lud.		98	
Kamp, Julia			1305
Kamp, N.	1305		
Katen, Annie			2111
Katen, John	1868		
Kauffmann, Phillipe L.	1523		
Kearney, Alice			2471
Kearney, Francis P.	2471		
Kearney, Louis Phillip			2471
Kearney, William J.	3514		
Kearns, Bernard	1602		
Kearns, James			1602
Kee, James		2385, 2400	
Keegan, Daisy I.			2790
Keegan, Dennis		2790	
Keegan, J. W.		2122, 2427	
Keegan, James			2790
Keegan, Lilly A.			2790

Name	Principal	Surety	Ward
Keegan, Maggie A.	2790		
Keegan, Mary E.		2790	
Keegan, Thomas P.		2122, 2327, 3259, 3532, 3818	
Kelley, Albert		807	
Kelley, Eddie			3757
Kelley, Gertie			3757
Kelley, Jacob	147		
Kelley, Maud			3757
Kelley, Willie			3757
Kellogg, A. S.	262		
Kelly, Francis Peter			3237
Kelly, J. W.		704, 1150	
Kelly, James W.		1324	
Kelsey, Alice F.			1933
Kelsey, Annie R.			1933
Kelsey, Benjamin		57	
Kelsey, Daniel M.			1933
Kelsey, Edwin J.			1933
Kelsey, Joseph			57
Kelsey, Mary	1933		
Kelsey, Mary H.		1933	
Kelsey, R. J.		1933	
Kelsey, Samuel	57		
Kelsey, Thomas H.			1933
Kelsey, William			57
Kelty, Anna L.			729
Kendall, Arthur			1736
Kendall, Homer			1736
Kendall, John	1736	88	
Kennedy, B. D.		3385	
Kennedy, George H.	937, 1079		
Kennedy, James		83	
Kennelly, J.		1381	
Kerbey, Ebenezer W.			3003
Kerbey, Sarah A.	3003		
Kerth, J. G.	3297		
Keyes, M. M.	1625		
Kidd, Daisy			2931
Kidd, F. A. (Mrs.)	2931		

Name	Principal	Surety	Ward
Kidd, William H.		4173	
Killberg, Peter		98	
Kimball, C. L.	1517	3014	
Kincaid, Oscar F.			789
King, Alice			924
King, Elnora C.	1896		
King, Fred		3229	
King, George F.		3694	
King, Henry Haight			1308
King, James		3007	
King, Mary E. (Mrs.)		2777	
King, Mathew Wallace, Jr.			3094
King, Matthew W.	1308		
King, N.	4203		
King, Thomas		3079	
King, William F.			1896
Kinne, Ethel S.			3448
Kinne, G. Newton			3448
Kinne, Mary F.			3448
Kinne, Seeley D.	3448		
Kinsell, Dudley	4242		
Kinslow, J. F.		3245	
Kinsmill, Thomas E.	98	98	
Kirby, E. C.			3003
Kirby, Sarah A.	3003		
Kirk, Alice J.			112
Kirkpatrick, T. F.		1829	
Kiser, Abraham		1172	
Kiser, Anton			2780
Kiser, Joseph			2780
Kiser, Josephine	2780		
Kiser, Theodore			2780
Kizer, John P.		475	
Klink, George E.			499
Klink, Margaret J.			499
Klink, Nicholas Ward			499
Klink, Stephen V. R.	499		
Klotz, C. G.		1472	
Knapp, Alice B.	2732		
Knapp, G. W.		940	

Name	Principal	Surety	Ward
Knapp, Hope Irene			2732
Knapp, Ida Lulu			2732
Knapp, W. D.		2931	
Knight, George			967
Knight, George W.			2305
Knowles, Clarence E.			2129
Knowles, D. C.		2129	
Knowles, David C.	341		
Knowles, J. H		494	
Knox, John T.	526		
Koch, Anna	1184		
Koenig, F.		2283	
Koenig, Frank		3694	
Kohle, A.		524	
Kohle, August		473, 572	
Kohlman, Solomon		1654	
Kopf, C. L.		3018, 3821	
Korbel, A.		3083	
Korbel, F.		3083	
Kraft, Violet			1611
Kreuz, Frank P.	2181		
Kreuz, Katharina			2181
Kroeger, F.		1960	
Kron, John		243	
Kruse, August			2463
Kruse, Edward P. E.		3099	
Kruse, Emil T.		3099	
Kruse, F. A.	2463		
Kruse, H. A.		4366	
Kruse, Louise J. (Mrs.)		2463	
Kruse, William H.			3099
Kuchler, Blaseus			1874
Kuchler, Carolina	1874		
Kuchler, Joseph			1874
Kuchler, Josephine			1874
Kuchler, Rosalie			1874
Kuffel, Isaac		376	
Kurtz, Fredericka		3796	
Kurtz, Lina		3796	
Lacque, B.		949	

Name	Principal	Surety	Ward
Lamb, John		88	
Lambert, Ellen A.			1878
Lambert, George F.			1878
Lambert, George Lee			1666
Lane, C. W.		4080	
Lane, Lincoln			1520
Langhorne, John W.		123	
Langley, Eliza			2849
Larison, Samuel		1042	
Larrison, Samuel			2796
Larsen, Anne C.	4179		
Larsen, Myrtle Lee			4179
Larsen, R.		4179	
Lastufka, John C.	3083		
Latapie, E.		704, 932	
Latimer, L. D.		391	
Laughlin, Cordelia G.	2305		
Laughlin, J. H.		2073	
Laughlin, James H.		321, 967, 1294	
Laughlin, John M.	967		
Laughlin, L.		345	
Laughlin, Lee		1567	
Lauritzen, Augusta			3007
Lauritzen, Clara	3007		
Lauritzen, Harold			3007
Lauteren, Antoinette M.	2480		
Lauteren, Anton J.			2480
Lauteren, Edgar F.			2480
Lauteren, Gertrude C.			2480
Laux, H.		2103	
Lavell, John	1666		
Lavine, Frank	724		
Lawler, John		2102, 3104	
Lawrence, H. E.		1402, 2085, 4203	
Lawrence, J. A.		1507	
Lawrence, James A.		120	
Lawrence, Manuel B.		3469	
Lawson, Mattie I.	3962		
Laymance, I. C.		414, 635	
Laymance, Isaac C.		127	

Name	Principal	Surety	Ward
Leak, Charles W.			526
Leak, John D.			526
Leavensworth, Thomas M.		1083	
LeBaron, H. M.		3460	
LeBaron, H. W.		3460	
Lee, W. H.		3642	
Lee, William H.		1983	
Leffingwell, J. L.		406	
Leffingwell, John Henry			1501
Leffingwell, Margaret	1501		
Leffingwell, William Charles			1501
Leiding, C. F.	1344		
Leigh, A. G.		811	
Leigh, Mary		811	
Leitch, Margaret G.			3240
Lemay, Edna			2434
Lemay, Elva			2434
Lemmons, James	123		
Lenz, Frederick W.			1184
Leonard, Charles W.			978
Leppo, D.		2485, 4232	
Leppo, D. H.		4232	
Leppo, O. F.	4232		
Leslie, Jonathan	88		
Letold, J. G.	1739		
Lewis, Catharine	22		
Lewis, Frank W.	1265, 1293		
Lewis, G. W.		2054	
Lewis, George			22
Lewis, George W.		1759	
Lewis, I. S.	3061		
Lewis, Isaac S.	3857		
Lewis, J. B.		1278	
Lewis, Jere		2797	
Lewis, John			22
Lewis, Joseph			22
Lewis, Leanna			60
Lewis, Lena May	2675		
Lewis, Maria			22
Lewis, Nevile			60

Name	Principal	Surety	Ward
Lewis, Prudie Mabel			2675
Lewis, R. E.	354	795	
Lewis, Seveir	60		
Lewis, Sophia			22
Lewis, Sylvester			60
Lichau, Albert E.			2346
Lichau, Archie C.			2346
Lichau, Arthur L.			2346
Lichau, Charles F.			2346
Lichau, Edward P.			2346
Lichau, Elmer C.			2346
Lichau, Henry Philip, Sr.	2346		
Lichau, Henry Phillip, Jr.			2346
Liddle, Lucinda			814
Light, E. H.		3562	
Lightner, Ella A.			1267
Lightner, John M.		174	
Lightner, Sarah J.	1267		
Lincoln, G. F.		4080	
Lind, Emma			473
Lind, John	473		
Lindemood, Israel		1477	
Lindsay, Adin A.			2421
Lindsay, Esther A.	2421		
Lindsay, Maggie F.			2421
Lindsay, Walter C.		2421	
Lingenfelter, Charley H.			3214
Lingenfelter, Jesse A.			3214
Lippitt, E. S.		1035, 1169	
Liter, W.		2002	
Little, J.		1305	
Litton, A. P.		2569	
Litton, H. B.	2569		
Litton, Ida Blanche			1557
Litton, Thomas G.			1557
Litzius, Louis		2165	
Lobenstein, Sol		3813	
Locke, Albert		2638	
Logan, Phebe H.			3253
Logan, Samuel	3253		

Name	Principal	Surety	Ward
Lohrmann, John		2013	
Long, M. A.		196	
Long, Marcus A.		89	
Longmore, Alexander			1402
Longmore, Thomas	1402		
Loomis, F. C.		3245	
Looney, Robert	843, 888		
Lopes, Manuel		1868, 2111	
Loranger, Frank			2504
Loranger, Hattie			2504
Loranger, Lillian E.	2504		
Loranger, William			2504
Loranger, Willie			2504
Lord, Edwin		2780	
Loucks, A. H.	729	725, 936, 1079	
Loughnane, James		475, 2266	
Lounibos, John		2941, 3679	
Lovejoy, A. P.		406	
Lovell, David J.		142	
Lowe, Celia K.	2721		
Lowery, Benjamin			926
Lowery, William			926
Lowrey, Mary J.	4001		
Lowrey, Robert L.		3605	
Lucas, John		148	
Lucas, Nellie B.			1807
Luce, Arthur S.	814		
Luce, Jirah	724½	814, 1557	
Luce, Mary	1178		
Luce, Milton Y.	1557		
Ludy, Catherine E.			4222
Ludy, Freda A.			4222
Ludy, G. H.			4222
Ludy, Selma E.			4222
Luff, Eva C.	4085		
Luff, Genevieve			4085
Luff, Hale			4085
Luttringer, J.		2657	
Lynch, Charles		1293	
Lynch, John		1287, 3339	

Name	Principal	Surety	Ward
Lyon, Robert B.		198	
Lyons, Dennis		608	
Lytakker, Rowland G.			3605
Lyttaker, F. E.	352, 1284, 3605		
Lyttaker, John T.			352
Lyttaker, Roland			1284
Lyttaker, Roland G.			1284
Mac, M. B.		2638	
Machado, Mary			1746
Macken, Jeremiah	995		
Macken, Robert			995
Maclay, Thomas	3886	4287	
Macy, Theora			194
Maddalena, Albert			4139
Maddalena, Charles		2383	4139
Madden, Adelia			2638
Maddocks, Irene		3293	
Maddocks, L. A.		3550	
Maddocks, Winthrop		1523	
Maddux, J. P.		278, 1294, 1828, 1877	
Maddux, James H.		1294	
Maddux, L. D.		931	
Madeira, F. A.	3776		
Madeira, Harry W.			2775
Maderas, Leopolinda			3597
Madler, Lizzie			1167
Madler, Margaretta			1168
Maede, August		873	
Magetti, Joseph			1181
Magetti, P.		1181	
Maggetti, G.	1181		
Maggetti, P.		2665	
Maggetti, Robert H.			4142
Magnes, R.		2543	
Magoon, H. K.		748, 748½	
Magoon, William H.	748		
Maher, M.		2627	
Maher, T. C.		724	
Mailer, J. C.		2106, 2270	

Name	Principal	Surety	Ward
Mailer, James C.		1512	
Maionchi, Leopold			3613
Manion, William		755	
Mann, Adelia A.			3052
Mardon, Henry		1411	
Markell, C. J. (Mrs.)		4032	
Markham, Andrew		2416, 2631, 2655, 2712, 2788, 2964, 3050	
Markley, John		3599	
Markwell, S.	1782		
Marsezell, Frank			3919
Marsezell, George			3919
Marsezell, Mary			3919
Marsezell, Samuel			3919
Marsezell, Thomas			3919
Marshall, A. S.		3456	
Marshall, Annabell			1315, 1398
Marshall, Charles			3625
Marshall, Domingo			2087
Marshall, Frank			2087
Marshall, Hugh A.	1962		
Marshall, James		1962	
Marshall, John		1004	2087, 3530
Marshall, Joseph			2087
Marshall, Manuel			2087
Marshall, Marian A.			1315
Marshall, Marion A.			1376
Marshall, Mary			2087
Marshall, Robert			3625
Marshall, Rosa			2087
Marshall, Sadie			3625
Marshall, Sarah A.	1315		
Marshall, William		3293	
Marti, M.		2103	
Martin, F. McG.	2767		
Martin, Fannie			1661
Martin, H. B.		152	
Martin, Horace B.		166	
Martin, James			1661

Name	Principal	Surety	Ward
Martin, Joseph L.			3289
Martin, Josiah Lewis			3907
Martin, Mary L.			3064
Martin, Nellie			3288
Martin, Rebecca Ann		2777	
Martin, S. M.		505	
Martin, Samuel B.		159	
Martin, Silas M.	34	34, 122	
Martin, Susan	3064		
Martinelli, Attilio C.	4222		
Mather, J.		3198	
Matheson, George G.			222
Matheson, Maria A.	222		
Matheson, Nettie			222
Matheson, Roderick			222
Mathews, C. W.		62	
Mathews, John		599	
Matthews, C. W.		252, 535	
Matthews, George Jones			2217
Matthews, Sarah H.			3226
Matthias, Edna Antoinette			3012
Matthias, Frances L.	3012		
Matthias, Frederick Leon			3012
Matthies, Heinrich	750		
Matthies, Henry			1378
Matthies, Lina	1378		
Matzenbach, W. B.		1267, 1990	
Maxwell, James G.		120	
Maynard, F. T.		122, 475, 1135, 1238, 1796, 2256	
Mayr, Johanna			3502
Mayr, Theresa			3502
McAnally, John		270	
McCabe, S. H.	2011		
McCarthy, D.		3496	
McChristian, Patrick		866	
McCleave, H. P.	2132		
McClellan, M. T.		711	
McClendon, William J.		2073	
McClish, J. N.		3452	

Name	Principal	Surety	Ward
McClish, James L.		321	
McClish, John		2588	
McClish, John N.	2073, 3288	3289, 3907	321
McClish, Thomas	321		
McConathy, Emma			2014
McConathy, F. A. (Mrs.)	2014		
McConnell, William E.		1440, 1664, 2305	
McCowen, Hale		3078	
McCown, Chester B.			3460
McCown, Elizabeth			3460
McCown, Ethel J.			3460
McCown, George M.	3460		
McCown, George R.			3460
McCoy, G. L.	327		
McCracken, Emma			949
McCracken, George F.			949
McCracken, Jasper	949	947	
McCray, W. L.		4108	
McCullough, David A.			503
McCullough, Mary L.			503
McCullough, Robert	503		
McCumiskey, Dasie E.			1820
McCumiskey, David J.			1820
McCumiskey, Florence I.			1820
McCumiskey, James			1820
McCumiskey, Levi			1820
McCumiskey, Raymond J.			1820
McCumiskey, Rose	1820		
McDermott, William		705	
McDonald, Alexander C.	85		
McDonald, J. R.		194	
McDonald, John		1324	
McDonald, M. L.		2416	
McDonald, Mark L.		1644	
McDonnell, Henry		2666	
McDonough, John		2611, 2775, 3714	
McDuffie, J. H.		3253	
McElarney, Frank		710	
McElwain, A. E.	3917		

Name	Principal	Surety	Ward
McElwain, Agnes			3917
McElwain, Augustus			3917
McElwain, Carrie B.			3917
McElwain, George			3917
McFarlane, George		4075	
McGee, Cerro Gordo (Mrs.)	1984		
McGee, Irene			1984
McGee, James H.	634, 1555, 1690		
McGee, Robert			490
McGee, William M.		1984	
McGrew, James C.			1744, 2959
McGrew, James G.	2959		
McGrew, Sophia		2959	
McGuire, Cora E.			866
McGuire, Cornelius		176	
McGuire, T.		1238	
McKamy, James W.		5	
McKeadney, Hugh			3425
McKeadney, Katie	3425		
McKinley, D. E.		1772	
McKinney, Katie			1990
McLaughlin, Michael		641	
McMackin, James		2780	
McMinn, Charles V.			931
McMinn, John		937, 1016	
McMinn, Joseph A.			931
McMinn, Mary F.			931
McNamara, B.		459	
McNamara, Elizabeth			3276
McNamara, Loretta			3277
McNamara, M.		1247	
McNear, Clara			1474
McNear, George P.	1474, 3131	1293, 2346, 2954, 3861, 3899, 3965, 4041, 4284	
McNear, John A.		1474	
McPeak, Anthony	911, 912		
McPherson, Annie E.			778
McPherson, Bertha M.			1176

Name	Principal	Surety	Ward
McPherson, Charles W.			1176
McPherson, Early			778
McPherson, Ewell			778
McPherson, Lycurgus	1004, 1176	790½, 976	
McPherson, Mary			778
McPherson, Stonewall			778
McReynolds, Dennis H.	3823		
McReynolds, Emma	3655		
McReynolds, Frank Cleveland			3655
McReynolds, Jacob		1095	
McReynolds, James	179	436, 704	
McReynolds, Marion Ralph			3655
McReynolds, Mary Frances			3614, 3655
McReynolds, Roy M.			3823
McReynolds, Samuel Floyd			3655
McReynolds, Vernon Clifford			3655
McReynolds, William		179	
McWilliams, Arthur			3202
McWilliams, Arthur C.			3202
McWilliams, J. H.		329	
Mead, Alice C.			725
Mead, Catherine	725		
Mead, James A.	2021	780, 1535, 1666, 1878, 2283, 2897	
Meador, E. M.		351	
Means, Thomas J.		60	
Mecham, Harrison		76, 112	
Mee, Ava C.	1472		
Mee, Belle			1472
Mee, Thomas			1472
Meeker, A. P.	1187		
Meeker, Charles E.			1187
Meeker, Clementina S.			383
Meeker, Estella			383
Meeker, Frank L.			1187
Meeker, Orion S.			383
Meeker, Ralph W.			1187
Meeker, Stephen A.		383	
Meeker, William N.	383		
Melendy, Henry		1477	

Name	Principal	Surety	Ward
Melton, Clymina			1006
Melton, Jacob Newton			329
Melton, James Benjamin			1006
Melton, John Nelson			329
Melton, Mary Catharine			329
Melton, Robert Wilson			1006
Melton, William Woodson			1006
Mendonca, J. J.		3596	
Menefee, Sarah			341
Meneray, P. A.		4001	
Merchant, Frederick H.			1035
Merchant, Joel	1035		
Merchant, T. S.		2611	
Meredith, J. H.		1647	
Meriwether, Elizabeth B.	3714		
Meriwether, H. D.	2611		
Meriwether, Herbert F.			2611
Meriwether, Herbert Francis			3714
Meriwether, Randolph			3714
Meriwether, Randolph M.			2611
Merritt, Clifford E.			3266
Merritt, E. C.		3250, 3482½	
Merritt, Edson C.	3266		
Merritt, John		2308	
Messersmith, Gertrude M.			3708
Messersmith, Mabel C.			3708
Meyer, Anton		750, 1933	
Meyer, Augusta			621
Meyer, Carolina Louisa			1523
Meyer, Catharina Bertha			1523
Meyer, F. A.	3502, 3899	1933, 2398, 3861, 4203	
Meyer, Frederick			620
Meyer, Gladys F.			2903
Meyer, Julia			621
Meyer, Kate	3351		
Meyer, Katy			621
Meyer, Lawrence			1523
Meyer, Linda Z.			2903
Meyer, Lorentz		1523	

Name	Principal	Surety	Ward
Meyer, Margaretha Salome			1523
Meyer, S.		778	
Meyer, Samuel		771	
Meyer, William			621
Meyer, William Jacob			1523
Meyerholtz, H.		1348	
Meyerholtz, Henry	1437	2013	
Michelson, George		3838	
Middleton, Walter V.			532
Milam, Benjamin L.			1981
Milam, M. S.		1981	
Milam, Thomas		1981	
Miles, T. W.		1140	
Millar, J. W.		3919	
Miller, Andrew			1989
Miller, Armelia M.			928
Miller, Bertha J.			1989
Miller, C. C.	135		
Miller, C. S.			4223
Miller, Caroline	1172		
Miller, Charles A.			1989
Miller, Charles C.	135, 136		
Miller, Daniel E.			135
Miller, Edmond H.			120
Miller, Frederick H.			940
Miller, G. T.		2176	
Miller, George		3626	
Miller, George E.			940
Miller, George K.			88
Miller, George Kay		135	
Miller, George T.		2588	
Miller, George W.		85	
Miller, J. R.		2611	
Miller, James R.			928
Miller, Jeanie M.			1989
Miller, John	1989		
Miller, John O.			1989
Miller, Lewis			1031
Miller, Lizzie E.			1172
Miller, Lucy P.			1989

Name	Principal	Surety	Ward
Miller, Mary		135, 136	
Miller, Mary A.			136
Miller, Mary J.			928
Miller, Mary Jane			120
Miller, Nannie E.			928
Miller, Rachel			928
Miller, Thomas		345	
Miller, Thomas B.		887	
Miller, Valentine			354
Miller, Wallace E.			1172
Miller, Zerilda	928		
Millington, Anna Electa			730
Millington, Buchanan			730
Millington, John			730
Millington, Nancy Maria	730		
Millington, Seth			730
Millington, Zachariah			730
Mills, A. J.		821	
Mills, Andrew		368	
Mills, George W.		1375	
Minetti, G. Perelli		3742	
Minetti, Jeanne Montalon	3742		
Mingus, Peter			929
Minoggio, Ambrogio			2192, 2971
Minoggio, Louis			2192, 2971
Minoggio, Mary	2192		
Miser, Frank S.			1535
Miser, Hannah	1535		
Miser, Mary E.			1535
Miser, Ross N.			1535
Mitchell, Armor W.			2909
Mitchell, Benjamin	25		
Mitchell, Evelyn D.			2909
Mitchell, Merle E.			2909
Mitchener, J.		1736, 2085	
Moan, Catherine			2308
Mobley, John Elmer	3408		
Mock, Eliza A.		1160	
Mock, Wesley	1168	515, 634, 1160	
Modini, Lorenzo	3613	2103, 2461, 2941	

Name	Principal	Surety	Ward
Moffet, John		1006	
Moland, John			2469
Molseed, Robert		1065	
Monahan, Ann	1209		
Monahan, Catharine Teressa			1233
Monahan, Catherine T.			1844
Monahan, Eugene		1209	
Monahan, Maggie A.		1209	
Monahan, Mary		1844	
Monahan, Mary L.			1209
Monahan, Mary Hanora			1233
Monahan, Patrick, Sr.	1233		
Monahan, Thomas F.	1844		
Monahan, Thomas Francis			1233
Monmonier, William B.		1557	
Moore, Charles			330, 790½, 1004
Moore, E.		651	
Moore, Elizabeth Ellen			330
Moore, Francis M.			330
Moore, Henrietta			330, 790½, 1004
Moore, Laura			330
Moore, Laura A.			790½
Moore, Luticia	330		
Moore, Myrta			1405
Moore, P.		3642	
Moore, P. L.	790½		
Moore, Perry			330
Moore, R. D.		3516	
Moore, Robert Drake		2631	
Moore, William T.			586
Mordecai, Eva T.	3671		
Mordecai, William			3671
Morin, Josiah	552		
Morris, H. B.		2901	
Morris, Joseph H. P.		1586, 2267	
Morris, W. H.		704	
Morrison, John		1329	
Morrow, John	3496		
Morrow, Samuel		5	

Name	Principal	Surety	Ward
Morse, A.	406	1501	
Morse, Amasa		1641	
Morton, W. H.		262	
Mosely, A. P.		2689	
Mothorn, Cashia S.		2675	
Mothorn, Cashia Sylvania (Mrs.)		2777	
Mothorn, David H.	2588		
Mothorn, Emily Dessie			2588
Mothorn, F. C.	3289, 3907	2675, 3288	
Mothorn, Lydia	2588		
Mothorn, P. D.		2675	
Mothorn, Sarah A.		2675, 3289, 3907	
Mothorn, Sarah Adaline		2777	
Mountjoy, Lula F.			770
Mountjoy, Mary L.	770		
Mountjoy, Mary L. P.	2010		
Mowbray, James R.		1042	
Mowbray, Mary J.		2796	
Moyer, John A.	2473		
Muldry, Martin		1233	
Mulgrew, J. F.		1824	
Mulgrew, John F.		1853	
Mullally, Patrick		1076	
Mullaly, John			1076
Muller, Amanda Louise			2712
Muller, Francis Leon			2712
Muller, Mary B.			2712
Muller, Mary Barbet			2712
Mulvehill, Ellen G.			2122
Mulvehill, M. (Mrs.)		3259	
Mulvehill, Margaret	2122		
Mulvenay, P.		995	
Munday, Alice			684
Munday, C. F.			684
Munday, Elizabeth	684		
Munday, Fanny			684
Munday, M. E. C.			684
Murdock, L. A.	1717		
Murphey, John	641, 705		
Murphy, Armidale			1657

Name	Principal	Surety	Ward
Murphy, George B.		3131, 4041	
Murphy, John		2308	
Murphy, William	1657		
Murray, Mary Alice			106
Muther, Frank		1455, 1836	
Mutz, Henry		722	
Myers, Dudley D.		129	
Nace, E. J.		416	
Nagle, F. G.		1217	
Nagle, William L.	1978		
Nalley, A. B.	1006	926, 1079, 1473	
Nason, John M.			475
Nason, Mary E.			475
Nason, Richard H.	475		
National Surety Company of New York		2954, 3857, 4149, 4150, 4243, 4318, 4344	
Nauert, Frederick A.		4373	
Neblett, Edward		529	
Necker, Bryant Taylor Earl			3283
Necker, Mary E.	3283		
Needham, Festus		826, 1065, 1287	
Needham, Jessie Ruby			300
Neeley, Edith Mabel			2777
Neeley, Keith Jacob			2777
Neeley, Lena May			2777
Neeley, Rachel Susan			2777
Neeley, William	2777		
Neeley, William Harten			2777
Neely, T. L.		1666	
Neil, James	124		
Neil, Katie			1439
Neil, Samuel		137	
Neil, Sarah C.			124
Neuburger, Morris		3502	
Nevill, Joseph N.		5	
Newberry, C. R.		3717	
Newburgh, E.		668, 808	
Newcom, Edgar			4140

Name	Principal	Surety	Ward
Newcom, Gertrude			4140
Newcom, Gesina	4140		
Newell, J. H.		3616	
Nichols, Martha Augusta (Mrs.)		2777	
Nickels, Thomas A.		1744	
Nisson, C.		2817	
Nisson, J.		2642	
Nobles, Harmon	3625	3626	
Noonan, George P.	485, 932, 2416	299, 1031, 1104, 1168, 1275, 1321, 1555, 1690, 1833, 1970, 2081, 2117	
Noonan, P. H.		1966	
Noonan, Patrick H.		1543, 2181	
Noonan, Paul M.			2416
Norris, Alferetta			3060
Norris, Basil S.			3060
Norton, Charles		2763	
Norton, E. M.		2290, 2537	
Norton, Eliza J.	2763		
Norton, Elizabeth Jane			2427
Norton, John Lewis			2427
Norton, L. A.		843½, 1006, 2021, 2537	
Norton, Lew A.		2290, 2616	
Nowell, John W.		4173	
Nuckolls, Nathaniel		174	
Nugent, Thomas		5	
Nunes, M. S.		3469	
Nye, B. M.	3562	1739	
Nye, B. Max			3562
Nye, Elsa H.			3562
Nye, Frances A.			3562
Nye, Helen			3562
Nye, Pauline P.			3562
O'Brien, J. C.		475	
O'Connor, Amy J.			3945
O'Connor, Edward W.			3945
O'Connor, Eleanor C.			3945

Name	Principal	Surety	Ward
O'Connor, Mary T.	3945		
O'Connor, Robert J.			3945
O'Farrell, Cathal			1203
O'Farrell, Florence			1203
O'Farrell, Gerald			1203
O'Farrell, John J.	1203		
O'Hara, John	1439	3945	
O'Leary, Patrick			826
O'Neale, W. T.		570	
O'Sullivan, Daniel		4247	
Oakes, Anthony G.		22	
Oates, James W.	1833, 2117, 3666		
Oettl, Bertha			1344
Oettl, Frank			1344
Oettl, Maria M.	1344		
Ogan, David P.			650
Ogan, Kittie V.			649
Ogan, Mary A.			648
Olson, Frederick Morris			3873
Ontis, John	344		
Ordway, Arah	333		
Ordway, Drucilla Helen			333
Ordway, Martha Jane			333
Ordway, Mary Abby			333
Ormsby, J. S.		152	
Orr, Charles			1105
Orr, John	1105		
Orr, Thomas D.		3078	
Orr, W. J. T.		2516, 2868, 3872	
Ortman, George E.	2953		
Ortman, Thomas			2953
Osborn, S. L.		1824	
Otis, Charles W.		3385	
Otis, Elizabeth	1189		
Otis, Frederick W.			1189
Otis, Isaac		1189	
Otis, Leonard			1189
Otis, Lewis S.			1189
Otterson, Agnes	175		

Name	Principal	Surety	Ward
Ottolini, Eda			3660
Ottolini, Henry			3660
Ottolini, Lily			3660
Ottolini, Maria	3660		
Overholser, Barton E.			1713
Overholser, W. R.	1713		
Overton, A. P.	704, 1031	422, 1168, 1555, 1690, 2081, 2334, 2589, 2788	
Overton, J. P.		2400, 2655, 2712, 2964, 3801, 3815	
Overton, John P.	1275, 2589	1104, 2305, 2631, 2997, 3050, 3189, 3283	
Owen, George E.		4085	
Owen, M. V.	980		
Owen, Thomas H.			980
Owens, James		2044	
Pacific Surety Company		3226, 3297, 3298, 3484, 3651	
Pacific Surety Company of California		3052	
Paddock, D. J.		3757	
Page, Charles E.			4292
Page, Robert C.		570	
Paine, Clara E.			515
Paine, Etta K.			515
Paine, Lula			515
Painter, J. M.		576	
Paivo, Mariano			4338
Palmer, James M.	918		
Palmer, Lottie Bertha			391
Palmer, Wales L.	940		
Palmer, William		641	
Palmer, William J.		3276, 3277	
Pangburn, Annie Eugenia			748
Parent, Arthur M.			4284
Parent, Arthur W.			4284
Parent, Hattie M.	4284		

Name	Principal	Surety	Ward
Parker, E. D.		396	
Parker, Freeman		1283	
Parker, George J.			2085
Parks, D. H.		540, 906	
Parks, H. G.		135	
Parks, S. L.		3202	
Parrent, Evermont		549	
Parsons, John I.		2909	
Parsons, Mary F.	2655		
Passalacqua, A. D.		2488, 2636, 3877	
Patchett, Dosha I.			4072
Patchett, John M.			4072
Patchett, Mary O.	4072		
Patchett, Roy C.			4072
Patchett, Ulysses A.			4072
Patchett, Walter C.			4072
Patten, Hugh	1532	85	
Patten, John D.		137	
Patten, Joseph		85	
Patten, Nettie			1532
Patten, Thomas B.	85, 141, 142	136, 140, 142	
Patterson, William	936		
Patteson, Addie		2117	
Patteson, William	2117		
Patton, Charles		182	
Patton, Mary A.	182		
Patton, Robert A.			182
Patty, L. H.	2115		
Paula, John A.		3596	
Paula, Manuel		1293	
Pauli, Albert F.			1083
Pauli, Caroline J.	1083		
Pauli, Eloisa F.			1083
Pauli, Emil H.			1083
Pauli, F. Albert	1083	698	
Pauli, G. T.	572	456, 524, 829	
Pauli, H. S.			572
Pauli, Robert J.			1083
Paxton, B. W.		3666	
Payne, Hannah			819

Name	Principal	Surety	Ward
Payne, Newton			819
Payne, William W.	819		
Pearce, George		216, 918, 1439	
Pechaco, George			1440
Peck, Mabel			1517
Peck, Mabel E.			1517
Pedigo, E. M.		1747	
Pedrotti, Luis		4051	
Peers, Alexander		1759	
Pepper, Clarence			4246
Pepper, Gertrude			4246
Pepper, John			4246
Pepper, May			4246
Pepper, Phebe		4284	
Percival, W. C.		940, 1420	
Pereira, Daniel A.		1293	
Perkins, G. R.		475	
Perrin, Robert		1647	
Perry, C. A.	1829		
Perry, Jeanette V.	2085		
Peters, Manuel		1746	
Petersen, Claus		4072	
Petersen, Hans P.		1951	
Petersen, Hans Peter		1951	
Peterson, A.		1150	
Peterson, Ann Frances			365
Peterson, Augustus			1150
Peterson, Dick			365
Peterson, Eleanor [Elmer R.]			1150
Peterson, Elizabeth	365		
Peterson, George W.		439	
Peterson, James C.			1150
Peterson, Jane Ellen			365
Peterson, John L.		3823	1150
Peterson, Lillie			2316
Peterson, Martha A.	1150	1284	
Peterson, Nathaniel Houston			365
Peterson, Pelina A.	2316		
Peterson, Thomas C.		439	
Peterson, William			1150

Name	Principal	Surety	Ward
Petery, Lillie			1217
Petray, C. B.	3633		
Petray, G. W.		250	
Petray, R. A.		3633	
Peugh, James A.		755	
Peugh, Jennie	1360		
Pezzaglia, Filippo		2192	
Pfalzgraf, Elsie			3846
Pfalzgraf, Eva			3846
Pfalzgraf, Justina L.			3846
Pfalzgraf, Lydia	3846		
Pfalzgraf, Oscar H.			3846
Pfalzgraf, Ruth			3846
Pfalzgraf, Theodore			3846
Pfau, John		270, 475, 750	
Pfister, C.		1808	
Pfister, Conrad		911, 912	
Phair, Carter Niles			4007
Phair, Lucinda			4007
Phair, Sara	4007		
Phillips, A. A.	2897		
Phillips, D. D.		1644	
Phillips, Fannie P.			3588
Phillips, George D.			2897
Phillips, Jacob		1507, 1713	
Phillips, John			485
Phillips, Lulu J.	3588		
Phillips, M. E.	2897		
Phillips, Maud R.			2897
Phillips, O. F.		1140	
Phillips, S. E.		2169	
Phillpot, Marion Jariat			188
Phillpot, William Addison			188
Pickle, C. J.		489	
Pickle, J. F.		789	
Pickle, J. R.		489	
Pieratt, John M.	1175		
Pierce, A. J.	604	399	
Pierce, Arthur L.			399
Pierce, Mary J.	1400		

Name	Principal	Surety	Ward
Pierce, Sarah C.	399		
Pierce, William S.			604, 1400
Pierson, Hiram		34	
Piezzi, S.		2342	
Piezzi, Victor		1837, 4051, 4196	
Pimm, Jacob	1398	1315	
Pina, Maria Antonia			216
Pinelli, A.		2941, 2971, 3613	
Pinschower, S.		3061	
Piper, John Jay		487	
Pipher, Philip		1739	
Pitkin, Alpha A.			3619
Pitkin, David W.	3619		
Pitkin, Sarah		3619	
Pitkin, Zelda			3619
Pitt, Charles W.			2270
Pitt, Ida			2270
Pitt, J. W.	2270		
Pitt, Maud			2270
Pitt, Ralph			2270
Plunket, John			2267
Poehlmann, C.		616, 709	
Poehlmann, Conrad	494, 2435	544, 750, 1749, 1834	
Poehlmann, Henry J.		2435, 3502	
Poehlmann, Martin		750	
Poggetto, Charles Dal	4318		
Polk, Charles Ephraim			2470
Polk, Edward Hubbard			2470
Polk, Ella Josephine			2470, 3784
Polk, William Clement			2470
Pollard, Thomas		1896	
Pometta, D.		4355	
Pometta, Deborah		4355	
Pond, Mary			368
Pool, Frank J.	3838		
Pool, Henry J.	83	238, 482, 607, 937	
Pooler, H. L.		490	

Name	Principal	Surety	Ward
Poppe, Catherine		1344	
Poppe, Julius A.		85	
Porter, Daniel J.		123	
Porter, H. J.		2569	
Porter, William W.		1281	
Pots, Martha A.			123
Potter, Joseph		2927	
Potter, Joseph H.		3881	
Powell, Jesse			1473
Powell, John		578	
Powell, Nettie			1473
Powell, R.	1473	778, 976, 1006, 1517, 1782	
Powell, Ransom		819	
Powers, D.		490	
Powers, David		729	
Powers, David P.	720		
Pozzi, Fillipo			4196
Pozzi, M. C.		2342	
Pozzi, Phillip			4196
Pozzi, Rafael	4196		
Prescott, George W.		1349	
Pressley, Emma W.	1281		
Pressley, James F.			1281
Pressley, John G.		1281	
Pressley, Louise W.			1281
Prewett, Francis G.			607
Prewett, Francis Graham			238
Prewett, George			238, 607
Prewett, James	238		
Prewett, Martha Ann			238
Prewett, Samuel		238	
Price, Henry Lucas			126
Price, John		506	
Price, Pitman Hardin			126
Pries, George		1976	
Prince, J. B.		2402	
Prindle, William		1096, 1850, 1966, 1996, 2827	
Procter, Charles E.		908	

Name	Principal	Surety	Ward
Proctor, T. J.	1499	1104	
Prows, D. W.			2636
Prows, Elizabeth	3127		
Prows, James F.			3127
Prows, Sylvester W.			3127
Puckett, C. W.	487		
Puckett, G. W.			487
Puckett, S. A.		487	
Pugh, James A.		62	
Pugh, Malvina			262
Pullen, Granville		2507	
Purcell, Matthias		17	
Purrine, A. S.		1187, 1390	
Purvine, Charles	122		
Purvine, Charles Francis			505
Purvine, J. C.		505	
Purvine, John C.	2408		
Purvine, Margaret J.			505
Purvine, Mary Jane	505		2408
Purvine, T. B.		1400, 2408	
Purvine, Thomas Byron			505
Purvine, Walter S.			505
Purvine, William			505
Purvine, William B.		2408	
Pyatt, George			1275
Pyne, Henry H.	2625		
Pyne, Willie H.			2625
Quartaroli, L.	3686		
Quinn, Stephen		270	
Raabe, M.		1745	
Raabe, M.		2957	
Rafael, A. J.	2087		
Rafael, J. E.		2111	
Rafael, M. E.	1746, 2111	1868, 2087	
Ragan, Joel		1532	
Ragsdale, J. W.		1984	
Rains, Gallant		131	
Rainsbury, Caroline		3673	
Rambo, Arden M.	3673		
Rambo, Ardon	3673		

Name	Principal	Surety	Ward
Rambo, Jacob		336	
Rambo, Mary E.			3550
Rambo, Ruby			3673
Rambo, William		3673	
Randolph, Isaac N.	5		
Rathcke, Floyd Cecil			3281
Rathcke, Fred	1747		
Rathcke, Fred C.	3281		
Rathcke, Henrietta			3281
Rathcke, Lewis Carl			3281
Rathcke, Walter Linton			3281
Rayner, A.		3694	
Rayner, Aaron		3662	
Rea, M. A.		4292	
Read, Bertha A.			1730
Read, Decker Jewett			1730
Read, Mary			1730
Read, Minnie I.	1730		
Reading, George J.		3564	
Redmond, Francis M.			1543
Redmond, Mary Jane	1543		
Redmond, Philip J.			1543
Reed, Charles H.			426
Reed, Emiline J.			426
Reichardt, Emma			299
Remmel, Charles		1009, 1028	
Remmel, George E.		3835	
Respini, Americo		3581	
Respini, Henry			3581
Respini, Leodina		3581	
Respini, Mariana	3581		
Revermann, Charles	3919		
Reynolds, Emma			1242
Reynolds, Margaret M.			4203
Reynolds, W. D.	1850, 3198	1780, 2849, 3666	
Rice, C. B.		475, 651	
Rice, J. H.		2459	
Rice, John E.		198	
Rice, Moses P.		198	
Richards, Curtis H.			2763

Name	Principal	Surety	Ward
Richards, Ethel M.			2763
Richards, Frank			1016
Richards, Harrison A.			2763
Richards, Jennie J.			2763
Richardson, Achillles		85	
Richardson, Holena E.			1690
Richardson, Mildred			3840
Richmond, F.		329	
Rickett, J. W.		2457	
Rickman, D. H.		435	
Rickman, Mary E.		2999	
Ricksecker, Helen Pearson			1682
Ricksecker, L. E.	1682		
Rideout, N. D.		1349	
Riedi, V.		1151, 3351	
Rien, George E.			1561
Rien, Nellie J.			1561
Riewerts, Christian C.			3180
Riewerts, Martha C.			3180
Riewerts, Mathilda (Mrs.)	3180		
Riewerts, Minnie H.			3180
Riewerts, Ocke M.			3180
Riley, B. H.			4080
Riley, E. H.			4080
Riley, Elizabeth	4080		
Roach, P.		3616	
Roach, Patrick	1076	3342	
Roach, Thomas		826	
Roan, John	17		
Robbins, George A.			4291
Roberts, Alonzo		2498	
Roberts, Charles	174	270	
Roberts, Frank		3942	
Roberts, Hugh		2266, 2721, 3509	
Roberts, Hugh J.		1265	
Roberts, John S.	515		
Robertson, James Calhoun			1670
Robertson, John		2045	
Robertson, Sarah Jessie			1670
Robertson, William A.	1670		

Name	Principal	Surety	Ward
Robinson, Ethel L.			3838
Robinson, George	1930		
Robinson, Roy L.			3838
Roche, John J.		1203	
Rochford, Josephine M.			3496
Rochford, Josephine Morrow			3189
Rodehaver, George W.	3784, 4223		
Rodgers, A. W.		124	
Rodgers, J. P.	1507		1868
Rogers, Frank			2111
Rogers, Hattie D.			2202
Rogers, Howard D.			2202
Rogers, James M.		503	
Rogers, Louisa M.	2202		
Rogers, W. K.		1083	
Rogers, William			2111
Rohrer, C. F.		4062	
Rohrer, Charles F.		3396	
Rohrer, Fred		85	
Roney, J. M.		532, 932, 1141, 1321, 1480, 1663, 1759, 1930, 2054	
Ronsheimer, John A.	2337		
Ronsheimer, Katy	1836		
Ronsheimer, Lizzie			1836
Ronsheimer, Mary			1836
Ronsheimer, Peter			1836
Ronsheimer, Tony			1836
Root, Jeremiah		122	
Rose, Fred		4239	
Rose, J. E. B.		2020	
Rose, J. W.	1141	2402	
Roseburgh, A.		1135	
Rosenberg, W.		986, 1517, 1535, 2829	
Rosenburg, W.		2829	
Rosenquest, Hans		2588	
Rosenthal, Joseph		771	
Ross, Benjamin F.	3662		

Name	Principal	Surety	Ward
Ross, D. L. B.		348	
Ross, Losson		3662	
Ross, Milburn		1284	
Rosseter, James H.		159	
Rowland, William		1141	
Rowlett, Henry			293
Rowlson, Eliza A.			3805
Rugg, J. T.			4340
Rule, C. H. S.		1833	
Rule, C. S.			570
Rule, E. J.			570
Rule, Elizabeth	570		
Rule, N. A.			570
Rule, William J.			570
Runyon, Charles D.			2902
Runyon, Charles E.			889
Runyon, Ella	2902		
Runyon, Emma			889
Runyon, Frederick M.			889
Runyon, Mary	889		
Runyon, Raleigh B.			2902
Runyon, S.		889	
Runyon, Solomon		889	
Rupe, Sam H.		85, 819	
Rupe, Samuel H.		98, 571, 635, 790½	
Russell, A. W.		117	
Russell, Mary A.			571
Russell, William F.			571
Rutherford, James A.			1186
Rutherford, Thomas			1186
Rutledge, Thomas		1440	
Ryan, Pierce			270
Ryland, Caius T.		3364	
Saare, Louis		3742	
Sackett, D. A.		475	
Sacry, D. S.		351	
Sales, John		1065, 3509	
Sales, W. L.	3509		
Salter, Eliza			2619

Name	Principal	Surety	Ward
Samuels, Thomas M.			4128
Sanborn, W. B.		1739	
Sandford, H. T.	978		
Sandford, Louis N.			557
Santos, Alfred			4025
Santos, Antonio	4025, 4338		4025
Santos, Ellen			4025
Santos, Gussie			3509
Santos, Jackson			4025
Santos, Philomena			4025
Santos, Sam			4025
Santos, William			4025
Sargent, Alvin Z.			1354, 1512
Sargent, Joshua C.	1354		
Sargent, Nanie E.			1354
Sargent, Nynie E.			1512
Sargent, Ruth			1354
Sargent, Ruth I.			1512
Sartori, Charles			2342
Sartori, Giuseppe	2342		
Savage, C. W.		1609, 2903	
Sawyer, Charles H.			1654
Sawyer, E. A.		1477	
Sawyer, Florence			1654
Sawyer, Lucy H.	1654		
Schaupp, Katherine	3796		
Scheibel, Theobald		1451	
Schetter, Otto		1175	
Schieck, John Gottfried		1240	
Schieffer, Albert A.			2071
Schieffer, C. H.	2071		
Schieffer, Clara H.			2071
Schieffer, Emma H.			2071
Schieffer, Frances C.			2071
Schieffer, Frederick H.			2071
Schieffer, Joseph C.			2071
Schieffer, Louis E.			2071
Schieffer, Millie I.			2071
Schieffer, Robert A.			2071
Schieffer, William H.			2071

Name	Principal	Surety	Ward
Schillingman, J. William		3397	
Schmitt, George	243	1348, 1378	
Schnittger, C. H.		1976, 2390	
Schnittger, Claus H.			2485
Schnittger, Friedericke (Mrs.)		2485	
Schocken, S.		2103, 3613	
Schroder, John		1794	
Schultz, Frederick O.			3104
Schultz, Otto		2903	
Schulze, Frederick O.			3104
Schumacher, Jessie M.	3881		
Schwab, F. J.		3519	
Schweitzer, Albert			1490
Schweitzer, William	1490		
Sciutti, Antonio			4318
Scoggan, John		2931	
Scoggan, John M.		2498	
Scott, B. W.	887		
Scott, Edna Bell			1477
Scott, Edna Belle			1477
Scott, Eli		3827	
Scott, George W.			3427
Scott, H. W.	1477		
Scott, J. C.		1641	
Scott, Lloyd A.			3427
Scott, Luke			887
Scott, Mary	3427		5
Scott, Pearl			3427
Scott, Sarah A.	2923		
Scott, Sylvester	1042		
Scoville, Benjamin			1664
Scudder, N. W.		1369	
Seaman, Jesse F.		222, 568	
Sears, Franklin		355	
Seavy, Laura V.			2435
Seavy, R.		604	
Seavy, Robert		525	
Seavy, Robert T.			2435, 3535
Seawell, David H.		627	
Seawell, William N.		627	

Name	Principal	Surety	Ward
Seegelken, E. A.		1794, 1836	
Seegelken, J. W.		2469, 3251	
Seeley, David			1586
Seibel, C. J.		3531	
Seibt, Gustav		1989	
Seibt, Mary		1989	
Seitz, Calvin		2014	
Sensibaugh, Alzirus			1663
Sensibaugh, Johnson			1663
Shafer, Ignitz			2232
Shafer, Sarah C.	2232		
Shane, Adam		755, 1052	
Sharon, Adelaide L.			540
Sharon, C. T. (Mrs.)		1114	
Sharon, Catharine T.	540		
Sharon, Edmund M.			540
Sharon, Margaretta R.			540
Sharp, Albert		3694	
Sharp, Solomon A.		130	
Shattuck, D. P.		98	
Shattuck, David O.	85		
Shattuck, Frank W.		85	
Shattuck, Richard		98	
Shaw, C. B.		3992, 4108	
Shaw, Ella L.			996
Shaw, Gertrude M.			4108
Shaw, I. E.		794	
Shaw, Isaac E.	996	3857	
Shaw, Mary H.	3440		
Shaw, Minerva M.	4108		
Shaw, N. R.		1187	
Shaw, S. H.		1405	
Shea, C.		1815	
Shea, Con		1820, 3189, 3526	
Shedd, Charles			1540
Shedd, Clarence			1540
Sheldon, D. B.		1682	
Shelford, Lorena L.			3078
Shelford, Mabel W.			3078
Shelford, P. L.	3078		

Name	Principal	Surety	Ward
Shelton, A. C.		2504, 3610	
Shepherd, J. S.		475	
Sheridan, James		1105	
Sherman, A.	3708		
Sherman, Allie A.	2681		
Sherman, C. J.		3708	
Sherman, Dell			2681
Sherman, Ellen			2681
Sherman, Franklin		3708	
Sherman, James G.			2681
Sherman, Sarah			2681
Sherry, Thomas		1305	
Sherwood, Effie			3678
Sherwood, Glen Milton			3678
Sherwood, Ruby A.	3678		
Shinn, A. J.			345
Shinn, Andrew J.			743
Shinn, Cynthia	345		
Shinn, E.			345
Shinn, E. J.			345
Shinn, Eliza J.			743
Shinn, J.			345
Shinn, J. O.		238	
Shinn, John Davis			743
Shinn, Mary Ellen			743
Shinn, Paul			3776
Shinn, R. F.			345
Shinn, Robert F.	743		
Shinn, S.			345
Shinn, S. M.		596	
Shinn, Shirley			3776
Shinn, Silas M.		1240	
Shoemake, Charley D.			2589
Shoemake, Ella C.			2589
Shores, Ida F.	4275		
Shores, Leander		2638	4275
Short, O. B.			2327
Shudy, John		3605	
Shuster, Jacob F.		1390	
Shuster, James E.		1390	

Name	Principal	Surety	Ward
Shuster, Josie			1390
Shuster, Marvin			1390
Shuster, Sarah E.	1390		
Sicotte, Fred			2516
Silberstein, J.		3714, 4140	
Silva, Charles J.		4025	
Silva, M. G.		1265	
Silva, Mary A.		3597	
Silver, Joseph		4015, 4338	
Silvia, A. J.	1293		
Silzle, Benjamin C.			2169
Silzle, George	2169		
Silzle, Kate A.			2169
Silzle, Lena A.			2169
Silzle, Minnie			2169
Silzle, Roy J.			2169
Silzle, William H.			2169
Simi, Alvira			3852
Simi, Isabella	3852		
Simi, Louis		3852	
Simmons, Charles			597
Simmons, Ida			597
Simmons, James S.			976
Simons, John S.	648, 649, 650		
Simpson, Alice M.			3818
Simpson, E. A.			368
Simpson, Philip A.			3818
Simpson, R. M.			368
Simpson, William B.			3818
Simpson, Willie B.	3818		
Singley, Charles E.	1661		
Sink, Daniel		996	
Sink, William D.		996	
Sioli, Victor		2169	
Skaggs, Alex, Jr.			2792
Skaggs, Alexander		127, 414	
Skaggs, E. W.	3147		
Skaggs, Eben	414		
Skaggs, Edward W.			2792
Skaggs, Emma L.			190

Name	Principal	Surety	Ward
Skaggs, Julia	2792		
Skaggs, Julia (Mrs.)		3147	
Skaggs, W. W.		3147	
Skiffington, John		641, 1533, 4324	
Skiffington, John R.		4072	
Skinner, Ada			1355
Skinner, L. T.	1286	1355	
Skinner, W. G.	1355	1286	
Slattery, William J.	639		
Sloan, Elizabeth R.			2927
Sloan, John R.			2927
Sloan, Maggie E.			2927
Slocum, George		1517	
Slusser, Bayard B.	1294		
Slusser, L. S. B.			1294
Slusser, Levi S. B.		238	
Slusser, Martin E.		1294	
Slusser, S. Effie	3214		
Slusser, Sarah		1294	
Slusser, William P.	1294	1294	
Smith, A. H.	436, 1870	436, 599	
Smith, Abbie			724
Smith, Adaline D.			416
Smith, Albert O.			416
Smith, Alexander H.	672		
Smith, Bertha E.	3835		
Smith, C. J.		3147	
Smith, C. P.	3610		
Smith, Charles B.			3061
Smith, Chauncey B.			416
Smith, Clifford F.			3835
Smith, Edmund	3484		
Smith, Elenora			137
Smith, Eliza			85
Smith, Everett R.			3835
Smith, Ezekiel			137
Smith, Frank	304		
Smith, George T.			634
Smith, George Taylor			634
Smith, George W.			98

Name	Principal	Surety	Ward
Smith, Governeur			304
Smith, H. W.		1068½, 2484	
Smith, Harry			932
Smith, Henry W.		1480	
Smith, I. P.		196	
Smith, Isaac			98
Smith, Isaac B.			98
Smith, Isaac P.	252		
Smith, J. P.		190, 436	
Smith, Jacob		159, 188	
Smith, James		665	159
Smith, James B.			137, 159
Smith, James F.		720	
Smith, James J.	98		
Smith, James M.			85
Smith, John			85
Smith, John B.		639	
Smith, John Henry			416
Smith, John K.		341	
Smith, John P.			85
Smith, L. M.	2129		
Smith, Louisa Ellen			85
Smith, Manuela			159
Smith, Manuella			159
Smith, Marion			3484
Smith, Martha J.			137
Smith, Napoleon B.			98
Smith, P. B.	634		
Smith, Preston B.		126	
Smith, R. Press., Jr.		532	
Smith, Roy E.			3484
Smith, Russell			3610
Smith, Salome			3610
Smith, Sarah C.			672
Smith, Sidney			3610
Smith, Stephen M.			159
Smith, Thomas U.	196		
Smith, Verna M.			3835
Smith, Violet E.			3835
Smith, W. J.		3857	

Name	Principal	Surety	Ward
Smith, W. T.	3835		
Smith, Wayne			3610
Smith, William J.	137		
Smithers, George E.		3605	
Smyth, T. U.		190	
Smyth, Thomas U.	436		
Snider, Ella			227
Snider, George R.			1140
Snider, Jane	1140		
Snider, Lucy B.			1140
Snider, Mary E.			1140
Snook, E. B.		3767	
Snyder, Dan Edger			1286
Soldate, Albert			2954
Soldate, John	2954		
Soldate, M. A.	2954		
Soldati, Alex		2954	
Solomon, Charles	866	864, 1477	
Somes, G. R.		2897	
Somes, Mary Ellen	2897		
Sommers, Louisa		3295	
Sommers, Mary	3295		
Sommers, Minnie			3295
Sondheimer, E.		227	
Soules, S.		819	
Soules, Stephen	571	795	
Sousa, M. C.		4025	
Sparks, George W.		1083	
Spencer, Charles			897
Spencer, George			897
Spencer, Nancy			897
Spencer, Rowena			897
Spencer, Shattuck			897
Spotswood, A.		1119	
Spotswood, Robert		587	
Springer, Christopf	1960		
Springer, Frank			1960
Springer, Lena			1960
Springer, Maria E.			1960
Sproule, George W.			808

Name	Principal	Surety	Ward
Squires, Harry			264
Squires, Harvy			264
Sroufe, John		124	
St. Clair, Estelle			2117
St. Clair, F. C.		1176	
St. Clair, Francis Marion			198
St. Clair, Frank C.	976		2117
St. Clair, Freddie			2117
St. Clair, James	198		
St. Clair, Mary E.		2117	
St. Clair, Mary Ellen			2117
St. Clair, Richardson			2117
St. Clair, William Wallace			198
Stacey, William			2102
Staedler, Elizabeth	1641		
Staedler, Harry			1641
Stafford, Edward P.			1278
Stafford, N. O.		100	
Stamer, Julius		2792	
Stanley, J. F.		3202	
Stanley, J. P.		505	
Stanly, A. J.		327	
Stapleton, Patrick	270		
Stapp, I. N.	107		
Starke, Francis			1603
Starke, Fred J.	1603		
Starke, Frederick	1135		
Starr, A. D.	1349		
Starr, Mary E.		2116	
Starr, William M.		1349	
Starr, Windfield			336
Starrett, Robert		3079	
Steadman, Amos		238	
Steadman, Amos D.		937	
Steadman, Charles			1079
Steadman, Grace			1079
Steadman, Ida M.			655
Steadman, Mabelle			1079
Steadman, Mary G. W.	937, 1079		
Steadman, Maud			1079

Name	Principal	Surety	Ward
Stearns, John P.			3364
Stearns, Martha T.	3364		
Stebbins, Emma (Mrs.)			4173
Stebbins, Lambert W.	4173		
Steel, James Henry			1829
Steel, Mabel			1626
Steiger, Edward	3679		
Steiger, Emma			3679
Steiger, Fritz			3679
Steiger, George			3679
Steiger, Herman			3679
Steiger, William			3679
Steiner, John R.	3044		
Steiner, John, Jr.			4150
Steiner, John, Sr.	4150		
Stengel, Christian		4164	
Stenzel, C.		2657	
Stephenson, John N.		3496	
Sterling, Carrie			1782
Sterling, Elizabeth			76
Sterling, James F.			1782
Stevens, William H.			272
Stewart, Abel		112	
Stewart, Ann	1834		
Stewart, Frank Lester			709
Stewart, Hannah M.	709		
Stewart, John A.			1834
Stewart, William Allen			709
Stites, A. H.		743, 1028	
Stites, Alex H.		1009	
Stockdale, Hugh	475		
Story, S. C.		655	
Stowell, Margaret R. E. A. B.			213
Stratton, F. W.		1697	
Straub, Anna C.		3858	
Stridde, Charles		3668, 3682	
Striening, M. J.		3064	
Strode, Charles			3633
Strode, George			3633
Strode, James			3633

Name	Principal	Surety	Ward
Strom, William	873	929	
Strong, John	3641	958	
Stryker, James A.			568
Stuart, A. McG.		2767, 3448	
Stump, J. A.		3733	
Stump, John Conrad			3872
Stump, Minnie S.	3872		
Stump, Vera V. G.			3872
Sullenger, Madison		60	
Sullivan, Catharine M.			705
Sullivan, Ellen F.			705
Sullivan, George E.			705
Sullivan, J. W.		1782	
Sullivan, John P.			705
Sullivan, Michael		270	
Sullivan, Robert Henry			709
Sutton, H. D.		305, 586	
Sutton, Hannah	2610		
Sutton, Hiram D.		641	
Swain, Georgia I.			724½
Swain, Mamie			1178
Swain, Mary D.			724½, 1178
Swain, R. M.		1996	
Swain, Susan I.			724½
Swank, J. W.		2316	
Sweeney, Jerry		705	
Sweetman, C. H.		327	
Sweetser, John A.		3488	
Swett, Frank H.	1512		
Swift, Granville P.		103, 355	
Swisher, J. R.	1824, 2626	1824, 2681, 2989, 3588	
Swisher, James R.		2989, 3962	
Switzer, Elizabeth			1082
Switzer, Henrietta			1082
Switzer, Henry			1082
Switzer, Viola			1082
Swygert, Isaac	2045	2044	
Swygert, John		2045	
Swygert, Sarah A.			2045

Name	Principal	Surety	Ward
Symonds, C. W.		1135	
Taft, Henry C.		738	
Talbot, Coleman	579		
Talbot, Courtney		333	
Talbot, Holeman		579	
Talbot, Holman		333	
Talbot, Kennedy B.			579
Talmadge, Samuel		2316, 2902, 2997	
Tarrant, Emily Augusta			1797
Tarrant, H. F.	1797		
Tarrant, Joseph Henry			1797
Tarrant, Rosalie			1797
Tarrant, Sophie A.			1797
Tarwater, Edward Lewis	3694		
Tate, A. F.		1867	
Tate, Alice	1867		
Tate, Augustine E.			103
Tate, Hazel D.			1867
Tate, J. H.		85	
Tate, Jesse T.			103
Tate, John H.			103
Tate, Josefa F.			103
Tate, Margaret A.			103
Tate, Minnie Ann			1867
Tate, Robert J.			1867
Tate, Thomas H.		85	
Taylor, Brown S.			3599
Taylor, John		216	81
Taylor, John S.		526, 1465, 1664, 1828, 1870, 2106, 2180, 3198, 3756, 3801	3599
Taylor, Nannie S.		3599	
Taylor, Palestine			81
Taylor, Putnam			81
Taylor, T. F.	3599	3835	
Taylor, Thomas Flint			3599
Taylor, Wayne			81
Teegarden, F. Josephine	1349		
Tempel, C.		1348, 1693	

Name	Principal	Surety	Ward
Tennent, Isabel Eva			552
Terschuren, G. F.		2715	
Thatcher, D.	790		
Thayer, Daniel S.		142	
The Aetna Indemnity Company of Hartford, Connecticut		4142, 4143	
The American Surety Company		3094	
The Title Guaranty and Surety Company		4275	
The Title Guaranty and Trust Company of Scranton, Pennsylvania		3868	
The United States Fidelity and Guaranty Company		3050, 3266, 3408, 3440, 3458, 3532, 3655, 3678, 3935, 3957, 3989, 4242	
Thielemann, Mary			243
Thielemann, Otto			243
Thilo, Anna	3297		
Thilo, C. A.			3297
Thomas, A.		426, 456	
Thomas, Alfred R.		3550	
Thomas, Bertha			2651
Thomas, Charles E.			1160
Thomas, David	490		
Thomas, Elsie	3942		
Thomas, Flora M.	1160		
Thomas, Henry R.	3550		
Thomas, Isaiah		336	
Thomas, Lorraine			3942
Thomas, Mabel			3942
Thomas, Oscar			2651
Thomas, Sylvia			2651
Thomas, W. E.	2651		
Thompson, Carrie A.			1609
Thompson, Charles H.	1609		
Thompson, Gertrude			2054
Thompson, J. J.		3427	
Thompson, Robert A.	1970		
Thompson, Rudolph	4287		
Thompson, Thomas L.	299	1970	

Name	Principal	Surety	Ward
Thompson, William A.		85	
Thompson, Wilmer			1970
Thurgood, Elizabeth M.			639
Thurgood, Margaret Elizabeth			233
Thurgood, Margaret G.	233		
Thurgood, Mary Ann			233, 639
Thurgood, William S.			639
Thurgood, William Sharp			233
Tighe, Kelly	826	639	
Timms, Ann			2914
Timms, Anthony			305
Timms, John H.	305		
Tivnen, John	1759	698	
Tivnen, Mary Clara			2282
Tobin, Patrick			168
Todd, Calvin	3298		
Todd, S. S.		125	
Tomasi, Alfonso M.		3710	
Tomasi, Americo L.		3710	
Tomasi, Fedela	3710		
Tomasi, Linda O.			3710
Tomasini, Americo F.	3066		
Tomasini, Juliet			1837
Tomasini, Lila			1837, 3066
Tomasini, Louis	1837		
Tomasini, Marino		3066	
Tomasini, Matteo	3066	1837	
Tomasini, Sabina		3066	
Tomasini, Waldo			1837
Tomasini, Waldo A.			1837, 3066, 4287
Tombs, Ann P.			2616
Torrance, S. H.	821		
Torrance, Sophia P.			3839
Torres, Manuel	159		
Totten, Edward			130
Totten, George Mansfield			130
Towey, Peter	1966, 3919	3532, 3919	
Towne, Beverly M.			2115
Towne, Lester B.		2115	
Towne, S. D.		684	

Name	Principal	Surety	Ward
Towne, Walter		2115	
Tracy, Charles			935
Tracy, Dora			935
Tracy, Eda			935
Tracy, Phoebe			935
Trask, Freeman		582	
Travers, Theodore O.			17
Travers, William M.			17
Traversi, Joseph		3066	
Treadway, Griffin		117	
Treadway, R. M.		117	
Trembley, A.		2181, 3818	
Trimble, George			950
Trimble, Louis			950
Trimble, Lucy E.			950
Trimble, Martha J.	950		
Trimble, William H.	535		
Trotter, R.		1284	
Truett, A. D.	2638		
Truett, M. K.	2638		
Truitt, J. W.		3917	
Truitt, John R.		780	
Trumbull, Luther			83
Tupper, G. A.		648, 649, 650, 721, 735, 1625, 1717, 2651	
Turner, Cornelius J.			176
Turner, G. J.		819	
Turner, James C.	176		
Turner, Jasper N.			176
Turner, John		908	
Turner, O. W.		3365	
Turner, R. W.	3104		
Turner, Sarepta A.			176
Turner, Serepta A.			176
Tuttle, Charles L.			2844, 3250
Tuttle, E. F.	4321		
Tuttle, Gladys Dexter			4321
Tuttle, Grace C.	3250		
Underhill, Charles		1345	

Name	Principal	Surety	Ward
Underhill, John Lee			1345
Underhill, Milley	1345		
Underhill, Neva			1345
Underhill, W. H.		1345	
Underwood, F. L.		525	
Underwood, Susanna M.			95
Ungewitter, H. W.	2516	3815	
Ungewitter, Mary	3815		
Unwiller, Lavinia		3876	
Unwiller, William		3876	
Upson, William A.		2636	
Urban, Frank			3083
Urban, Joseph			3083
Urban, Martha			3083
Urton, W. L.		755	
Vail, Anna B.	807		
Vail, Nellie			807
Valentine, Harrison	168		
Van Buren, E.		3427	
Van Doren, John S.		1540	
Vance, James M.		1472	
Vance, Robbin			2010, 2627
Vance, Stewart			2010, 2627
Vanderhoof, M. V.	2358		
Vanderleith, Elise	3813		
Vanderleith, Violet			3813
Vanwinkle, Thomas B.		126	
Vasques, P. J.		5, 85	
Vasquez, P. J.		85	
Vassar, Benjamin			1042
Vassar, Jacob			1042
Vaughan, Marvin T.	4273		
Vaughn, Bertha			1028
Vaughn, Daniel	188	85	
Vaughn, Spencer			1028
Vaughn, William			1028
Veal, William	316		
Veale, W. R.	3805	2102, 2470	
Veale, William R.		2610	
Veron, P. A.			1264

Name	Principal	Surety	Ward
Violetti, Angolina	2850		
Violetti, Joseph			2850
Vitaes, F. Perera		1746	
Vitoes, F. P.		3597	
Voss, Anna K.	4366		
Voss, Arthur Edwin			4366
Voss, Claus		2463	
Wade, Elizabeth			4273
Wade, Ina B. (Mrs.)		940	
Wade, John D.			4273
Wagele, Charles		3779	1976
Wagele, Dorris	1976		
Wailes, Elbert S.			3822
Wailes, Eugene A.			3822
Wailes, J. A.	3822		
Wailes, Jessie L.			3822
Wailes, Lulu M.			3822
Walker, E. S.			2021
Walker, J. G.		634	
Walker, J. L.	2631	1657	
Walker, J. M.		2117	
Walker, J. P.		264	
Walker, John		552, 1586, 1682	
Walker, John Cecil			2631
Walker, John L.		3823	
Walker, L. F.		3839	
Walker, Mary E.	3839		
Walker, Nathaniel			355
Walker, Nellena			2631
Walker, O. V.		616	
Walker, Rudolphus			1480
Walker, Water Lawrence			2631
Wall, H. C.		546	
Wallace, W. H.		889	
Walliser, Carl	2684		
Walliser, Carl Alfred			2684
Walliser, Emily Constance			2684
Walliser, Lucie deB.		2684	
Walls, David	1283	2779	
Walsh, M.	1247		

Name	Principal	Surety	Ward
Walsh, Mary E.			3514
Walsh, Thomas E.			3514
Walters, Solomon		3452	
Wambold, D. M.		3061	
Wambold, Daniel M.		2796	
Warboys, J. W.		1609, 2202, 3562	
Ward, A.		709	
Ward, Franklin Arthur			3228
Ward, Harry B.			3989
Ward, Phil Demill			3989
Warfield, George			1276
Warfield, George H.		3852	
Warfield, R. H.	1276, 1517, 2176	1376	
Warmcastle, F. M.		34	
Warner, A. L.		2588	
Warner, Alma	2116		
Warner, Augusta L.	2829		
Warner, Frederick A.			2829
Warner, G.		300, 505	
Warner, Gustavus	34	34	
Warner, Henrietta			2116
Warner, James		1422	
Warner, Oscar E.			2829
Warner, William E.			2116
Warren, John B.			3717
Warren, Mary E.	3717		
Warren, W. P.		1176, 2666	
Warth, Claiborne	710		
Washer, Johanna M.			936
Waters, James			1287
Waters, Mary	1287		
Watson, Alexander	3240		
Watt, John	3999		
Watt, Mary E.			3999
Watt, May			3999
Weaver, C. W.	2290, 3516	2021, 2488, 2611, 2625, 2897, 3767, 3846	
Webber, L. Ross			3662

Name	Principal	Surety	Ward
Weber, Alma P.			2923, 3396
Weber, Clara A. B.			2923, 3396
Weber, Franklin B.			2923
Weber, H.		4373	
Weber, Henry		3679	
Weber, Mary E.			2923
Weber, Richard B. F.			2923
Weeks, Braddock		2257	
Weeks, Frank P.		1962	
Weeks, Horace		4075	
Wegener, Julius		2165	
Wegner, Ed		2103, 2282	
Weigand, Charles			3528
Weigand, Christina	3528		
Weigand, George Washington			3528
Weigand, Mary	1065		
Weigand, William Francis			1065
Weise, C.	524	1797	
Weise, Charles			524
Weise, Eliza			524
Weise, Frederick			524
Weise, Henrietta			524
Weise, Henry			524
Weisshand, August		1960	
Welling, Charles		3813	
Welling, John		475	
Wells, Ellen S.	3614		
Wendt, Fred	1808		
Wensinger, F. S.		1203	
Wescoatt, Effie E.		2654	
Wescoatt, Glenn			2654
Wescoatt, Nelson		2654	
Wescoatt, O.		3375	
Wescoatt, O. K.	2654		
West, Carlos			62
West, Charles			1833
West, Eddie			937
West, Fred			1833
West, Genevieve			62
West, Guelermo			62

Name	Principal	Surety	Ward
West, Henry			1833
West, Juan			62
West, Maria del Carmen			62
West, Nellie			937
West, Samuel		60	
Westfall, John	95		
Weston, Elizabeth P.			3630
Weston, Gecrge	3630		
Weston, H. L	1520		
Weston, Robert W.			3630
Weyl, H.		2282	
Weyl, Henry		2029, 2165, 2941	
Weymouth, Mary A.	1018		
Weymouth, Minnie C.			1018
Wheeler, David R.			1104
Wheeler, George W.			1104
Wheeler, Ira E.			1104
Wheeler, Jacob	1104	3064	
Wheeler, Jacob F.			1104
Whitaker, G. N.		947, 1763	
Whitaker, J. P.		1763	
White, Harrison		1729	
White, Henry M.	1027		
White, Maggie			771
White, T. H.		494	
White, W. P.	771		
White, William	2927		
Whitehill, W. W.	4246		
Whitlock, Annie S.			1097
Whitlock, Charles J.			1097
Whitlock, Joel R.			1097
Whitlock, Mary J.	1097		
Whitlock, William M.			1097
Whitman, G. W.	456		
Whitman, Lillie			456
Whitman, N. A.	456		
Whitney, A. P.		525, 616, 924	
Whitney, W. B.		1878, 3675	
Whitney, William B.		1824, 2625	
Wickersham, F. A.		2954	

Name	Principal	Surety	Ward
Wickersham, I. G.	557	1697, 1796	
Wickersham, Jesse C.		557, 924	
Wiers, James		1119	
Wightman, Lulu			3642
Wilcox, Sidney B.	1981		
Wiley, Edith			3050
Wiley, Maud C.	3050		
Wilfley, Samuel	546		
Wilkins, Emily	439		
Wilkins, Henrietta C.			439
Wilkins, Maria S.			439
Wilkins, William			439
Wilkinson, Alfred			2921
Wilkinson, Bertha			2892
Wilkinson, Henry Dean			2921
Wilkinson, Mattie V.	2921		
Williams, George E.	112		
Williams, John A.	2788		
Williams, Sarah J.	3786		
Williams, W. H.		1355	
Williamson, Thomas D.		98	
Williamson, William M.		175	
Williges, Elize			1437
Willis, T. N.		426, 597, 648, 649, 650	
Wills, J. P.		3776	
Willy, J. W.		1439	
Wilsey, A.		935	
Wilsey, Amasa		576	
Wilsey, Frankie Jane			1314
Wilsey, H.		1314	
Wilsey, Hayes			1314
Wilsey, Henry Martin			1314
Wilsey, Mary Elizabeth			1314
Wilsey, Sarah M.	1314		
Wilson, Albert C.			935
Wilson, Celia A.			935
Wilson, Charles S.		1083	
Wilson, Daydawn			2103
Wilson, E.		95	

Name	Principal	Surety	Ward
Wilson, Ellen P.	2909		
Wilson, Gaston			935
Wilson, George B.			935
Wilson, Isaac E.			935
Wilson, John B.	1146		
Wilson, John G.		473	
Wilson, Joseph Percy			2103
Wilson, Leland			935
Wilson, M. A.	190		
Wilson, Matthew Alexander	2295		
Wilson, Robert J.			2103
Wilson, Thomas B.	2103		
Wilson, Valentine	935		
Wilson, William	336		
Winans, J. L.		3003	
Winder, Edward C.			1725, 4032
Winder, Elizabeth	4032		
Winder, Joseph		1725	
Winder, Mary A.	1725		
Winder, Robert J.			1725
Wines, W. F.	2931, 3409		
Winkler, Arthur S.		3786	
Winkler, Florence E.			3786
Winkler, John J.			873
Winkler, Oliver M.		3786	
Winkler, Walter S.			3786
Winn, Helen Augusta			131
Winn, Lydia Francis			131
Winters, Dennis	2266		
Winters, Joseph			2266
Wise, Henry		422, 529, 735, 829, 1054, 1083	
Wisecarver, Elizabeth	2484		
Wisecarver, J. R.		743	
Wisecarver, Joseph R.		1329	
Wiseman, Ella			377
Wiseman, Susan			377
Wiswell, Nelson	3861		
Witbro, Ernest H.			3779
Witbro, Henry			3779

Name	Principal	Surety	Ward
Witbro, Kate B.	3779		
Withrow, William		503	
Witt, J. G. William			958
Wohlers, Winifred	3528		
Wolf, Charles		1827	
Wolfe, George W.		95	
Wooden, Joseph		884	
Woodley, George		4324	
Woods, George E.	3790		
Woods, James A.			3790
Woods, James S.		137	
Woods, Jonas S.	85		
Woods, Lillie B.			3790
Woods, Mary Alice			1507
Woodward, E. F.		2358	
Woodworth, Abby H.	3226		
Woolsey, C. F.			4075
Woolsey, E. W.	3482½		
Woolsey, Martha A.			3482½
Woolsey, Nellie C.	4075		
Woolsey, W. E.	3482½		
Worth, Claiborne	710		
Wright, Amelia A.			582
Wright, Arthur Gordon			1962
Wright, Daisy A.			1853
Wright, Ernest Walter			1962
Wright, Esther			3801
Wright, Ethel Audrey			1962
Wright, Girault S.			3756, 3801
Wright, Isaac		475	
Wright, James A.			582
Wright, John A.			582
Wright, Myrtle J.			1853
Wright, Olive B.			3756, 3801
Wright, S. B.		3919	
Wright, Sampson B.	3756, 3801		
Wright, Sarah E.			582
Wright, Winfield R.			3756, 3801
Wright, Winfield S. M.		89	
Wyatt, Melvin J.			3899

Name	Principal	Surety	Ward
Wyatt, Raymond			3899
Wyman, William Henry			2507
Yarbrough, Frederic C.			2868
Yarbrough, R. L.	2868		
Yarbrough, R. Lee	2569		
Yates, Amy	2987		
Yates, Florence			2987
Yates, J. W.		190, 252	
Yordi, A. H.	3333		
Yordi, Alice C.			3333
Yordi, Nellie E.			3333
York, Louis			2767
Young, Amelia	2989		
Young, Clarence			2989
Young, Clarence Henry			2989
Young, Clement C.			1850
Young, George C.	1990		
Young, George E.	2989	2989	
Young, Hazel L.			3827
Young, Herbert E.			3962
Young, Hiram		141, 142	
Young, J. M.		3214	
Young, J. N.		3214	
Young, James B.		936	
Young, James M.		3214	
Young, James N.		3214	
Young, Lena C.			1850
Young, Lena May (Mrs.)		2777	
Young, Mariah E.			2180
Young, Mary R.		1850	
Young, N. A.		978	
Zartman, William	100	2132	
Zeller, H. J.		1184	
Zimmerman, George		641	
Zimmerman, George H.		2383	
Zimmerman, William W.	3094		
Zimmermann, F. W.	3965		
Zimmermann, Frederick			3965
Zimmermann, William			3965

Bonds of Guardians

Case #	Principals	Sureties	Bound to	Amount ($)	Type	Date	Book	Page(s)
5	Randolph, Isaac N.	Brockman, Israel; Nugent, Thomas; Vasques, P. J.	Scott, Mary (heir of W. W. Scott, dec'd)	3,000	Minor	7 Apr 1852		
5	Randolph, Isaac N.	Morrow, Samuel; Hiland, O. A.	Scott, Mary (heir of W. W. Scott, dec'd)	3,000	Minor	6 Jun 1853		
5	Randolph, Isaac N.	Morrow, Samuel; McKamy, James W.	Scott, Mary (heir of W. W. Scott, dec'd)	3,000	Minor	17 Jun 1853		
5	Cooke, Martin E.	Nevill, Joseph N.; Brockman, Israel; Brunner, Christian	Scott, Mary (heir of W. W. Scott, dec'd)	11,000	Minor	20 Jun 1853		
17	Roan, John	Purcell, Matthias; Campbell, Peter	Travers, William M.; Travers, Theodore O. (children of Sergt. Travers, dec'd)	1,000	Minors	27 Apr 1852		
22	Lewis, Catharine	Oakes, Anthony G.; Ellis, William	Lewis, Maria; Lewis, George; Lewis, Sophia; Lewis, John; Lewis, Joseph (heirs of John Lewis, dec'd)	2,000	Minors	2 Oct 1858		
25	Mitchell, Benjamin	Brockman, Israel; Carriger, Nicholas	Carriger, Solomon	8,000	Insane person	26 Mar 1853		
34	Warner, Gustavus	Pierson, Hiram; Gilbert, Jacob	Camron, Oliver P.; Camron, Mary E. (heirs of Thomas P. Camron, dec'd)	6,000	Minors	29 Mar 1855		
34	Martin, Silas M.	Warner, Gustavus; Bonham, B. N.	Camron, David E. (heir of Thomas P. Camron, dec'd)	3,000	Minor	29 Mar 1855		
34	Camron, John M.	Martin, Silas M.; Bonham, B. N.; Warner, Gustavus	Camron, Alva U. (heir of Thomas P. Camron, dec'd)	3,000	Minor	29 Mar 1855		
34	Brown, Thomas A.	Warmcastle, F. M.; Brown, Warren	Cameron, William W. (heir of T. P. Cameron, dec'd)	3,000	Minor	[?] [?] 1855; filed 29 Apr 1855		
41	Carrillo de Fitch, Josepha	Carrillo, Julio; Fitch, Henry Edward; Fitch, Frederick	Fitch, Joseph; Fitch, Josephine; Fitch, John; Fitch, Isabel; Fitch, Charles; Fitch, Anna (heirs of Henry D. Fitch, dec'd)	10,000	Minors	8 Jan 1856		
57	Kelsey, Samuel	Kelsey, Benjamin; Hubbard, William	Kelsey, William; Kelsey, Joseph (heirs of Samuel Kelsey, dec'd)	5,000	Minors	27 Jan 1855		
60	Lewis, Seveir	Means, Thomas J.; West, Samuel	Lewis, Sylvester; Lewis, Nevile; Lewis, Leanna (heirs of George W. Lewis, dec'd)	300	Minors	31 Jul 1855		
60	Lewis, Seveir	Sullenger, Madison; Commary, P.	Lewis, Sylvester; Lewis, Nevile; Lewis, Leanna (heirs of George W. Lewis, dec'd)	300	Minors	30 Nov 1857		
62*	Holmes, Henderson P.	Clark, James P.; Hahman, F. G.	West, Juan (heir of William Mark West, dec'd)	2,400	Minor	8 May 1862	A	67
62*	Holmes, Henderson P.	Hendley, John; Boyce, John F.	West, Carlos (heir of William Mark West, dec'd)	2,400	Minor	8 May 1862	A	68
62*	Holmes, Henderson P.	Hendley, John; Boyce, John F.	West, Genevieve (heir of William Mark West, dec'd)	2,400	Minor	8 May 1862	A	69
62*	Holmes, Henderson P.	Clark, James P.; Hahman, F. G.	West, Maria del Carmen (heir of William Mark West, dec'd)	2,400	Minor	8 May 1862	A	70
62*	Holmes, Henderson P.	Arnold, G. W.; Mathews, C. W.; Pugh, James A.; Coulter, S. T.	West, Guelermo (heir of William Mark West, dec'd)	2,000	Minor	19 Dec 1863	A	120-121
76	Greening, William	Mecham, Harrison; Crow, John L.	Sterling, Elizabeth (heir of Charles B. Sterling, dec'd)	3,500	Minor	22 Oct 1855		

Case #	Principals	Sureties	Bound to	Amount ($)	Type	Date	Book	Page(s)
81	Derrick, J. C.	Camron, John M.; Huff, John G.	Taylor, John; Taylor, Putnam; Taylor, Wayne; Taylor, Palestine (heirs of Eli and Margaret Taylor, dec'd)	800	Minors	24 Jul 1854		
83	Pool, Henry J.	Kennedy, James; Hartman, J. W.	Trumbull, Luther	1,000	Incompetent person	19 Sep 1856		
85	Shattuck, David O.	Shattuck, Frank W.; Miller, George W.	Smith, Louisa Ellen (heir of Hiram Smith, dec'd)	1,000	Minor	20 May 1853		
85	Patten, Thomas B.	Patten, Hugh; Vaughn, Daniel	Smith, John (son of Hiram Smith, dec'd)	1,000	Minor	16 May 1853		
85	Patten, Thomas B.	Brockman, Israel; Blakeney, J. C.; Patten, Joseph; Vasques, P. J.; Tate, Thomas H.; Chambers, T. K.	Smith, John P. (son of Hiram Smith, dec'd)	6,000	Minor	17 Jun 1854		
85	Bishop, Tennessee C.	Blakeney, J. C.; Ellis, William; Vasquez, P. J.; Tate, J. H.; Rupe, Sam H.; Thompson, William A.; Rohrer, Fred; Beasley, Jesse; Johnson, C. A.	State of California; The Probate Court of Sonoma County appointed Tennessee C. Bishop the guardian of the person and the estate of John P. Smith, minor.	10,000	Minor	2 Feb 1857		
85	Woods, Jonas S.	Tate, Thomas H.; Cassebohm, William; Bishop, T. C.; Hendley, John	Smith, John P. (heir of Hiram Smith, dec'd)	10,000	Minor	17 Aug 1857		
85	Brockman, Israel	Hendley, John; Brewster, John A.	Smith, James M. (son of Hiram Smith, dec'd)	1,000	Minor	16 May 1853		
85	Brockman, Israel	Beasley, Jesse; Ingram, John; Carrillo, Julio; Richardson, Achilles	Smith, James M. (heir of Hiram Smith, dec'd)	6,000	Minor	7 Nov 1854		
85	McDonald, Alexander C.	Bruns, Harmann; Davies, Jonathan; Poppe, Julius A.; Akers, Stephen; Cassebohm, William	Smith, James M.	10,000	Minor	30 Nov 1857		
85	Brockman, Israel	Beasley, Jesse; Ingram, John; Carrillo, Julio; Richardson, Achilles	Smith, Eliza (heir of Hiram Smith, dec'd)	6,000	Minor	7 Nov 1854		
87	Hill, John H.	Cooke, Martin E.; Beck, Robert; Cooper, James	Burns, William	15,000	Incompetent person	20 Dec 1854		
87	Hill, John H.	Hill, William McPherson; Hoen, Berthold; Carrillo, Julio	Burns, William K.	15,000	Incompetent person	6 Jan 1858		
88	Leslie, Jonathan	Lamb, John; Kendall, John	Miller, George K. (heir of Daniel Miller, dec'd)	3,500	Minor	[?] Nov 1857; approved and filed 20 Nov 1857		
89	Clark, Jarena	Griggs, Joseph H.; Wright, Winfield S. M.; Long, Marcus A.	Clark, William T. (child of William T. Clark, dec'd)	8,000	Minor	17 Nov 1857		
93	Bidwell, Thomas J.	Bedwell, Ira; Gird, Henry S.	Brooks, Thomas (heir of James Brooks, dec'd)	200	Minor	18 Feb 1860		
93	Bidwell, Ira	Bidwell, Thomas J.; Gird, Henry S.	Bidwell, Nancy (heir of James Brooks, dec'd)	200	Minor	18 Feb 1860		
93	Bedwell, Ira	Bidwell, Thomas J.; Gird, Henry S.	Bedwell, James (heir of James Brooks, dec'd)	200	Minor	18 Feb 1860		
95	Westfall, John	Wolfe, George W.; Wilson, E.	Underwood, Susanna M. (daughter of Benjamin E. Underwood, dec'd)	1,000	Minor	14 Nov 1857		

112

Case #	Principals	Sureties	Bound to	Amount ($)	Type	Date	Book	Page(s)
98	Berggren, John Fr.	Kamp, Harold Lud; Brockman, Israel	Smith, Isaac; Smith, Napoleon B.; Smith, George W. (children of George Smith, dec'd)	600	Minors	9 Oct 1857		
98	Kinsmill, Thomas E.	Jacobson, Jacob; Williamson, Thomas D.	Smith, George W. (child of George Smith, dec'd)	300	Minor	20 May 1860		
98	Kinsmill, Thomas E.	Rupe, Samuel H.; Shattuck, Richard/D. P.	Smith, Isaac B. (child of George Smith, dec'd)	800	Minor	28 May 1860		
98	Smith, James J.	Kinsmill, Thomas E.; Killberg, Peter	Smith, Napoleon B. (child of George Smith, dec'd)	400	Minor	19 Nov 1860		
100	Zartman, William	Fritsch, John; Stafford, N. O.; Carrillo, Julio	Judkins, L. M.	2,000	Insane person	9 Jan 1858		
103	Bowles, Joseph M.	Swift, Granville P.; Fine, I. Holt	Tate, Jesse T.	1,000	Minor	19 Feb 1861		
103	Bowles, Joseph M.	Swift, Granville P.; Fine, I. Holt	Tate, Margaret A.	1,000	Minor	19 Feb 1861		
103	Bowles, Joseph M.	Swift, Granville P.; Fine, I. Holt	Tate, John H.	1,000	Minor	19 Feb 1861		
103	Bowles, Joseph M.	Swift, Granville P.; Fine, I. Holt	Tate, Augustine F.	1,000	Minor	19 Feb 1861		
103	Bowles, Joseph M.	Swift, Granville P.; Fine, I. Holt	Tate, Josefa F.	1,000	Minor	19 Feb 1861		
106	Carroll, James	Gordon, Joseph; Carroll, Patrick	Murray, Mary Alice (daughter of Patrick Murray)	200	Minor	25 Mar 1858		
107	Stapp, I. N.	Bloom, Joseph; Cook, J. W.	Dillingham, William K.; Dillingham, Susan M.; Dillingham, Mary E.; Dillingham, Sarah E.; Dillingham, John J. L. (children of John Dillingham, dec'd)	500	Minors	20 May 1868		
112	Williams, George E.	Stewart, Abel; Mecham, Harrison	Kirk, Alice J.	2,400	[Minor]	15 Apr 1858		
117	Freeland, Nancy M.	Russell, A. W.; Beaver, Henry; Carrillo, Julio; Treadway, R. M.; Treadway, Griffin	Freeland, Albert Clark (son of A. C. Freeland, dec'd)	10,600	Minor	No date; approved and filed 14 Jun 1858		
120	Holman, John H.	Lawrence, James A.; Maxwell, James G.	Miller, Edmond H.; Miller, Mary Jane (children of John M. Miller, dec'd)	800	Minors	22 Jul 1858		
122	Purvine, Charles	Martin, Silas M.; Augustine, Albert	Johnson, William A. (mistakenly given as Johnson, William L. in bond)	2,000	Minor	25 Aug 1858		
122	Purvine, Charles	Root, Jeremiah; Blackburn, Charles	Johnson, Charles	2,000	Minor	23 Aug 1858		
122	Colton, F. D.	Maynard, F. T.; Cavanagh, John	Johnson, William A.	600	Minor	30 Apr 1870		
123	Lemmons, James	Langhorne, John W.; Porter, Daniel J.	Pots, Martha A. (child of Dickerson A. Pots and Eliza Jane, his wife, both dec'd)	500	Minor	29 May 1858		
124	Neil, James	Sroufe, John; Rodgers, A. W.	Neil, Sarah C. (heir of Ezekial W. Smith, dec'd)	1,500	Minor	10 Aug 1858		
125	Cook, John B.	Farmer, William; Todd, S. S.	Cook, John H.; Cook, William Y.; Cook, Jesse G.; Cook, James W.; Cook, Mary Ann; Cook, Lucinda E.; Cook, Finess Lee	2,000	Minors	24 Aug 1858		

113

Case #	Principals	Sureties	Bound to	Amount ($)	Type	Date	Book	Page(s)
126	Givens, Elisha	Smith, Preston B.; Vanwinkle, Thomas B.	Price, Henry Lucas (child and heir of Phillip H. Price, dec'd)	700	Minor	25 Sep 1858		
126	Givens, Elisha	Smith, Preston B.; Vanwinkle, Thomas B.	Price, Pitman Hardin (child and heir of Phillip H. Price, dec'd)	700	Minor	25 Sep 1858		
127	Grover, Thomas J.	Skaggs, Alexander; Laymance, Isaac C.	Grover, James M.	3,000	[Minor]	16 Oct 1858		
129	Holloway, Lyscomb [Lipscomb] C.	Beaver, Henry; Myers, Dudley D.	Holloway, Henrietta; Holloway, Mary E.; Holloway, George W. (children of Archibald D. and Elizabeth E. Holloway, both dec'd)	3,000	Minors	22 Nov 1858		
130	Haven, Joshua P.	Sharp, Solomon A.; Bosworth, John H.	Totten, Edward (child of George Mansfield Totten, dec'd, and Julia K. Totten)	200	Minor	29 Nov 1858		
130	Haven, Joshua P.	Sharp, Solomon A.; Bosworth, John H.	Totten, George Mansfield (child of George Mansfield Totten, dec'd, and Julia K. Totten)	200	Minor	29 Nov 1858		
131	Dodge, L. C.	Rains, Gallant; Clyman, Lancaster	Winn, Helen Augusta	400	Minor	8 Mar 1861		
131	Dodge, L. C.	Rains, Gallant; Clyman, Lancaster	Winn, Lydia Francis	400	Minor	8 Mar 1861		
132	Bell, William T.	Bell, James S.; Bell, George K.; Bell, Margaret	Bell, Henry H.; Bell, Albert K.; Bell, John W.; Bell, Louisa F. (heirs of Samuel Bell, dec'd)	8,000	Minors	20 Dec 1858		
135	Miller, Charles C.	Miller, Mary; Carr, Nelson	Miller, Daniel E. (heir of Daniel Miller, dec'd)	3,500	Minor	14 Nov 1857		
135	Miller, Charles C.	Miller, George Kay; Hughes, John; Cook, Valentine B.; Cook, James G.; Groshong, Uriah	Miller, Daniel E. (heir of Daniel Miller, dec'd)	3,500	Minor	11 May 1861		
135	Miller, C. C.	Miller, George Kay; Parks, H. G.	Miller, Daniel E. (heir of Daniel Miller, dec'd)	3,500	Minor	10 Jan 1863		
136	Miller, Charles C.	Miller, Mary; Patten, Thomas B.; Copeland, Alexander	Miller, Mary A. (heir of Daniel Miller, dec'd)	3,500	Minor	18 Nov 1857		
137	Smith, William J.	Woods, James S.; Blakeney, J. C.; Brockman, Israel; Ellis, William; Beasly, Jesse; Neil, Samuel; Patten, John D.	Smith, James B.; Smith, Martha J.; Smith, Elenora; Smith, Ezekiel (children of Ezekiel W. Smith, late of Andrew County, Missouri, dec'd)	7,000	Minors	25 Jan 1858		
140	Crane, Richard H.	Patten, Thomas B.; Crane, Joel	Edmunson, Richard P.	1,200	Minor	1 Apr 1859		
141	Patten, Thomas B.	Young, Hiram; Crane, Richard H.	Edmunson, Thomas Jefferson	1,200	Minor	9 Apr 1859		
142	Edmunson, Thomas J.	Chamberlain, David; Hearn, James	Edmunson, Emma (daughter of Rufus C. Edmunson, late of Sonoma County, California, dec'd)	500	Minor	27 Apr 1864	A	147-148
142	Edmunson, Thomas J.	Chamberlain, David; Hearn, James	Edmunson, Hugh R. (son of Rufus C. Edmunson, late of Sonoma County, California, dec'd)	500	Minor	27 Apr 1864	A	149-150
142*	Edmunson, Thomas J.	Crane, Richard H.; Lovell, David J.	Edmunson, William F. (son of Rufus C. Edmunson, late of Sonoma County, California, dec'd)	500	Minor	27 Apr 1864	A	151-152
142	Edmunson, John C.	Patten, Thomas B.; Collier, Ira	Edmunson, Hugh R.	800	Minor	15 Feb 1862	A	54-55
142	Edmunson, John C.	Patten, Thomas B.; Thayer, Daniel S.	Edmunson, Emily	800	Minor	15 Feb 1862	A	56-57

Case #	Principals	Sureties	Bound to	Amount ($)	Type	Date	Book	Page(s)
142	Patten, Thomas B.	Isom, Hugh; Young, Hiram	Edmunson, Hugh R.	1,200	Minor	1 Apr 1859		
142	Patten, Thomas B.	Hershberger, Jeremiah; Harvey, Thomas J.	Edmunson, Emily	1,200	Minor	9 Apr 1859		
142	Patten, Thomas R.	Crane, Richard H.; Crane, Joel	Edmunson, William F.	1,200	Minor	1 Apr 1859		
143	Crane, Joel	Farmer, William; Crane, Richard H.	Edmunson, John C.	1,200	Minor	1 Apr 1859		
147	Kelley, Jacob	Dickey, S. R.; Isom, H.	Cox, John W.; Cox, Henry F.	1,200	Minors	10 Sep 1859		
148	Andrews, John	Green, C. C.; Lucas, John	Crabtree, Mary J.	1,600	Minor	30 Sep 1859		
152	Holman, John H.	Ormsby, J. S.; Green, C. C.; Martin, H. B.	Arnold, George W.	5,000	Insane person	7 Dec 1859		
159	Curtis, Tyler	Smith, Jacob; Rosseter, James H.	Smith, Stephen M.	1,000	Minor	1 Aug 1861	A	26-27
159	Curtis, Tyler	Smith, Jacob; Rosseter, James H.	Smith, James	1,000	Minor	1 Aug 1861	A	25-26
159	Curtis, Tyler	Smith, Jacob; Rosseter, James H.	Smith, Manuela	1,000	Minor	1 Aug 1861	A	24-25
159	English, John M.	Martin, Samuel B.; Atkinson, Louis	Smith, James B.	15,000	Minor	11 Sep 1873		
159	Torres, Manuel	Braly, M. A.; Carrillo, Julio	Smith, Manuella	6,000	Minor	14 Jan 1860		
159	Torres, Manuel	Braly, M. A.; Carrillo, Julio	Smith, James (son of Stephen Smith, late of Bodega, dec'd)	6,000	Minor	14 Jan 1860		
159	Torres, Manuel	Braly, M. A.; Carrillo, Julio	Smith, Stephen M.	6,000	Minor	14 Jan 1860		
166	Bidwell, Thomas J.	Crane, G. L.; Gird, Richard; Martin, Horace B.	Gird, Henry S.	10,000	Insane person	12 May 1860		
168	Valentine, Harrison	Emerson, Henry; Hood, Thomas B.	Tobin, Patrick	1,000	Minor	5 Jun 1860		
174	Roberts, Charles	Lightner, John M.; Cohn, Isaac H.; Nuckolls, Nathaniel	Crook, J. J.	3,000	Insane person	1 Sep 1860		
175	Otterson, Agnes	Auser, Elijah W.; Blyth, James	Crisp, William H.	500	Minor	8 Sep 1860		
175	Otterson, Agnes	Williamson, William M.; Blyth, James	Crisp, William H. (child of John Crisp, dec'd)	500	Minor	1 May 1861		
176	Turner, James C.	Gilliam, Mitchel; McGuire, Cornelius	Turner, Sarepta/Serepta A.	400	Minor	16 Sep 1861	A	17-18
176	Turner, James C.	Gilliam, Mitchel; McGuire, Cornelius	Turner, Jasper N.	420	Minor	16 Sep 1861	A	14-15
176	Turner, James C.	Gilliam, Mitchel; McGuire, Cornelius	Turner, Cornelius J.	400	Minor	16 Sep 1861	A	19-20
179	McReynolds, James	McReynolds, William; Clyman, Lancaster	Gauldin, Willis Wilson	1,400	Minor	5 Nov 1860		
179	McReynolds, James	McReynolds, William; Clyman, Lancaster	Gauldin, Martha Anne	1,400	Minor	5 Nov 1860		
179	McReynolds, James	McReynolds, William; Clyman, Lancaster	Gauldin, Benjamin F.	1,400	Minor	5 Nov 1860		
179	McReynolds, James	McReynolds, William; Clyman, Lancaster	Gauldin, John V.	1,400	Minor	5 Nov 1860		
182	Crane, Richard H.	Patton, Charles; Carrillo, Julio	Patton, Robert A.	1,000	Minor	12 Feb 1861		
182	Patton, Mary A.	Crane, Richard H.; Davis C. E.	Patton, Robert A.	1,000	Minor	28 Dec 1860		

Case #	Principals	Sureties	Bound to	Amount ($)	Type	Date	Book	Page(s)
186	Adamson, Jacob	Galusha, D. A.; Cooper, William M.	Adamson, Mary E.	1,000	Minor	6 Mar 1861		
188	Vaughn, Daniel	Smith, Jacob; Andrews, John	Phillpot, William Addison	1,000	Minor	9 May 1861		
188	Vaughn, Daniel	Smith, Jacob; Andrews, John	Phillpot, Marion Jariat	1,000	Minor	9 May 1861		
190	Wilson, M. A.	Grove, David; Yates, J. W.; Smith, J. P.; Smyth, T. U.	Skaggs, Emma L. (child of Elijah S. Skaggs, dec'd)	4,000	Minor	7 Oct 1865	A	207-208
194	Hutton, Charles E.	McDonald, J. R.; Fike, N.	Macy, Theora	3,000	Minor	13 May 1868		
196*	Smith, Thomas U.	Heald, Thomas T.; Long, M. A.; Hudson, T. W.; Aull, A. B.; Espy, John; Espy, G. T.; Smith, I. P.	Heald, George William	18,000	Minor	7 Aug 1861	A	1-2
198	St. Clair, James	Akers, Stephen; Lyon, Robert B.	St. Clair, Francis Marion	1,000	Minor	7 Sep 1861	A	10-11
198	St. Clair, James	Akers, Stephen; Lyon, Robert B.	St. Clair, William Wallace	1,000	Minor	7 Sep 1861	A	8-9
198	St. Clair, James	Rice, John E.; Rice, Moses P.	St. Clair, Francis Marion; St. Clair, William Wallace (children of David St. Clair, dec'd)	1,000	Minors	22 Oct 1857		
213	Fike, Nathan	Hall, D. W.; Haigh, John	Stowell, Margaret R. E. A. B.	2,000	Minor	8 May 1862	A	65
216	Fitch, William	Pearce, George; Taylor, John	Pina, Maria Antonia	200	Minor	7 Sep 1864	A	177-178
222	Matheson, Maria A.	Seaman, Jesse F.; Hertel, R.	Matheson, Roderick; Matheson, Nettie; Matheson, George G.	1,000	Minors	19 Sep 1866		
227	Aull, A. B.	Hudson, T. W.; Sondheimer, E.	Snider, Ella	2,500	Minor	12 Sep 1864	A	174
233	Thurgood, Margaret G.	Bloom, D.; Constoll, F.	Thurgood, William Sharp	200	Minor	31 Aug 1866		
233	Thurgood, Margaret G.	Bloom, D.; Constoll, F.	Thurgood, Mary Ann	200	Minor	31 Aug 1866		
233	Thurgood, Margaret G.	Bloom, D.; Constoll, F.	Thurgood, Margaret Elizabeth	200	Minor	31 Aug 1866		
238	Prewett, James	Grove, David; Shinn, J. O.	Prewett, Francis Graham (son and heir of John and Mary Prewett, late of Sonoma County, dec'd)	800	Minor	13 Jun 1864	A	162
238	Prewett, James	Slusser, Levi S. B.; Steadman, Amos	Prewett, Martha Ann (daughter and heir of John and Mary Prewett, late of Sonoma County, dec'd)	800	Minor	13 Jun 1864	A	164
238	Prewett, James	Esmond, Cornwell; Carlton, Austin	Prewett, George (son and heir of John and Mary Prewett, late of Sonoma County, dec'd)	800	Minor	13 Jun 1864	A	163
238	Prewett, James	Pool, Henry J.; Prewett, Samuel	Prewett, Francis Graham	800	Minor	3 Nov 1866		
243	Schmitt, George	Bliss, William D.; Kron, John	Thielemann, Otto; Thielemann, Mary	4,000	Minors	8 Jan 1870		
250	Jacobs, George H.	Petray, G. W.; Caldwell, Hugh	Caldwell, John G.	500	Minor	28 Apr 1864	A	142-143
250	Jacobs, George H.	Petray, G. W.; Caldwell, Hugh	Caldwell, Samuel T.	500	Minor	25 Apr 1864	A	145-146
252	Bedwell, Franklin	Matthews, C. W.; Yates, J. W.	Crisp, Sarah Judith (daughter of John W. Crisp, dec'd)	300	Minor	1 Aug 1864	A	167
252	Smith, Isaac P.	Hendley, John; Farmer, E. T.	Crisp, John B. (son of John W. Crisp, dec'd)	400	Minor	6 Aug 1864	A	169-170
262	Kellogg, A. S.	Morton, W. H.; Bostwick, N. W.	Pugh, Malvina	350	Minor	2 Sep 1864	A	

116

Case #	Principals	Sureties	Bound to	Amount ($)	Type	Date	Book	Page(s)
264	Johnson, J. J.	Carson, R. W.; Walker, J. P.	Squires, Harry/Harry	1,400	Insane person	9 Nov 1864	A	181
270	Stapleton, Patrick	Sullivan, Michael; Pfau, John	Ryan, Pierce	2,000	Insane person	22 Jun 1866		
270	Stapleton, Patrick	Roberts, Charles; Gallagher, John	Ryan, Pierce	1,600	Insane person	6 Aug 1866		
270	Stapleton, Patrick	Burns, John; Campbell, George W.	Ryan, Pierce	1,600	Insane person	29 Sep 1866		
270	Crilly, Nicholas	Quinn, Stephen; McAnally, John	Ryan, Pierce	1,600	Insane person	15 Mar 1865	A	190
272	Fike, Nathan	Allison, George; Brown, A. M.	Stevens, William H.	1,000	Minor	13 Mar 1865	A	187
278	Garrow, Edward	Maddux, J. P.; Giannini, Henry G.	Hurn, Sibbie; Hurn, William; Hurn, Solomon; Hurn, John; Hurn, Seth	1,500	Minors	1 May 1865	A	194
281*	Grove, David	Hood, T. B.; Farmer, E. T.	Directors of the Insane Asylum of California; The Probate Court of Sonoma County appointed David Grove the guardian of Harry Campbell, an insane person, on 17 May 1865. This bond insured that David Grove would pay the $15 per month board and medical attendance charges for his ward and supply his clothing while he was confined in the State Insane Asylum.	400	Insane person	17 May 1865	A	196
283	Hardin, Lucinda	Ellis, John J.; Hardin, James A.; Doyle, M.	Hardin, George M.; Hardin, Stonewall J. (heirs of W. Jefferson Hardin, Jr., dec'd)	1,000	Minors	31 Jul 1865	A	201
293	Darrow, J. O.	Allison, George; Fike, N.	Rowlett, Henry	500	Minor	29 Sep 1865		
296	Grant, John D.	Hassett, J. D.; Bloom, D.	Grant, Henry D. F.	1,000	Minor	[?] Jan 1866		
299*	Thompson, Thomas L.	Atterbury, William B.; Noonan, George P.	Reichardt, Emma	1,000	Minor	4 Dec 1865	A	211
300	Frasler, D. S.	Jewell, Jesse; Warner, G.	Needham, Jessie Ruby	4,900	Minor	7 Dec 1869		
304	Smith, Frank	Barnes, A. N.	Smith, Governeur	500	Minor	29 Apr 1867		
305	Timms, John H.	Sutton, H. D.; Harmon, H. H.	Timms, Anthony	1,000	Incompetent person	2 Jan 1866		
316	Veal, William	Crane, R. H.; Barnes, Jehu	Corban, Margaret Ann Kelly	1,000	Minor	16 Jul 1866		
321	McClish, Thomas	McClish, James L.; Laughlin, James H.	McClish, John N.	800	Minor	10 Sep 1866		
327	McCoy, G. L.	Stanly, A. J.; Sweetman, C. H.	Fine, Abraham	200	Minor	4 Oct 1866		
327	McCoy, G. L.	Stanly, A. J.; Sweetman, C. H.	Fine, Emsly	200	Minor	4 Oct 1866		
327	McCoy, G. L.	Stanly, A. J.; Sweetman, C. H.	Fine, Emiline/Emeline	200	Minor	4 Oct 1866		
329	Annis, William O.	Richmond, F.; McWilliams, J. H.	Melton, Jacob Newton	250	Minor	19 Dec 1866		

Case #	Principals	Sureties	Bound to	Amount ($)	Type	Date	Book	Page(s)
329	Annis, William O.	Richmond, F.; McWilliams, J. H.	Melton, Mary Catharine	250	Minor	19 Dec 1866		
329	Annis, William O.	Richmond, F.; McWilliams, J. H.	Melton, John Nelson	250	Minor	19 Dec 1866		
330	Moore, Luticia	Dittemore, Theodore; Jacobs, G. H.	Moore, Charles (son and heir of Elisha Moore, dec'd)	200	Minor	15 Dec 1866		
330	Moore, Luticia	Dittemore, Theodore; Jacobs, G. H.	Moore, Elizabeth Ellen (daughter and heir of Elisha Moore, dec'd)	200	Minor	15 Dec 1866		
330	Moore, Luticia	Dittemore, Theodore; Jacobs, G. H.	Moore, Perry (son and heir of Elisha Moore, dec'd)	200	Minor	15 Dec 1866		
330	Moore, Luticia	Dittemore, Theodore; Jacobs, G. H.	Moore, Henrietta (daughter and heir of Elisha Moore, dec'd)	200	Minor	15 Dec 1866		
330	Moore, Luticia	Dittemore, Theodore; Jacobs, G. H.	Moore, Francis M. (son and heir by a former wife of Elisha Moore, dec'd)	200	Minor	15 Dec 1866		
330	Moore, Luticia	Dittemore, Theodore; Jacobs, G. H.	Moore, Laura (daughter of Elisha Moore, dec'd)	200	Minor	15 Dec 1866		
333	Ordway, Arah	Talbot, Courtney; Talbot, Holman	State of California; The Probate Court of Sonoma County recognized and confirmed the appointment of Arah Ordway as the guardian of Mary Abby Ordway, Martha Jane Ordway, and Drucilla Helen Ordway, minor children of William Ordway, dec'd, and Arah Ordway, by the last will and testament of William Ordway, dec'd.	2,500	Minors	14 Jan 1868		
336	Wilson, William	Rambo, Jacob; Thomas, Isaiah	Alley, Charles W.	300	Minor	20 Jan 1868		
336	Wilson, William	Rambo, Jacob; Thomas, Isaiah	Starr, Windfield	300	Minor	20 Jan 1868		
341	Knowles, David C.	Hood, T. B.; Smith, John K.	Menefee, Sarah	600	Incompetent person	3 Jun 1867	A	231
344	Ontis, John	Caldwell, William; Cook, Charles	Cathey, John; Cathey, James; Cathey, George; Cathey, Paralee (heirs of David Cathey, dec'd)	500	Minors	23 Jul 1867		
345	Shinn, Cynthia	Laughlin, L.; Miller, Thomas	Shinn, R. F.; Shinn, S.; Shinn, A. J.; Shinn, E. J.; Shinn, J.; Shinn, E.	350	Minors	1 Jun 1868		
348*	Hunt, Charles	Atterbury, William B.; Ross, D. L. B.	Flege, Henry	2,000	Insane person	6 Aug 1867	A	234
351	Brown, John	Meador, E. M.; Sacry, D. S.	Domingan, Isabel	300	Minor	8 Mar 1865		
352	Lyttaker, F. E.	Frick, George W.; Huie, George W.	Lyttaker, John T.	500	[Minor]	12 Aug 1867		
354	Lewis, R. E.	Allison, George; Berry, James	Miller, Valentine	1,600	Incompetent person	10 Sep 1867	A	238
355	Jones, Frederick S.	Swift, Granville P.; Sears, Franklin	Walker, Nathaniel	4,000	Minor	30 Sep 1867	A	240
358	Campbell, Margaret Jane	Clark, James P.; Campbell, James A.	Campbell, George Samuel	210	Minor	14 Sep 1867		
365	Peterson, Elizabeth	Black, Houston; Farmer, E. T.	Peterson, Jane Ellen	2,000	Minor	7 Dec 1867		

118

Case #	Principals	Sureties	Bound to	Amount ($)	Type	Date	Book	Page(s)
365	Peterson, Elizabeth	Black, Houston; Farmer, E. T.	Peterson, Ann Frances	2,000	Minor	7 Dec 1867		
365	Peterson, Elizabeth	Black, Houston; Farmer, E. T.	Peterson, Nathaniel Houston	2,000	Minor	7 Dec 1867		
365	Peterson, Elizabeth	Black, Houston; Farmer, E. T.	Peterson, Dick	2,000	Minor	7 Dec 1867		
368	Brandon, Joseph R.	Mills, Andrew; Cavanagh, John	Pond, Mary; Simpson, R. M.; Simpson, E. A.	300	Minors	5 Feb 1868		
376	Fruits, Jacob	Fulton, James; Kuffel, Isaac	Fruits, Robert F.	120	Minor	6 Apr 1868		
376	Fruits, Jacob	Fulton, James; Kuffel, Isaac	Fruits, John S.	120	Minor	6 Apr 1868		
377	Fulton, David	Fulton, James; Gray, James	Wiseman, Susan	200	Minor	6 Apr 1868		
377	Fulton, David	Fulton, James; Gray, James	Wiseman, Ella	200	Minor	6 Apr 1868		
383	Meeker, William N.	Meeker, Stephen A.; Howe, Edwin A.	Meeker, Clementina S.; Meeker, Estella; Meeker, Orion S.	600	Minors	3 Aug 1868		
391	Fowler, James E.	Eliason, W. A.; Latimer, L. D.	Palmer, Lottie Bertha	100	Minor	7 Sep 1868		
396	Coon, James M.	Coon, Robert W.; Parker, E. D.	Coon, Hugh	100	Minor	21 Aug 1869		
399	Pierce, Sarah C.	Pierce, A. J.; Jewell, I. R.	Pierce, Arthur L.	14,000	Minor	3 Jan 1870		
406	Morse, A.	Lovejoy, A. P.; Leffingwell, J. L.	Flynn, Patrick	200	Insane person	9 Apr 1869		
414	Skaggs, Eben	Skaggs, Alexander; Laymance, I. C.	Easley, Amanda M.; Easley, William P.; Easley, Sarah F.	1,200	Minors	14 Jul 1869		
416	Greene, Shadrack	Nace, E. J.; Berger, M.	Smith, Adaline D.	100	Minor	16 Jul 1869		
416	Greene, Shadrack	Nace, E. J.; Berger, M.	Smith, Albert O.	100	Minor	16 Jul 1869		
416	Greene, Shadrack	Nace, E. J.; Berger, M.	Smith, John Henry	100	Minor	16 Jul 1869		
416	Greene, Shadrack	Nace, E. J.; Berger, M.	Smith, Chauncey B.	100	Minor	16 Jul 1869		
422	Boyce, John F.	Wise, Henry; Overton, A. P.	Clark, Florence B.	400	Minor	29 Sep 1869		
422	Boyce, John F.	Wise, Henry; Overton, A. P.	Clark, Mary Alice	400	Minor	29 Sep 1869		
422	Boyce, John F.	Wise, Henry; Overton, A. P.	Clark, Charles P.	400	Minor	29 Sep 1869		
426	Hardin, James T.	Thomas, A.; Willis, T. N.	Reed, Charles H.	480	Minor	8 Oct 1869		
426	Hardin, James T.	Thomas, A.; Willis, T. N.	Reed, Emiline J.	480	Minor	8 Oct 1869		
435	Brown, Elizabeth J.	Rickman, D. H.; Hausch, Christian	Brown, Mary R.; Brown, Calvin H.; Brown, Thomas L.; Brown, Oliver; Brown, Orrin	1,000	Minors	26 Feb 1870		
436	Smith, A. H.	Griggs, J. H.; McReynolds, James	Aull, George	2,000	Minor	17 Nov 1876		
436	Smyth, Thomas U.	Smith, J. P.; Smith, A. H.	Aull, Laura	1,000	Minor	[4 Dec 1871]		
436	Smyth, Thomas U.	Smith, J. P.; Smith, A. H.	Aull, George	1,000	Minor	4 Dec 1871		
439	Wilkins, Emily	Peterson, George W.; Peterson, Thomas C.	Wilkins, Maria S.; Wilkins, William; Wilkins, Henrietta C.	300	Minors	10 Jun 1870	A	255-256

Case #	Principals	Sureties	Bound to	Amount ($)	Type	Date	Book	Page(s)
444	Farquhar, Mary A.	Abbey, Richard; Judson, Egbert	Farquhar, Nora; Farquhar, Winnifred	11,040	Minors	24 Jun 1870	A	262-263
456	Whitman, G. W.; Whitman, N. A.	Pauli, G. T.; Thomas, A.	Whitman, Lillie	500	Minor	8 Oct 1870		
457	Clyman, Lancaster	Gregson, James; Fix, Jesse K.	Clyman, Frances M.	200	Minor	7 Nov 1870		
457	Clyman, Lancaster	Gregson, James; Fix, Jesse K.	Clyman, Alice C.	200	Minor	7 Nov 1870		
457	Clyman, Lancaster	Gregson, James; Fix, Jesse K.	Clyman, James I.	200	Minor	7 Nov 1870		
459	Driscol, John	Duffy, Thomas; McNamara, B.	Burk, Margaret	100	Minor	12 Oct 1870		
461	Burrus, G. W.	Hassett, John D.; Hudson, T. W.	Burrus, Mary C.	100	Minor	7 Nov 1870		
461	Burrus, G. W.	Hassett, John D.; Hudson, T. W.	Burrus, James A.	100	Minor	7 Nov 1870		
473	Lind, John	Kohle, August; Wilson, John G.	Lind, Emma	276	Minor	4 Feb 1871		
475	Nason, Richard H.	Welling, John; Fernald, J.; Case, A. B.; Brown, Daniel; Shepherd, J. S.; Kizer, John P.; Perkins, G. R.; Cheeseman, F. S.; Rice, C. B.; Dinwiddie, J. L.; Pfau, John; Sackett, D. A.; Hurd, Washington; Loughnane, James; Hasbrouck, H. B.; Wright, Isaac	Nason, Mary E.; Nason, John M.	8,000	Minors	15 Dec 1873		
475	Nason, Richard H.	O'Brien, J. C.; Foreman, William R.	Nason, John M.	3,000	Minor	14 May 1878		
475	Stockdale, Hugh	Fritsch, John; Hasbrouck, H. B.; Derby, A. B.; Comstock, William; Maynard, F. T.	Nason, Mary E.; Nason, John M.	10,000	Minors	7 Mar 1871		
482	Carter, Mary E.	Dickenson, William N.; Hembree, Andrew T.	Carter, Nancy V.	134	Minor	22 May 1871		
482	Carter, Mary E.	Dickenson, William N.; Hembree, Andrew T.	Carter, Margaret L.	134	Minor	22 May 1871		
482	Carter, Mary E.	Dickenson, William N.; Hembree, Andrew T.	Carter, Andrew Jackson	134	Minor	22 May 1871		
482	Carter, Mary E.	Pool, Henry J.; Campbell, James A.	Carter, Nancy V.	1,000	Minor	4 Dec 1871		
482	Carter, Mary E.	Pool, Henry J.; Campbell, James A.	Carter, Margaret L.	1,000	Minor	4 Dec 1871		
482	Carter, Mary E.	Pool, Henry J.; Campbell, James A.	Carter, Andrew J.	1,000	Minor	4 Dec 1871		
482	Carter, Mary E.	Pool, Henry J.; Davis, L. T.	Carter, Nancy V.	225	Minor	16 Aug 1875		
482	Carter, Mary E.	Pool, Henry J.; Davis, L. T.	Carter, Margaret L.	225	Minor	16 Aug 1875		
482	Carter, Mary E.	Pool, Henry J.; Davis, L. T.	Carter, Andrew J.	225	Minor	16 Aug 1875		
485	Noonan, George P.	Brown, John; Abelbeck, F. D.	Phillips, John	1,000	Insane person	15 May 1871		
487	Puckett, C. W.	Piper, John Jay; Puckett, S. A.	Puckett, G. W.	1,200	Insane person	30 May 1871		
488	Brush, D. C.	Gerkhardt, H. F.; Champlain, E.	Hilby, Agatha M.	50	Minor	24 Jun 1871		
488	Brush, D. C.	Gerkhardt, H. F.; Champlain, E.	Hilby, Francis M.	50	Minor	24 Jun 1871		

120

Case #	Principals	Sureties	Bound to	Amount ($)	Type	Date	Book	Page(s)
489	Badger, Joseph	Pickle, C. J.; Pickle, J. R.	Hughes, Josephine	200	Minor	6 Jul 1865		
490	Carr, James	Brians, William; Hassett, James H.	McGee, Robert	600	Insane person	5 Jun 1871		
490	Thomas, David	Pooler, H. L.; Powers, D.	McGee, Robert	500	Insane person	7 June 1875		
494	Ackermann, B. Henry	White, T. H.; Hartman, J. W.	Ackermann, Louis Dan	2,000	Minor	8 Nov 1865	A	218
494	Poehlmann, Conrad	Knowles, J. H; Cutter, J. S.	Ackermann, Louis Dan	2,000	Minor	8 Aug 1871		
499	Klink, Stephen V. R.	Canan, William S.; Fike, Nathan	Klink, Margaret J.; Klink, Nicholas Ward; Klink, George E.	500	Minors	3 Aug 1871		
503	McCullough, Robert	Withrow, William; Rogers, James M.	McCullough, David A.	800	Minor	4 Sep 1871		
503	McCullough, Robert	Withrow, William; Rogers, James M.	McCullough, Mary L.	800	Minor	4 Sep 1871		
504	Gill, Ann	Gill, George Q.; Baralli, Joseph	Gill, Antonette	3,000	Minor	18 Nov 1871		
505	Purvine, Mary Jane	Martin, S. M.; Warner, G.	Purvine, Margaret J.	622	Minor	[14] Oct 1871		
505	Purvine, Mary Jane	Purvine, J. C.; Stanley, J. P.	Purvine, Charles Francis	622	Minor	[14 Oct 1871]		
505	Purvine, Mary Jane	Purvine, J. C.; Stanley, J. P.	Purvine, Thomas Byron	622	Minor	[14] Oct 1871		
505	Purvine, Mary Jane	Martin, S. M.; Warner, G.	Purvine, William	622	Minor	[14] Oct 1871		
505	Purvine, Mary Jane	Purvine, J. C.; Stanley, J. P.	Purvine, Walter S.	622	Minor	[14 Oct 1871]		
506	Hendrick, E. W.	Field, James; Price, John	Coston, Addie	1,000	Minor	5 Oct 1871		
515	Roberts, John S.	Mock, Wesley; Howard, John F.	Paine, Etta K.	100	Minor	28 Dec 1871		
515	Roberts, John S.	Mock, Wesley; Howard, John F.	Paine, Clara E.	200	Minor	28 Dec 1871		
515	Roberts, John S.	Mock, Wesley; Howard, John F.	Paine, Lula	100	Minor	28 Dec 1871		
524	Weise, C.	Pauli, G. T.; Kohle, A.	Weise, Eliza; Weise, Frederick; Weise, Henrietta; Weise, Henry; Weise, Charles (children of C. Weise)	200	Minors	9 Feb 1872		
525	Dickson, D. S.	Whitney, A. P.; Seavy, Robert	Hunter, Wilbur L.	150	Minor	18 Nov 1872		
525	Dickson, D. S.	Whitney, A. P.; Seavy, Robert	Hunter, Olin M.	150	Minor	18 Nov 1872		
525	Cross, John L.	Underwood, F. L.	Cross, Cynthia J., infant heir-at-law of Elizabeth A. Hunter, late of Sonoma County, California, dec'd; This is a Muscatine County, Iowa, Circuit Court document; Also included is a certified copy of John L. Cross's Guardian's Letters for Cynthia J. Cross dated 31 Dec 1873, which is also a Muscatine County, Iowa, Circuit Court document.	600	Minor	31 Jan 1873		

Case #	Principals	Sureties	Bound to	Amount ($)	Type	Date	Book	Page(s)
526	Knox, John T.	Brown, John; Taylor, John S.	Leak, John D.; Leak, Charles W.	3,000	Minors	4 Mar 1872		
529	Hudson, Elizabeth	Neblett, Edward; Wise, Henry	Hudson, Henry W.	1,000	Minor	15 Mar 1872		
530	Benson, Josiah H.	Green, G. D.; Chapman, T. M.	Benson, Henry; Benson, William; Benson, Josiah; Benson, Nathaniel; Benson, Laura; Benson, Louis E.; Benson, Martha	2,800	Minors	4 Mar 1872		
532	Johnson, Melville	Roney, J. M.; Smith, R. Press., Jr.	Middleton, Walter V.	2,000	Minor	18 Mar 1872		
535	Trimble, William H.	Matthews, C. W.; Brown, A. M.	Fike, Stephen Spencer	1,500	Minor	3 May 1872		
540	Sharon, Catharine T.	Parks, D. H.; Canfield, William D.	Sharon, Edmund M.	800	Minor	13 May 1872		
540	Sharon, Catharine T.	Parks, D. H.; Canfield, William D.	Sharon, Margaretta R.	800	Minor	13 May 1872		
540	Sharon, Catharine T.	Parks, D. H.; Canfield, William D.	Sharon, Adelaide L.	800	Minor	13 May 1872		
544	Edwards, Hannah	Chapman, L.; Poehlmann, Conrad	Edwards, George	300	Minor	7 Jun 1872		
544	Edwards, Hannah	Chapman, L.; Poehlmann, Conrad	Edwards, Joseph	300	Minor	7 Jun 1872		
544	Edwards, Hannah	Chapman, L.; Poehlmann, Conrad	Edwards, Mary	300	Minor	7 Jun 1872		
546	Wilfley, Samuel	Wall, H. C.; Archer, John	Covey, George; Covey, Mary	1,600	Minors	13 May 1872		
549	Collier, Susan	Adams, John; Parrent, Evermont	Collier, Shedrick F.	100	Minor	3 Jun 1872		
552	Morin, Josiah	Walker, John; Dougherty, John	Tennent, Isabel Eva	100	Minor	4 Jun 1872		
557	Wickersham, I. G.	Atwater, H. H.; Wickersham, Jesse C.	Sandford, Louis N.	2,000	Minor	10 Jul 1872		
564	Hunt, Benjamin W.	Hardin, James A.; Forsyth, Robert	Hunt, Sarah C.; Hunt, Charles W.; Hunt, James B.; Hunt, Francis W.; Hunt, Lottie E.	300	Minors	27 Aug 1872		
568	Hockman, Jacob	Jacobs, George H.; Seaman, Jesse F.	Stryker, James A.	400	Minor	7 Sep 1872		
570	Rule, Elizabeth	O'Neale, W. T.; Page, Robert C.	Rule, N. A.	250	Minor	26 Aug 1872		
570	Rule, Elizabeth	O'Neale, W. T.; Page, Robert C.	Rule, E. J.	250	Minor	26 Aug 1872		
570	Rule, Elizabeth	O'Neale, W. T.; Page, Robert C.	Rule, C. S.	250	Minor	26 Aug 1872		
570	Rule, Elizabeth	O'Neale, W. T.; Page, Robert C.	Rule, William J.	250	Minor	26 Aug 1872		
571	Soules, Stephen	Church, A. M.; Bloom, Joseph	Russell, Mary A.	3,428	Minor	12 Sep 1872		
571	Soules, Stephen	Rupe, Samuel H.; Grater, J. F.	Russell, William F.	3,428	Minor	[12 Sep] 1872		
572	Pauli, G. T.	Hahman, F. G.; Kohle, August	Pauli, H. S.	500	Insane person	3 Sep 1872		
576	Fullagar, William	Fullagar, Alfred; Painter, J. M.; Hutchinson, Richard; Wilsey, Amasa	Fullagar, Elizabeth	500	Minor	5 Oct 1872		
578	Davis, Ira	Humphries, Charles; Powell, John	Armstrong, Rosanna	200	Minor	26 Oct 1872		

122

Case #	Principals	Sureties	Bound to	Amount ($)	Type	Date	Book	Page(s)
579	Talbot, Coleman	Hendley, John; Talbot, Holeman	Talbot, Kennedy B.	1,000	Insane person	12 Nov 1872		
582	Hunter, John	Boyd, George W.; Trask, Freeman	Wright, John A.; Wright, Sarah E.; Wright, James A.; Wright, Amelia A.	250	Minors	27 Dec 1872		
584	Finley, John	Hitchcock, Hollis; Findley, Elizabeth; Goodman, L. S.	Findley, David; Findley, Katharine; Findley, Elizabeth; Findley, Samuel; Findley, Harvey	7,000	Minors	2 Jan 1873		
586	Howell, Stephen T.	Chenoweth, Miles H.; Sutton, H. D.	Moore, William T.	300	Minor	14 Dec 1872		
587	Jackson, Jane	Ayers, William; Spotswood, Robert	Jackson, Abraham Joseph; Jackson, Mary Jane; Jackson, Margaret; Jackson, Gideon; Jackson, Fanny Victoria	500	Minors	26 Dec 1872		
596	Howard, Mary Ellen	Shinn, S. M.; Davis, Ira	Hatfield, Joseph A.; Hatfield, Francis A.; Hatfield, William P.; Hatfield, Rebecca	100	Minors	23 Mar 1873		
597	Baird, Mary E.	Willis, T. N.; Farmer, E. T.	Simmons, Charles	400	Minor	[7 Mar 1873]		
597	Baird, Mary E.	Willis, T. N.; Farmer, E. T.	Simmons, Ida	400	Minor	7 Mar 1873		
599	Heald, Jacob G.	Smith, A. H.; Mathews, John	Heald, John Edson	600	Minor	14 Mar 1873		
604	Pierce, A.J.	Haskell, W. B.; Seavy, R.	Pierce, William S.	2,500	Minor	21 Apr 1873		
607	Brooks, William	Pool, Henry J.; Clark, Benjamin	Prewett, Francis G.	800	Minor	16 Apr 1873		
607	Brooks, William	Pool, Henry J.; Clark, Benjamin	Prewett, George	900	Minor	16 Apr 1873		
608	Harrington, John F.	Lyons, Dennis; Flood, Michael	Baylis, Theodore	500	Minor	4 Mar 1874		
616	Brackett, J. S.	Walker, O. V.; Fairbanks, H. T.	Burbank, Caleb	1,000	Insane person	29 May 1873		
616	Burbank, Samuel F.	Whitney, A. P.; Poehlmann, C.	State of California; The Probate Court of Sonoma County appointed Samuel F. Burbank the guardian of the person and the estate of Caleb Burbank, an insane person, on 19 Oct 1874 and directed letters of guardianship to issue to him upon his executing this bond.	500	Insane person	26 Oct 1874		
620	Bates, H. F.	Adler, Lewis; Clark, George W.	Meyer, Frederick	400	Minor	19 Jun 1873		
621	Dorman, William	Adler, Lewis; Bates, H. F.	Meyer, Augusta; Meyer, Julia; Meyer, William; Meyer, Katy	8	Minors	19 Jun 1873		
623	Jones, Elizabeth A.	Boyce, J. F.; Allen, O. S.	Jones, Minnie; Jones, Fred (children of Willard D. Jones, dec'd)	1,000	Minors	27 Jun 1873		
627	Castens, Henrey	Seawell, William N.; Seawell, David H.	Hegeler, Gerhard	1,000	Minor	28 Jul 1873		
627	Castens, Henrey	Seawell, William N.; Seawell, David H.	Castens, Sophia	1,000	Minor	28 Jul 1873		

123

Case #	Principals	Sureties	Bound to	Amount ($)	Type	Date	Book	Page(s)
634	Smith, P. B.	Mock, Wesley; Walker, J. G.	State of California; The Probate Court of Sonoma County appointed P. B. Smith the guardian of the estate of George Taylor Smith, a minor, on 25 Aug 1873 and directed letters of guardianship to issue to him upon his executing this bond.	800	Minor	1 Sep 1873		
634	McGee, James H.	Holman, John H.; Davis, Preston	State of California; The Probate Court of Sonoma County appointed James H. McGee the guardian of the person and the estate of George T. Smith, a minor, on 17 Nov 1873 and directed letters of guardianship to issue to him upon his executing this bond.	800	Minor	15 Dec 1873		
635	Hausch, Christian	Rupe, Samuel H.; Laymance, I. C.	Hausch, Charles H. J.	400	Minor	25 Aug 1873		
635	Hausch, Christian	Rupe, Samuel H.; Laymance, I. C.	Hausch, Henery Etta	400	Minor	25 Aug 1873		
635	Hausch, Christian	Rupe, Samuel H.; Laymance, I. C.	Hausch, Ellsey	400	Minor	25 Aug 1873		
635	Hausch, Christian	Rupe, Samuel H.; Laymance, I. C.	Hausch, Hannah May	400	Minor	25 Aug 1873		
635	Hausch, Christian	Rupe, Samuel H.; Laymance, I. C.	Hausch, Flora	400	Minor	25 Aug 1873		
635	Hausch, Christian	Rupe, Samuel H.; Laymance, I. C.	Hausch, Anna Bell	400	Minor	25 Aug 1873		
639	Slattery, William J.	Tighe, Kelly; Smith, John B.	Thurgood, Elizabeth M.	600	Minor	23 Oct 1876		
639	Slattery, William J.	Tighe, Kelly; Smith, John B.	Thurgood, Mary Ann	600	Minor	23 Oct 1876		
639	Slattery, William J.	Tighe, Kelly; Smith, John B.	Thurgood, William S.	600	Minor	23 Oct 1876		
641	Barry, Julia	Hopes, E.; Bailey, James B.	Barry, William	500	Minor	3 Jan 1882		
641	Murphey, John	Skiffington, John; Sutton, Hiram D.	Barry, William	1,000	Minor	21 Mar 1876	C	320
641	Murphey, John	McLaughlin, Michael; Palmer, William	Barry, Thomas	1,000	Minor	18 Mar 1876	C	321
641	Barry, Julia M.	Hynes, James; Zimmerman, George	Barry, Thomas; Barry, Ellen Agnes; Barry, Julia; Barry, Mary Elizabeth; Barry, William; Barry, Susan Ann	2,400	Minors	6 Sep 1873	C	348
648	Simons, John S.	Tupper, G. A.; Willis, T. N.	Ogan, Mary A.	300	Minor	1 Oct 1873		
649	Simons, John S.	Tupper, G. A.; Willis, T. N.	Ogan, Kittie V.	300	Minor	1 Oct 1873		
650	Simons, John S.	Tupper, G. A.; Willis, T. N.	Ogan, David P.	300	Minor	1 Oct 1873		
651	Field, J. C.	Rice, C. B.; Moore, E.	Fader, Kate A.	100	Minor	13 Jan 1877		
651	Field, J. C.	Rice, C. B.; Moore, E.	Fader, Victor V.	100	Minor	13 Jan 1877		
651	Field, J. C.	Rice, C. B.; Moore, E.	Fader, Helen M.	100	Minor	13 Jan 1877		
651	Field, J. C.	Cassidy, J. W.; Moore, E.	Fader, Victor V.	475	Minor	19 Apr 1878		
651	Field, J. C.	Cassidy, J. W.; Moore, E.	Fader, Helen M.	1,330	Minor	19 Apr 1878		
651	Field, J. C.	Cassidy, J. W.; Moore, E.	Fader, Kate A.	785	Minor	19 Apr 1878		

Case #	Principals	Sureties	Bound to	Amount ($)	Type	Date	Book	Page(s)
651	Field, J. C.	Hill, William; Moore, E.	Fader, Annie K.; Fader, Katie H.; Fader, Victor V.; Fader, Helen M.	1,600	Minors	6 Aug 1875	C	273
651	Field, J. C.	Hill, William; Case, A. B.	Fader, Anna H.; Fader, Katie A.; Fader, Victor V.; Fader, Helen M.	4,500	Minors	4 Mar 1875		
652	Bicknell, Elizabeth	Donahue, John; Carpenter, L. F.	Bicknell, Ida; Bicknell, Anna; Bicknell, Charles	500	Minors	29 Oct 1873		
655	Clawson, Charles	Story, S. C.; Burnham, John H.	State of California; The Probate Court of Sonoma County appointed Charles Clawson the guardian of the person of Ida M. Steadman, a minor, on 3 Nov 1873 and directed letters of guardianship to issue to him upon his executing this bond.	250	Minor	3 Nov 1873		
665	Chinn, Lewis F.	Hood, Thomas B.; Smith, James	State of California; The Probate Court of Sonoma County appointed Lewis F. Chinn the guardian of the estate and the person of Amanda Metcaliffe, a minor, on 12 Jan 1874 and directed letters of guardianship to issue to him upon his executing this bond.	1,000	Minor	12 Jan 1874		
668	Freeman, John M.	Kahn, Achilla; Newburgh, E	Cashdollar, Alҏia Beatrice	250	Minor	24 Jan 1874		
672	Smith, Alexander H.	Heald, Thomas T.; Bumpus, C. H.	Smith, Sarah C.	250	Minor	25 Feb 1874		
675	Fowler, James E.	Gaver, Andrew P.; Jones, William	Fowler, Edgar J.	4,500	Minor	24 Mar 1874	C	173-174
675	Fowler, James E.	Gaver, Andrew P.; Jones, William	Fowler, William Warren	4,500	Minor	24 Mar 1874	C	172-173
675	Fowler, James E.	Joy, Benjamin; Acker, R. W.	Fowler, William Warren	4,500	Minor	14 Jul 1875		
675	Fowler, James E.	Joy, Benjamin; Acker, R. W.	Fowler, Edgar J.	4,500	Minor	14 Jul 1875		
677	Davis, Charles M.	Jones, Reuben A.; Bagley, J. W.	Davis, Henry	500	Minor	21 Mar 1874	C	176-178
677	Davis, Charles M.	Jones, Reuben A.; Bagley, J. W.	Davis, Ella	500	Minor	21 Mar 1874	C	174-176
677	Davis, Charles M.	Jones, Reuben A.; Bagley, J. W.	Davis, Edwin	500	Minor	21 Mar 1874	C	178-180
684	Munday, Elizabeth	Towne, S. D.; Bernhard, Isaac	Munday, M. E. C.; Munday, C. F.; Munday, Alice; Munday, Fanny	800	Minors	8 May 1874	C	184-185
698	Burris, David	Tivnen, John; Pauli, F. Albert	Hardcastle, Job	300	Insane person	18 Jun 1874	C	201-202
704	Carrillo, Henry G.	Carrillo, Lizzie; Carrillo, Joaquin	Carrillo, Mary F.	400	Minor	24 Aug 1874	C	214-215
704	Carrillo, Henry G.	Carrillo, Lizzie; Carrillo, Joaquin	Carrillo, Louisa A.	400	Minor	24 Aug 1874	C	212-214
704	Carrillo, Henry G.	Carrillo, Lizzie; Carrillo, Joaquin	Carrillo, Amelia C.	400	Minor	24 Aug 1874	C	209-210
704	Carrillo, Henry G.	Carrillo, Lizzie; Carrillo, Joaquin	Carrillo, Frederick A.	400	Minor	24 Aug 1874	C	206-207
704	Carrillo, Henry G.	Carrillo, Lizzie; Carrillo, Joaquin	Carrillo, Frank J.	400	Minor	24 Aug 1874	C	207-209
704	Carrillo, Henry G.	Carrillo, Lizzie; Carrillo, Joaquin	Carrillo, Catherine A.	400	Minor	24 Aug 1874	C	211-212
704	Carrillo, Henry G.	Carrillo, Elizabeth; Dougherty, John	Carrillo, Fred A.	400	Minor	13 Aug 1875	C	277-278

Case #	Principals	Sureties	Bound to	Amount ($)	Type	Date	Book	Page(s)
704	Carrillo, Henry G.	Carrillo, Elizabeth; Dougherty, John	Carrillo, Amelia C.	400	Minor	13 Aug 1875	C	280-281
704	Carrillo, Henry G.	Carrillo, Elizabeth; Dougherty, John	Carrillo, Frank J.	400	Minor	13 Aug 1875	C	276-277
704	Carrillo, Henry G.	Carrillo, Elizabeth; Dougherty, John	Carrillo, Mary F.	400	Minor	13 Aug 1875	C	279-280
704	Carrillo, Henry G.	Carrillo, Elizabeth; Dougherty, John	Carrillo, Louisa A.	400	Minor	13 Aug 1875	C	281-282
704	Carrillo, Henry G.	Carrillo, Elizabeth; Dougherty, John	Carrillo, Catherine A.	400	Minor	13 Aug 1875	C	278-279
704	Overton, A. P.	Kelly, J. W.; McReynolds, James	Carrillo, Amelia C.	600	Minor	5 Oct 1877		
704	Overton, A. P.	Kelly, J. W.; McReynolds, James	Carrillo, Catherine A.	600	Minor	5 Oct 1877		
704	Overton, A. P.	Kelly, J. W.; McReynolds, James	Carrillo, J. Frank	500	Minor	5 Oct 1877		
704	Overton, A. P.	Kelly, J. W.; McReynolds, James	Carrillo, Fred. A.	800	Minor	5 Oct 1877		
704	Overton, A. P.	Kelly, J. W.; McReynolds, James	Carrillo, Fannie B.	600	Minor	5 Oct 1877		
704	Overton, A. P.	Kelly, J. W.; McReynolds, James	Carrillo, Louisa A.	600	Minor	5 Oct 1877		
704	Overton, A. P.	Latapie, E.; Carter, J. W.	Carrillo, Catherine A.	600	Minor	13 May 1879		
704	Carrillo, Joaquin	Hood, George; Morris, W. H.	Carrillo, Catherine A.	600	Minor	6 Nov 1882		
705	Murphey, John	Sweeney, Jerry; McDermott, William	Sullivan, Ellen F.; Sullivan, John P.; Sullivan, George E.; Sullivan, Catharine M.	500	Minors	[?] Oct 1874	C	216-217, 282-283
709	Stewart, Hannah M.	Ward, A.; Poehlmann, C.	Stewart, William Allen; Stewart, Frank Lester; Sullivan, Robert Henry	3,000	Minors	19 Oct 1874	C	218-219, 285
710	Warth/Worth, Claiborne	McElarney, Frank; Crigler, William E.	Cox, George W.	1,600	Minor	30 Oct 1874	C	220, 286
711	Fisk, Clara S.	Fisk, J. C.; McClellan, M. T.	Fisk, Frank	2,400	Minor	28 Dec 1876		
711	Fisk, Clara S.	Fillebrown, Almira B.; Fisk, John C.	Fisk, Frank	3,000	Minor	4 Aug 1884		
720	Powers, David P.	Jewell, D. H.; Smith, James F.; Hoag, O. H.	Churchman, William (child of William Churchman, dec'd)	1,200	Minor	4 Jan 1875	C	225-227
721	Downs, Vernon	Boyce, J. F.; Tupper, G. A.	Churchman, John	1,200	Minor	4 Jan 1875	C	227-230
722	Downs, Vernon	Mutz, Henry; Gregg, Isaac	Churchman, Maggie	1,200	Minor	27 May 1876		
724	Lavine, Frank	Maher, T. C.; Dunning, E. B.	Smith, Abbie	500	Minor	5 Jan 1875	C	230-231
724½	Luce, Jirah	Hassett, J. D.; Hassett, A.	Swain, Georgia I.; Swain, Susan I.; Swain, Mary D.	4,000	Minors	21 Jan 1875	C	232
725	Mead, Catherine	Caldwell, F. M.; Loucks, A. H.	Mead, Alice C.	500	Minor	7 Jan 1875	C	233-234
726	Dozier, Melville	Dozier, E. C.; Dozier, L. F.	Dozier, Roland	2,000	Minor	25 Jan 1875	C	234-235
729	Loucks, A. H.	Brown, John; Powers, David	Kelty, Anna L.	500	Minor	15 Feb 1875		
730	Millington, Nancy Maria	Duncan, James P.; Duncan, Daniel	Millington, Buchanan	300	Minor	15 Feb 1875		

Case #	Principals	Sureties	Bound to	Amount ($)	Type	Date	Book	Page(s)
730	Millington, Nancy Maria	Duncan, James P.; Duncan, Daniel	Millington, Zachariah	300	Minor	15 Feb 1875		
730	Millington, Nancy Maria	Duncan, James P.; Duncan, Daniel	Millington, John	300	Minor	15 Feb 1875		
730	Millington, Nancy Maria	Duncan, James P.; Duncan, Daniel	Millington, Seth	300	Minor	15 Feb 1875		
730	Millington, Nancy Maria	Duncan, James P.; Duncan, Daniel	Millington, Anna Electa	300	Minor	15 Feb 1875	C	248-249
735	Clark, James P.	Wise, Henry; Tupper, G. A.	Clark, James M.	500	Minor	10 Mar 1875	C	247-248
735	Clark, James P.	Wise, Henry; Tupper, G. A.	Clark, Gertrude	500	Minor	10 Mar 1875	C	245-246
735	Clark, James P.	Wise, Henry; Tupper, G. A.	Clark, Estella	500	Minor	10 Mar 1875	C	246-247
735	Clark, James P.	Wise, Henry; Tupper, G. A.	Clark, Frederick W.	500	Minor	10 Mar 1875	C	249-250
735	Clark, James P.	Wise, Henry; Tupper, G. A.	Clark, Margaret E.	500	Minor	10 Mar 1875	C	253, 256
738	Hurd, G. W.	Dalton, William H.; Taft, Henry C.	Hurd, George Henry	250	Minor	23 Mar 1875	C	252-253
738	Hurd, G. W.	Dalton, William H.; Taft, Henry C.	Hurd, Charlotte Psyche	250	Minor	23 Mar 1875	C	251-252
738	Hurd, G. W.	Dalton, William H.; Taft, Henry C	Hurd, Lizzie J. T.	250	Minor	23 Mar 1875	C	261
743	Shinn, Robert F.	Stites, A. H.; Wisecarver, J. R.	Shinn, Eliza J.	100	Minor	3 May 1875	C	258
743	Shinn, Robert F.	Stites, A. H.; Wisecarver, J. R.	Shinn, Andrew J.	100	Minor	3 May 1875	C	260
743	Shinn, Robert F.	Stites, A. H.; Wisecarver, J. R.	Shinn, Mary Ellen	100	Minor	3 May 1875	C	259
743	Shinn, Robert F.	Stites, A. H.; Wisecarver, J. R.	Shinn, John Davis	100	Minor	3 May 1875	C	267
746	Gallaway, A. J.	Dittemore, J. Wallace; Hassett, Aaron	Galaway, Amanda A.	200	Minor	24 May 1875	C	264
746	Gallaway, A. J.	Dittemore, J. Wallace; Hassett, Aaron	Galaway, Allen R.	200	Minor	24 May 1875	C	266
746	Gallaway, A. J.	Dittemore, J. Wallace; Hassett, Aaron	Galaway, A. J., Jr.	200	Minor	24 May 1875	C	265
746	Gallaway, A. J.	Dittemore, J. Wallace; Hassett, Aaron	Galaway, Nancy E.	200	Minor	24 May 1875	C	269
748	Magoon, William H.	Gossage, Z.; Magoon, H. K.	Pangburn, Annie Eugenia	500	Minor	7 Jun 1875	C	
748½	Hager, George D.	Hall, L. B.; Magoon, H. K.	State of California; The Probate Court of Sonoma County appointed George D. Hager the guardian of Ella Harvey, a minor, on 30 Jul 1875 and letters of guardianship were directed to him upon the execution of this bond.	200	Minor	30 Jul 1875		
750	Matthies, Heinrich	Poehlmann, Conrad; Poehlmann, Martin	Held, Henrietta Georgina	3,000	Minor	17 May 1879		
750	Matthies, Heinrich	Pfau, John; Meyer, Anton	Held, Henrietta Georgina	3,000	Minor	14 Jul 1875	C	270
755	Elder, J. W.	Shane, Adam; Davis, Levi; Gentry, J. C.; Peugh, James A.; Manion, William; Urton, W. L.	Elder, John M.; Elder, Monroe C.; Elder, Madison L.; Elder, Charles G.; Elder, Jessie M.; Elder, Hellena M. (heirs of William Elder and his wife Phebe A. Elder, dec'd)	5,000	Minors	24 Jul 1875	C	289-290

Case #	Principals	Sureties	Bound to	Amount ($)	Type	Date	Book	Page(s)
770	Mountjoy, Mary L.	Justice, S. A.; Henley, Barclay	Mountjoy, Lula F.	100	Minor	27 Sep 1875	C	299-300
770½	Godwin, Phebe A.	Dickinson, Charles; Drummond, Donald	Godwin, Frederick Oscar	400	Minor	9 Oct 1875	C	300-301
770½	Godwin, Phebe A.	Dickinson, Charles; Drummond, Donald	Godwin, Henry Talmond	400	Minor	9 Oct 1875	C	301-302
770½	Godwin, Phebe A.	Dickinson, Charles; Drummond, Donald	Godwin, Hiram Ladd	400	Minor	9 Oct 1875	C	302-303
771	White, W. P.	Meyer, Samuel; Rosenthal, Joseph	White, Maggie	200	Minor	19 Aug 1876		
778	Hall, L.J.	Powell, R.; Hassett, A.	McPherson, Annie E.	5,000	Minor	3 Mar 1884		
778	Hall, L.J.	Powell, R.; Hassett, A.	McPherson, Mary	5,000	Minor	3 Mar 1884		
778	Hall, L.J.	Powell, R.; Hassett, A.	McPherson, Early	5,000	Minor	3 Mar 1884		
778	Gird, Henry S.	Brown, H. K.; Barnes, E. H.	McPherson, Stonewall	8,000	Minor	3 Mar 1884		
778	Gird, Henry S.	Powell, R.; Meyer, S.	McPherson, Early	1,000	Minor	3 Mar 1884		
778	Gird, H. S.	Hall, L. J.; Powell, R.	McPherson, Ewell	10,000	Incompetent person	29 Aug 1888	1	85
778	Gird, Henry S.	Powell, R.; Meyer, S.	McPherson, Ewell	8,000	Minor	3 Mar 1884		
780	Hassett, Aaron	Mead, James A.; Truitt, John R.	Brown, Daniel	200	Minor	1 Dec 1875		
780	Hassett, Aaron	Mead, James A.; Truitt, John R.	Brown, Martha E.	200	Minor	1 [Dec] 1875		
780	Hassett, Aaron	Mead, James A.; Truitt, John R.	Brown, James W.	200	Minor	1 Dec 1875		
789	Eikenbery, John S.	Bell, Albert K.; Pickle, J. F.	Kincaid, Oscar F.	1,400	Minor	25 Jan 1876	C	312-313
790	Thatcher, D.	Ensign, J. C.; Gill, H.	Herron, Amy	250	Minor	25 Jan 1876	C	314-315
790	Thatcher, D.	Ensign, J. C.; Gill, H.	Herron, Belle	250	Minor	25 Jan 1876	C	313-314
790½	Moore, P. L.	McPherson, Lycurgus; Rupe, Samuel H.	Moore, Henrietta	75	Minor	31 Jan 1876	C	317-318
790½	Moore, P. L.	McPherson, Lycurgus; Rupe, Samuel H.	Moore, Charles	75	Minor	31 Jan 1876	C	315-316
790½	Moore, P. L.	McPherson, Lycurgus; Rupe, Samuel H.	Moore, Laura A.	75	Minor	31 Jan 1876	C	316
794	Atherton, Isaac W.	Gerkhardt, H. F.; Shaw, I. E.	Atherton, Albert W.	500	Minor	29 Mar 1876	C	330-331
794	Atherton, Isaac W.	Gerkhardt, H. F.; Shaw, I. E.	Atherton, Dwight C.	500	Minor	29 Mar 1876	C	331-332
795	Goddard, Jane M.	Soules, Stephen; Lewis, R. E.	Goddard, Albert D.	300	Minor	7 Feb 1876	C	324-325
795	Goddard, Jane M.	Soules, Stephen; Lewis, R. E.	Goddard, Frank W.	300	Minor	7 Feb 1876	C	325-326
795	Goddard, Jane M.	Soules, Stephen; Lewis, R. E.	Goddard, Wellman	300	Minor	7 Feb 1876	C	326-327
795	Goddard, Jane M.	Soules, Stephen; Lewis, R. E.	Goddard, Jesse P.	300	Minor	7 Feb 1876	C	323-324
807	Vail, Anna B.	Button, I. V.; Kelley, Albert	Vail, Nellie	100	Minor	[19] Apr 1876	C	336-337
808	Cavanagh, John	Newburgh, E.; Atwater, H. H.	Sproule, George W.	500	Minor	21 Apr 1876	C	337-338
811	Evans, Mary Ellen	Leigh, Mary; Leigh, A. G.	Evans, Charles William	100	Minor	10 May 1876	C	338-339

Case #	Principals	Sureties	Bound to	Amount ($)	Type	Date	Book	Page(s)
811	Evans, Mary Ellen	Leigh, Mary; Leigh, A. G.	Evans, John Wirt	100	Minor	10 May 1876	C	340-341
811	Evans, Mary Ellen	Leigh, Mary; Leigh, A. G.	Evans, Lucy Jane	100	Minor	10 May 1876	C	339-340
814	Luce, Arthur S.	Luce, Jirah; Bailhache, John N.	Liddle, Lucinda	600	Minor	20 May 1876	C	343-344
819	Hassett, John D.	Powell, Ransom; Hassett, Aaron	Payne, Newton	3,500	Minor	13 Aug 1880		
819	Hassett, John D.	Powell, Ransom; Hassett, Aaron	Payne, Hannah	3,500	Minor	13 Aug 1880		
819	Payne, William W.	Grove, David; Turner, G. J.	Payne, Newton	2,700	Minor	20 Jun 1876		
819	Payne, William W.	Rupe, Sam H.; Soules, S.	Payne, Hannah	2,700	Minor	20 Jun 1876		
821	Torrance, S. H.	Mills, A. J.; Haskins, M. D.	Hill, Amos	100	Insane person	15 Jan 1877		
826	Tighe, Kelly	Needham, Festus; Roach, Thomas	O'Leary, Patrick	600	Insane person	27 Jul 1876	C	354
829	Gerkhardt, H. F.	Pauli, G. T.; Wise, Henry	Gropp, Charles	2,000	Insane person	29 Jun 1876		
843	Looney, Robert	Doty, A.; Cheney, T. H.	Hood, Mary	200	Minor	5 Dec 1876	C	364
843	Looney, Robert	Doty, A.; Cheney, T. H.	Hood, Albert	200	Minor	5 Dec 1876	C	366
843	Looney, Robert	Doty, A.; Cheney, T. H.	Hood, Sarah	200	Minor	5 Dec 1876	C	365
843½	Bledsoe, A. C.	Johnson, George A.; Norton, L. A.	Byrns, James W.	400	Minor	7 May 1878		
863	Beatty, William	Cooper, Richard; Beatty, Mary	Hopper, Emma Belle	100	Minor	17 Apr 1877	C	389
863	Beatty, William	Cooper, Richard; Beatty, Mary	Hopper, Eugene	100	Minor	17 Apr 1877	C	390
863	Beatty, William	Cooper, Richard; Beatty, Mary	Hopper, Climama	100	Minor	17 Apr 1877	C	388
863	Beatty, William	Cooper, Richard; Beatty, Mary	Hopper, Edward	100	Minor	17 Apr 1877	C	387
864	Johnson, Rachel	Solomon, Charles; Emerson, Henry	Epperley, Levi Oliver	100	Minor	22 Jan 1877	C	391
866	Solomon, Charles	Johnson, Rachel; Dougherty, John	McGuire, Cora E.	3,650	Minor	22 Jan 1877	C	393
866	Johnson, Rachel	Gillam, Mitchel; Branscom, B. F.; McChristian, Patrick	McGuire, Cora E.	3,500	Minor	11 Aug 1877		
873	Strom, William	Maede, August; Boyce, J. F. (Dr.)	Winkler, John J.	1,000	Incompetent person	10 Apr 1877	C	397
884	Ackerman, Nannie	Gibbs, Henry; Wooden, Joseph	Ackerman, Harriet Bell	800	Minor	12 May 1877		
884	Ackerman, Nannie	Gibbs, Henry; Wooden, Joseph	Ackerman, Mary Bell	800	Minor	12 May 1877		
884	Ackerman, Nannie	Gibbs, Henry; Wooden, Joseph	Ackerman, Rebecca Jane	800	Minor	12 May 1877		
887	Scott, B. W.	Barney, M. W.; Miller, Thomas B.	Scott, Luke	100	Minor	14 Apr 1877		
888	Looney, Robert	Doty, A.; Cheney, T. H.	Hood, Stella Blanche	100	Minor	20 Apr 1877		
889	Runyon, Mary	Runyon, Solomon; Brown, Arthur	Runyon, Emma	10,000	Minor	4 Aug 1877		

Case #	Principals	Sureties	Bound to	Amount ($)	Type	Date	Book	Page(s)
889	Brown, Arthur	Wallace, W. H.; Runyon, S.	Runyon, Frederick M.	10,000	Minor	28 Aug 1877		
889	Brown, Arthur	Wallace, W. H.; Runyon, S.	Runyon, Charles E.	10,000	Minor	28 Aug 1877		
897	Burris, David	Fulkerson, Richard; Farmer, Elijah T.	Spencer, Nancy (child of Charles Spencer, dec'd)	600	Minor	3 Jul 1877	C	417
897	Burris, David	Fulkerson, Richard; Farmer, Elijah T.	Spencer, Shattuck (child of Charles Spencer, dec'd)	600	Minor	3 Jul 1877	C	416
897	Burris, David	Fulkerson, Richard; Farmer, E. T.	Spencer, Rowena (child of Charles Spencer, dec'd)	600	Minor	3 Jul 1877	C	418
897	Burris, David	Fulkerson, Richard; Farmer, Elijah T.	Spencer, George (child of Charles Spencer, dec'd)	600	Minor	3 Jul 1877	C	420
897	Burris, David	Fulkerson, Richard; Farmer, Elijah T.	Spencer, Charles (child of Charles Spencer, dec'd)	600	Minor	3 Jul 1877	C	419
906	Hickman, John E.	Parks, D. H.; Hickman, B. F.	Fiscus, George W.	800	Minor	15 Oct 1877		
908	Goddard, W. H.	Turner, John; Procter, Charles E.	Field, Effa	1,750	Minor	22 Oct 1877	C	423
908	Goddard, W. H.	Hudson, T. W.; Gilbride, R.	Field, Erma	1,750	Minor	8 Dec 1877	C	424
911	McPeak, Anthony	Irwin, Thomas N.; Pfister, Conrad	Bates, Laura	800	Minor	21 Dec 1877		
911	McPeak, Anthony	Irwin, Thomas N.; Pfister, Conrad	Bates, Neely	800	Minor	21 Dec 1877		
912	McPeak, Anthony	Irwin, Thomas N.; Pfister, Conrad	Blakeley, Martin L.	400	Minor	21 Dec 1877		
912	McPeak, Anthony	Irwin, Thomas N.; Pfister, Conrad	Blakeley, Eugene	400	Minor	21 Dec 1877		
912	McPeak, Anthony	Irwin, Thomas N.; Pfister, Conrad	Blakeley, Unity	400	Minor	21 Dec 1877		
918	Palmer, James M.	Pearce, George; Doyle, M.	Hinkston, Nancy	4,000	Incompetent person	16 Feb 1878		
919	Isaacs, Esther	Bloom, Jonas; Cohn, Samuel	Isaacs, Louis	2,000	Minor	26 Nov 1877	C	435
919	Isaacs, Esther	Bloom, Jonas; Cohn, Samuel	Isaacs, Marks	2,000	Minor	26 Nov 1877	C	436
924	Blackburn, Charles	Whitney, A. P.; Wickersham, Jesse C.	King, Alice	2,000	Minor	2 Oct 1877		
926	Barnes, E. H.	Nalley, A. B.; Johnson, George A.	Lowery, William	300	Minor	28 Jan 1878	C	439
926	Barnes, E. H.	Nalley, A. B.; Johnson, George A.	Lowery, Benjamin	300	Minor	28 Jan 1878	C	438
928	Miller, Zerilda	Gallaway, A. J.; Hotchkiss, B.	Miller, Armelia M.	1,700	Minor	24 Dec 1877	C	430
928	Miller, Zerilda	Gallaway, A. J.; Hotchkiss, B.	Miller, Nannie E.	1,700	Minor	24 Dec 1877	C	428
928	Miller, Zerilda	Gallaway, A. J.; Hotchkiss, B.	Miller, Mary J.	1,700	Minor	24 Dec 1877	C	429
928	Miller, Zerilda	Gallaway, A. J.; Hotchkiss, B.	Miller, Rachel	1,700	Minor	24 Dec 1877	C	431
928	Miller, Zerilda	Gallaway, A. J.; Hotchkiss, B.	Miller, James R.	1,700	Minor	24 Dec 1877	C	432
929	Heisel, Paul	Johnson, Peter; Strom, William	Mingus, Peter	2,000	Insane person	19 Feb 1878		
931	Ferguson, Russel	Maddux, L. D.; Baber, B. F.	McMinn, Mary F.	300	Minor	29 Aug 1877		
931	Ferguson, Russel	Maddux, L. D.; Baber, B. F.	McMinn, Joseph A.	300	Minor	29 Aug 1877		

Case #	Principals	Sureties	Bound to	Amount ($)	Type	Date	Book	Page(s)
931	Ferguson, Russel	Maddux, L. D.; Baber, B. F.	McMinn, Charles V.	300	Minor	29 Aug 1877		
932	Noonan, George P.	Latapie, E.; Roney, J. M.	Smith, Harry	600	Minor	29 Sep 1877		
935	Wilson, Valentine	Cheney, R. J.; Drummond, Donald	Wilson, Gaston	50	Minor	3 Oct 1877		
935	Wilson, Valentine	Cheney, R. J.; Drummond, Donald	Wilson, Isaac E.	50	Minor	3 Oct 1877		
935	Wilson, Valentine	Cheney, R. J.; Drummond, Donald	Wilson, Albert C.	50	Minor	3 Oct 1877		
935	Wilson, Valentine	Cheney, R. J.; Drummond, Donald	Wilson, Leland	50	Minor	3 Oct 1877		
935	Wilson, Valentine	Cheney, R. J.; Drummond, Donald	Wilson, Celia A.	50	Minor	3 Oct 1877		
935	Wilson, Valentine	Wilsey, A.; Cheney, D.	Wilson, George B.	200	Minor	6 Oct 1877		
935	Wilson, Valentine	Cheney, R. J.; Drummond, Donald	Tracy, Phoebe	50	Minor	3 Oct 1877		
935	Wilson, Valentine	Cheney, R. I.; Drummond, Donald	Tracy, Charles	50	Minor	3 Oct 1877		
935	Wilson, Valentine	Cheney, R. J.; Drummond, Donald	Tracy, Eda	50	Minor	3 Oct 1877		
935	Wilson, Valentine	Wilsey, A.; Cheney, D.	Tracy, Dora	200	Minor	6 Oct 1877		
936	Patterson, William	Young, James B.; Loucks, A. H.	Wasler, Julianna M.	500	Minor	27 Aug 1877		
937	Kennedy, George H.	Pool, Henry J.; Steadman, Amos D.	West, Nellie	2,500	Minor	19 Sep 1877	C	426
937	Kennedy, George H.	Pool, Henry J.; Steadman, Amos D.	West, Eddie	2,500	Minor	19 Sep 1877	C	427
937	Steadman, Mary G. W.	Gaines, Crockett; Pool, Henry J.; McMinn, John	West, Nellie	2,400	Minor	25 Mar 1879		
937	Steadman, Mary G. W.	Gaines, Crockett; Pool, Henry J.; McMinn, John	West, Eddie	2,400	Minor	25 Mar 1879		
940	Palmer, Wales L.	Wade, Ina B. (Mrs.); Harmon, Samuel H.	Miller, George E.	7,500	Minor	14 Nov 1877		
940	Palmer, Wales L.	Wade, Ina B. (Mrs.); Harmon, Samuel H.	Miller, Frederick H.	7,500	Minor	14 Nov 1877		
940	Cannon, J. P.	Knapp, G. W.; Cannon, L. L.; Percival, W. C.	Miller, George E.	5,200	Minor	31 Dec 1883		
947	Hughes, John	Whitaker, G. N.; McCracken, Jasper	Hershberger, Charles	250	Minor	8 Apr 1878	C	447
947	Hughes, John	Whitaker, G. N.; McCracken, Jasper	Hershberger, Frank	250	Minor	8 Apr 1878	C	446
949	McCracken, Jasper	Lacque, B.; Hughes, John	McCracken, George F.	250	Minor	8 Apr 1878	C	450
949	McCracken, Jasper	Lacque, B.; Hughes, John	McCracken, Emma	250	Minor	8 Apr 1878	C	449
950	Trimble, Martha J.	Ferguson, John N.; Beeson, William S.; Hertel, R.	Trimble, Louis	1,000	Minor	27 May 1878	C	453
950	Trimble, Martha J.	Ferguson, John N.; Beeson, William S.; Hertel, R.	Trimble, Lucy E.	1,000	Minor	27 May 1878	C	451
950	Trimble, Martha J.	Ferguson, John N.; Beeson, William S.; Hertel, R.	Trimble, George	1,000	Minor	27 May 1878	C	452
958	Farmer, J. A.	Strong, John; Farmer, C. C.	Witt, J. G. William	600	Minor	6 Jun 1878	C	458
967	Laughlin, John M.	Laughlin, James H.; Dinwiddie, J. L.	Knight, George	700	Minor	26 Aug 1878	C	467
976	St. Clair, Frank C.	McPherson, Lycurgus; Hassett, J. D.	Simmons, James S.	3,000	Minor	9 Nov 1878	C	471
976	Hall, L. J.	Powell, R.; Hassett, A.	Simmons, James S.	3,000	Minor	3 Mar 1884		

Case #	Principals	Sureties	Bound to	Amount ($)	Type	Date	Book	Page(s)
978	Sandford, H. T.	Young, N. A.; Curtiss, J. H.	Leonard, Charles W.	1,800	Insane person	9 Dec 1878		472-473
980	Owen, M. V.	Allen, Samuel J.; Cannon, R. B.	Owen, Thomas H.	500	Incompetent and insane person	21 Dec 1878	C	472-473
986	Fitch, Joseph	Brown, H. K.; Rosenberg, W.	Fitch, Natalia	325	Minor	23 Jan 1879	C	476-477
986	Fitch, Joseph	Brown, H. K.; Rosenberg, W.	Fitch, William C.	325	Minor	23 Jan 1879	C	478-479
986	Fitch, Joseph	Brown, H. K.; Rosenberg, W.	Fitch, Herman	325	Minor	23 Jan 1879	C	477-478
986	Fitch, Joseph	Brown, H. K.; Rosenberg, W.	Fitch, Clara	325	Minor	23 Jan 1879	C	479-480
995	Macken, Jeremiah	Mulvenay, P.; Heavey, B. J.	Macken, Robert	750	Minor	6 Feb 1879	C	485-486
996	Shaw, Isaac E.	Sink, Daniel; Sink, William D.	Shaw, Ella L.	1,000	Minor	27 Mar 1879	C	486-487
1004	McPherson, Lycurgus	Marshall, John; Fried, Henry	Moore, Charles	100	Minor	24 Mar 1879	C	490-491
1004	McPherson, Lycurgus	Marshall, John; Fried, Henry	Moore, Henrietta	100	Minor	24 Mar 1879	C	491-492
1006	Nalley, A. B.; Barnes, E. H.	Powell, R.; Moffet, John	Melton, William Woodson	20,000	Minor	25 Mar 1879	C	493-494
1006	Nalley, A. B.; Barnes, E. H.	Norton, L. A.; Farmer, E. T.	Melton, Clymina	20,000	Minor	2 Apr 1879	C	495-496
1006	Nalley, A. B.; Barnes, E. H.	Norton, L. A.; Farmer, E. T.	Melton, James Benjamin	20,000	Minor	2 Apr 1879	C	496-497
1006	Nalley, A. B.; Barnes, E. H.	Powell, R.; Moffet, John	Melton, Robert Wilson	20,000	Minor	2 Apr 1879	C	494-495
1009	Bosworth, C. M.	Stites, Alex H.; Remmel, Charles	Bosworth, Fannie L.	200	Minor	28 May 1879	C	501
1009	Bosworth, C. M.	Stites, Alex H.; Remmel, Charles	Bosworth, James O., Jr.	200	Minor	28 May 1879	C	502
1009	Bosworth, C. M.	Stites, Alex H.; Remmel, Charles	Bosworth, Climena D.	200	Minor	28 May 1879	C	498
1009	Bosworth, C. M.	Stites, Alex H.; Remmel, Charles	Bosworth, Viola	200	Minor	28 May 1879	C	498-499
1009	Bosworth, C. M.	Stites, Alex H.; Remmel, Charles	Bosworth, Lorinda W.	200	Minor	28 May 1879	C	500-501
1009	Bosworth, C. M.	Stites, Alex H.; Remmel, Charles	Bosworth, Albert H.	200	Minor	28 May 1879	C	499-500
1016	Hoag, O. H.	McMinn, John; Harris, Jacob	Richards, Frank	1,000	Minor	9 Jun 1879	C	509
1018	Weymouth, Mary A.	Henley, Barclay; Ames, C. G.	Weymouth, Minnie C.	1,000	Minor	5 Jul 1879	C	510-511
1027	White, Henry M.	Bell, Henry; Clark, Benjamin	Carter, Andrew J.	600	Minor	6 Oct 1879	C	515-516
1028	Crowell, Albert	Stites, A. H.; Remmel, Charles	Vaughn, William	500	Minor	[?] Sep 1879	C	516-517
1028	Crowell, Albert	Stites, A. H.; Remmel, Charles	Vaughn, Spencer	500	Minor	[?] Sep 1879	C	518
1028	Crowell, Albert	Stites, A. H.; Remmel, Charles	Vaughn, Bertha	500	Minor	[?] Sep 1879	C	517
1031	Overton, A. P.	Noonan, George P.; Hahman, F. G.	Miller, Lewis	1,200	Minor	15 Oct 1879	C	520-521

132

Case #	Principals	Sureties	Bound to	Amount ($)	Type	Date	Book	Page(s)
1035	Merchant, Joel	Lippitt, E. S.; Campbell, Joseph	Merchant, Frederick H.	250	Minor	13 Nov 1879	C	523-524
1042	Scott, Sylvester	Larison, Samuel; Mowbray, James R.	Vassar, Jacob	300	Minor	1 Dec 1879	C	528-529
1042	Scott, Sylvester	Larison, Samuel; Mowbray, James R.	Vassar, Benjamin	300	Minor	1 Dec 1879	C	526-527
1052	Dibble, P. K.	Gentry, J. C.; Shane, Adam; Fulton, James	State of California; The Probate Court of Sonoma County appointed P. K. Dibble the guardian of Ida B. Ewing, minor heir of James M. Ewing, dec'd, on [?] Dec 1879 and letters of guardianship were directed to be issued to him upon his executing this bond.	2,200	Minor	31 Dec 1879		
1054	Bloom, Jonas	Wise, Henry; Cohn, Samuel	Cohen, Nettie	3,000	Minor	12 Jan 1880	C	534
1054	Bloom, Jonas	Wise, Henry; Cohn, Samuel	Cohen, Rosa	3,000	Minor	12 Jan 1880	C	534-535
1058	Forsyth, Benjamin	Carithers, D. N.; Clark, D.	State of California; The Superior Court of Sonoma County appointed Benjamin Forsyth the guardian of Henry Mizer Forsyth, minor, on 17 Jan 1880 and letters of guardianship were directed to be issued to him upon his executing this bond.	1,000	Minor	17 Jan 1880	C	538-539
1065	Weigand, Mary	Carroll, Patrick; Needham, Festus	Weigand, William Francis	1,400	Minor	28 Feb 1880	C	541-542
1065	Weigand, Mary	Sales, John; Molseed, Robert	Weigand, William Francis	1,400	Minor	11 Dec 1880	C	542-543
1068½	Goodspeed, Anson	Ferguson, H. O.; Smith, H. W.	State of California; The Superior Court of Sonoma County appointed Anson Goodspeed the guardian of Willerton T. Goodspeed, minor child of C. J. Goodspeed, dec'd, on 29 Mar 1880 and letters of guardianship were directed to be issued to him upon his executing this bond.	500	Minor	30 Mar 1880	C	545-546
1068½	Goodspeed, Anson	Ferguson, H. O.; Smith, H. W.	State of California; The Superior Court of Sonoma County appointed Anson Goodspeed the guardian of Charles A. Goodspeed, minor child of C. J. Goodspeed, dec'd, on 29 Mar 1880 and letters of guardianship were directed to be issued to him upon his executing this bond.	500	Minor	30 Mar 1880	C	546-547
1076	Roach, Patrick	Mullally, Patrick; Hinshaw, E. C.	Mullally, John	5,000	Insane person	26 Apr 1880	C	
1079	Steadman, Mary G. W.	Fisher, A. L.; Loucks, A. H.	Steadman, Grace	300	Minor	15 Jun 1880	C	550-551
1079	Steadman, Mary G. W.	Fisher, A. L.; Loucks, A. H.	Steadman, Maud	300	Minor	15 Jun 1880	C	551
1079	Steadman, Mary G. W.	Fisher, A. L.; Loucks, A. H.	Steadman, Mabelle	300	Minor	15 Jun 1880	C	551-552
1079	Kennedy, George H.	Barnes, E. H.; Nalley, A. B.	Steadman, Charles	300	Minor	1 Sep 1880	C	552-553
1082	Farmer, E. T.	Farmer, C. C.; Cocke, W. E.	Switzer, Viola	350	Minor	28 Jun 1880	C	554-555
1082	Farmer, E. T.	Farmer, C. C.; Cocke, W. E.	Switzer, Henry	350	Minor	28 Jun 1880	C	555-556

Case #	Principals	Sureties	Bound to	Type	Amount ($)	Date	Book	Page(s)
1082	Farmer, E. T.	Farmer, C. C.; Cocke, W. E.	Switzer, Henrietta	Minor	350	28 Jun 1880	C	556-557
1082	Farmer, E. T.	Farmer, C. C.; Cocke, W. E.	Switzer, Elizabeth	Minor	350	28 Jun 1880	C	557-558
1083	Pauli, F. Albert	Wilson, Charles S.; Rogers, W. K.	Pauli, Robert J.	Minor	1,667	29 May 1880	C	558-559
1083	Pauli, F. Albert	Cornelius, George H.; Sparks, George W.	Pauli, Albert F.	Minor	1,667	29 May 1880	C	559-560
1083	Pauli, F. Albert	Carriger, Nicholas; Leavensworth, Thomas M.	Pauli, Emil H.	Minor	1,667	29 May 1880	C	560-561
1083	Pauli, Caroline J.	Hahman, F. G.; Wise, Henry	Pauli, Eloisa F.	Minor	1,667	1 Jun 1880	C	561-562
1092*	Gaston, Hugh	Gaver, A. P.; Gaston, Hamilton	Gaston, Dora E.	Minor	6,500	21 Jul 1880	C	566-567
1095*	Canfield, William D.	Baker, Bloomer; McReynolds, Jacob	Bartlett, John	Minor	1,300	6 Nov 1880	C	569-570
1096*	Gray, J. W.	Prindle, William; Clark, D.	Harvey, Charles A.	Minor	2,000	16 Aug 1880	C	570-571
1096*	Gray, J. W.	Prindle, William; Clark, D.	Harvey, Sarah V.	Minor	2,000	16 Aug 1880	C	571-572
1097*	Whitlock, Mary J.	Jones, Charles; Baker, A. M.	Whitlock, Annie S.	Minor	100	17 Aug 1880	C	572
1097*	Whitlock, Mary J.	Jones, Charles; Baker, A. M.	Whitlock, Charles J.	Minor	100	17 Aug 1880	C	573
1097*	Whitlock, Mary J.	Jones, Charles; Baker, A. M.	Whitlock, William M.	Minor	100	17 Aug 1880	C	573-574
1097*	Whitlock, Mary J.	Jones, Charles; Baker, A. M.	Whitlock, Joel R.	Minor	100	17 Aug 1880	C	574-575
1104	Wheeler, Jacob	Noonan, George P.; Overton, John P.; Proctor, T. J.	Wheeler, George W.	Minor	250	30 Aug 1880	C	583-584
1104	Wheeler, Jacob	Noonan, George P.; Overton, John P.	Wheeler, Jacob F.	Minor	250	30 Aug 1880	C	584-585
1104	Wheeler, Jacob	Noonan, George P.; Overton, John P.	Wheeler, David R.	Minor	250	30 Aug 1880	C	585-586
1104	Wheeler, Jacob	Noonan, George P.; Overton, John P.; Proctor, T. J.	Wheeler, Ira E.	Minor	250	30 Aug 1880	C	586-587
1105	Orr, John	Duncan, A.; Sheridan, James	Orr, Charles	Minor	2,000	27 Aug 1880	C	587-588
1114	Bartlett, Mary Jane	Bartlett, Harris; Sharon, C. T. (Mrs.)	Bartlett, Lydia A.	Minor	2,500	12 Oct 1880	C	593-594
1119	Hardin, W. J.	Wiers, James; Spotswood, A.	Graham, Arthur W.	Minor	100	3 Dec 1880	C	596-597
1119	Hardin, W. J.	Wiers, James; Spotswood, A.	Graham, Ida J.	Minor	100	3 Dec 1880	C	597-598
1126	Johnson, Elizabeth (Mrs.)	Baker, Henry; Clark, J. P.	Johnson, Bertha	Minor	4,200	20 Dec 1880	C	602-603
1135	Starke, Frederick	Roseburgh, A.; Symonds, C. W.	Dahlman, Martha	Minor	1,350	19 Nov 1881	C	607-608
1135	Starke, Frederick	Creghino, Antonio [Cereghino, Antonio]; Hess, Frederick	Dahlman, Frederick S.	Minor	1,350	19 Nov 1881	C	608-609
1135	Starke, Frederick	Maynard, F. T.; Fairbanks, H. T.	Dahlman, Henry	Minor	1,350	19 Nov 1881	C	609
1135	Dahlmann, Augusta	Dahlmann, Henry; Dahlmann, Martha	Dahlmann, Frederick S.	[Minor]	2,500	26 May 1885	C	
1140	Snider, Jane	Phillips, O. F.; Miles, T. W.	Snider, Mary E.	Minor	100	25 Mar 1881	C	610-611
1140	Snider, Jane	Phillips, O. F.; Miles, T. W.	Snider, George R.	Minor	100	25 Mar 1881	C	611-612

Case #	Principals	Sureties	Bound to	Amount ($)	Type	Date	Book	Page(s)
1140	Snider, Jane	Phillips, O. F.; Miles, T. W.	Snider, Lucy B.	100	Minor	25 Mar 1881	C	612-613
1141	Fitch, Joseph, Sr.	Crane, R.; Roney, J. M.	Fitch, Joseph	500	Minor	[?] Mar 1881	C	613-614
1141	Rose, J. W.	Rowland, William; Grant, John D.	Fitch, Joseph, Jr.	4,000	Minor	3 Oct 1883		
1146	Wilson, John B.	Daniel, H. H.; Cowan, William	Hatfield, Rebecca	100	Minor	14 May 1881	C	616-617
1146	Wilson, John B.	Daniel, H. H.; Cowan, William	Hatfield, Francis J.	100	Minor	14 May 1881	C	617-618
1146	Wilson, John B.	Daniel, H. H.; Cowan, William	Hatfield, William P.	100	Minor	14 May 1881	C	618-619
1146	Wilson, John B.	Daniel, H. H.; Cowan, William	Hatfield, Joseph A.	100	Minor	14 May 1881	C	619-620
1150	Peterson, Martha A.	Peterson, A.; Kelly, J. W.	Peterson, William	100	Minor	16 May 1881	D	6-7
1150	Peterson, Martha A.	Peterson, A.; Kelly, J. W.	Peterson, Eleanor [Elmer R.]	100	Minor	16 May 1881	D	2-3
1150	Peterson, Martha A.	Peterson, A.; Kelly, J. W.	Peterson, John L.	100	Minor	16 May 1881	D	5-6
1150	Peterson, Martha A.	Peterson, A.; Kelly, J. W.	Peterson, James C.	100	Minor	16 May 1881	D	3-4
1150	Peterson, Martha A.	Peterson, A.; Kelly, J. W.	Peterson, Augustus	100	Minor	16 May 1881	D	7-8
1151	Connolly, B. F.	Ferguson, John J.; Riedi, V.	Connolly, Frank	100	Minor	21 May 1881	D	11-13
1151	Connolly, B. F.	Ferguson, John J.; Riedi, V.	Connolly, Theodore	100	Minor	21 May 1881	D	10-11
1151	Connolly, B. F.	Ferguson, John J.; Riedi, V.	Connolly, Thomas	100	Minor	21 May 1881	D	8-9
1157	Hamm, Mary A.	Guay, John B.; Guldager, Louis	Hamm, Ellen E.	700	Minor	6 Jul 1881	D	15-16
1160	Thomas, Flora M.	Mock, Eliza A.; Mock, Wesley	Thomas, Charles E.	5,000	Minor	2 Jun 1888	D	336-337
1160	Thomas, Flora M.	Mock, Eliza A.; Armstrong, James	Thomas, Charles E.	2,000	Minor	13 Aug 1881	D	17-18
1167	Freeman, W. D.	Haskins, Thomas J.; Freeman, E. R.	Madler, Lizzie	1,800	Minor	1 Aug 1881	D	21-22
1168	Mock, Wesley	Overton, A. P.; Noonan, George P.	Madler, Margaretta	1,800	Minor	11 Jan 1882	D	22-23
1169	Bryant, Thomas H.	Cassiday, J. W.; Lippitt, E. S.	Bryant, Thomas P.	1,600	Minor	12 Sep 1881	D	24-25
1169	Bryant, Thomas H.	Cassiday, J. W.; Lippitt, E. S.	Bryant, Ann Augusta	1,600	Minor	12 Sep 1881	D	25-26
1169	Bryant, Thomas H.	Cassiday, J. W.; Lippitt, E. S.	Bryant, John E.	1,600	Minor	12 Sep 1881	D	23-24
1172	Miller, Caroline	Kiser, Abraham; Cox, W. E.	Miller, Wallace E.	200	Minor	16 Aug 1881	D	29-30
1172	Miller, Caroline	Kiser, Abraham; Cox, W. E.	Miller, Lizzie E.	200	Minor	16 Aug 1881	D	28-29
1175	Pieratt, John M.	Carriger, Nicholas; Agnew, S. J.	Fowler, Robert F.	2,600	Incompetent person	28 Sep 1881	D	31-32
11/5	Fowler, Robert B.	Schetter, Otto; Craig, O. W.	Fowler, Robert F.	1,000	Incompetent person	19 Jul 1882		
11/b	McPherson, Lycurgus	St. Clair, F. C.; Warren, W. P.	McPherson, Bertha M.	100	Minor	24 Sep 1881	D	34-35
1176	McPherson, Lycurgus	St. Clair, F. C.; Warren, W. P.	McPherson, Charles W.	100	Minor	24 Sep 1881	D	32-33

Case #	Principals	Sureties	Bound to	Amount ($)	Type	Date	Book	Page(s)
1178	Luce, Mary	Allen, W. T.; Alexander, Charles	Swain, Mary D.	200	Minor	26 Nov 1881	D	36-37
1178	Luce, Mary	Cook, J.; Alexander, Charles	Swain, Mamie	3,300	Minor	18 Aug 1882		
1181	Maggetti, G.	Magetti, P.; Atwater, H. H.	Magetti, Joseph	1,000	Incompetent person	7 Nov 1881	D	38-40
1184	Koch, Anna	Hall, E. G.; Zeller, H. J.	Lenz, Frederick W.	2,800	Minor	13 Jun 1885	1	23
1186*	Davidson, John	Davidson, James; Bryant, Charles G.	Rutherford, James A.	2,500	Minor	11 Nov 1881	D	41-42
1186	Davidson, John	Davidson, James; Bryant, Charles G.	Rutherford, Thomas	2,500	Minor	11 Nov 1881	D	42-43
1187	Meeker, A. P.	Purrine, A. S.; Shaw, N. R.	Meeker, Charles E.	500	Minor	23 Nov 1881	D	47-48
1187	Meeker, A. P.	Purrine, A. S.; Shaw, N. R.	Meeker, Ralph W.	500	Minor	23 Nov 1881	D	45-47
1187	Meeker, A. P.	Purrine, A. S.; Shaw, N. R.	Meeker, Frank L.	500	Minor	23 Nov 1881	D	43-45
1189	Otis, Elizabeth	Otis, Isaac; Abshier, J. H.	Otis, Leonard	800	Minor	29 Apr 1882	D	94-95
1189	Otis, Elizabeth	Otis, Isaac; Abshier, J. H.	Otis, Frederick W.	800	Minor	29 Apr 1882	D	97-98
1189	Otis, Elizabeth	Otis, Isaac; Abshier, J. H.	Otis, Lewis S.	800	Minor	29 Apr 1882	D	95-96
1198	Glover, Delia	Carmody, Patrick; Carmody, James	Glover, Josephine M.	400	Minor	23 Feb 1882	D	99-101
1198	Glover, Delia	Carmody, Patrick; Carmody, James	Glover, Albert B.	400	Minor	15 Feb 1882	D	98-99
1203	O'Farrell, John J.	Wensinger, F. S.; Roche, John J.	O'Farrell, Florence	100	[Minor]	24 Feb 1882	D	56-57
1203	O'Farrell, John J.	Wensinger, F. S.; Roche, John J.	O'Farrell, Gerald	100	[Minor]	24 Feb 1882	D	53-54
1203	O'Farrell, John J.	Wensinger, F. S.; Roche, John J.	O'Farrell, Cathal	100	[Minor]	24 Feb 1882	D	54-55
1209	Monahan, Ann	Monahan, Eugene; Monahan, Maggie A.	Monahan, Mary L.	600	Minor	13 Feb 1882	D	61-62
1217	Hall, J. E.	Nagle, F. G.; Forsyth, Robert	Blucher, Lillie (otherwise known as Petery, Lillie)	100	Minor	6 Mar 1882	D	66-67
1233	Monahan, Patrick, Sr.	Agnew, S. J.; Muldry, Martin	Monahan, Mary Hanora	1,400	Minor	20 May 1882	D	82-83
1233	Monahan, Patrick, Sr.	Agnew, S. J.; Muldry, Martin	Monahan, Catharine Teressa	1,400	Minor	20 May 1882	D	81-82
1233	Monahan, Patrick, Sr.	Agnew, S. J.; Muldry, Martin	Monahan, Thomas Francis	1,400	Minor	20 May 1882	D	79-80
1238	Bryan, Elizabeth	Maynard, F. T.; McGuire, T.	Bryan, Fred J.	250	Minor	13 Jun 1882	D	104-105
1238	Bryan, Elizabeth	Maynard, F. T.; McGuire, T.	Bryan, Mary	250	Minor	13 Jun 1882	D	105-106
1238	Bryan, Elizabeth	Maynard, F. T.; McGuire, T.	Bryan, Katy	250	Minor	13 Jun 1882	D	107-108
1238	Bryan, Elizabeth	Maynard, F. T.; McGuire, T.	Bryan, William	250	Minor	13 Jun 1882	D	112-114
1238	Bryan, Elizabeth	Maynard, F. T.; McGuire, T.	Bryan, John Leo	250	Minor	13 Jun 1882	D	114-115
1238	Bryan, Elizabeth	Maynard, F. T.; McGuire, T.	Bryan, Annie	250	Minor	13 Jun 1882	D	108-109
1238	Bryan, Elizabeth	Maynard, F. T.; McGuire, T.	Bryan, Joseph	250	Minor	13 Jun 1882	D	110-111
1238	Bryan, Elizabeth	Maynard, F. T.; McGuire, T.	Bryan, Rosa	250	Minor	13 Jun 1882	D	111-112

Case #	Principals	Sureties	Bound to	Amount ($)	Type	Date	Book	Page(s)
1240	Bruning, Henry W.	Shinn, Silas M.; Schieck, John Gottfried	Bruning, Caroline	1,000	Insane person	10 Aug 1882	D	115-116
1242	Farrar, M. C.	Harris, R. F.; Buckle, Thomas	Reynolds, Emma	200	Minor	18 Jul 1882	D	118-119
1247	Walsh, M.	McNamara, M.; Cavanagh, John	Hynes, John P.	4,500	Minor	16 Sep 1882	D	122-123
1264	Juilliard, C. F.	Guerne, George E.; Glenn, Robert	Veron, P. A.	3,000	Incompetent person	17 Oct 1882	D	137-138
1265*	Lewis, Frank W.	Roberts, Hugh J.; Silva, M. G.	Hunt, Katie	800	Incompetent person	12 Oct 1882	D	139-140
1267	Lightner, Sarah J.	Matzenbach, W. B.; Haskins, T. J.	Lightner, Ella A.	1,400	Minor	27 Nov 1882	D	140-141
1275	Overton, John P.	Hahman, F. G.; Noonan, George P.	Pyatt, George	800	Minor	27 Nov 1882	D	148-149
1276	Warfield, R. H.	Gaines, W. C.; Barnes, E. H.	Warfield, George	688	Minor	27 Nov 1882	D	150-151
1278	Fritsch, John	Lewis, J. B.; Cox, W. E.	Stafford, Edward P.	800	Minor	18 Dec 1882	D	152-153
1281	Pressley, Emma W.	Pressley, John G.; Porter, William W.	Pressley, Louise W.	140	Minor	2 Jan 1883	D	156-158
1281	Pressley, Emma W.	Pressley, John G.; Porter, William W.	Pressley, James F.	110	Minor	2 Jan 1883	D	155 156
1283	Hynes, Alma R.	Parker, Freeman; Cowen, Philip	Hynes, Wildric	1,400	Minor	10 Feb 1883	D	158-159
1283	Hynes, Alma R.	Parker, Freeman; Cowen, Philip	Hynes, Laura	1,400	Minor	10 Feb 1883	D	159-160
1283	Walls, David	Bryant, C. G.; Cowen, Philip	Hynes, Laura A.	750	Minor	18 Jun 1888	1	82
1283	Walls, David	Bryant, C. G.; Cowen, Philip	Hynes, Wildric F.	750	Minor	18 Jun 1888	1	82
1284	Lyttaker, F. E.	Trotter, R.; Ross, Milburn	Lyttaker, Roland	1,000	Incompetent person	19 Mar 1883	D	161-162
1284	Hendrix, E. U.	Peterson, Martha A.; Hendrix, Lewis	Lyttaker, Roland G.	1,000	Incompetent person	17 Apr 1886	1	36
1286	Skinner, L. T.	Skinner, W. G.; Davis, M. S.	Snyder, Dan Edger	1,000	Minor	22 Jan 1883	D	162-163
1287	Waters, Mary	Needham, Festus; Lynch, John	Waters, James	2,000	Minor	25 Jan 1883	D	163-165
1292	Gibbs, Elizabeth A.	Grosse, Guy E.; Armstrong, J. B.	Grosse, Joseph E.	2,000	Minor	19 Feb 1883	D	170-171
1293	Lewis, Frank W.	McNear, George P.; Lynch, Charles	Hunt, Jane Doe	5,000	Minor	2 Apr 1883	D	172-173
1293	Silvia, A. J.	Paula, Manuel; Pereira, Daniel A.	Hunt, Jane Doe	2,000	Minor	22 Apr 1884	D	
1294	Slusser, Bayard B.	Slusser, Sarah; Slusser, Martin E.; Slusser, William P.; Hopper, Thomas; Farmer, E. T.; Laughlin, James H.; Espey, John H.; Maddux, James H.; Forsythe, Robert A.	Slusser, L. S. B.	20,000	Insane person	9 Mar 1883	D	173-175
1294	Slusser, William P.	Slusser, Martin E.; Hopper, Thomas; Farmer, E. T.; Laughlin, James H.; Espey, John H.; Maddux, J. P.; Forsythe, Robert A.	Slusser, L. S. B.	20,000	Incompetent person	27 Oct 1884	D	

137

Case #	Principals	Sureties	Bound to	Amount ($)	Type	Date	Book	Page(s)
1296	Dabner, Mary	Dabner, William; Dabner, Anton	Dabner, Frank	1,000	Minor	27 Feb 1883	D	175-176
1296	Dabner, Mary	Dabner, William; Dabner, Anton	Dabner, Manuel	1,000	Minor	27 Feb 1883	D	177-178
1305	Kamp, N.	Little, J.; Sherry, Thomas	Kamp, Julia	400	[Minor]	18 Apr 1883	D	187-188
1308	King, Matthew W.	Abraham, Caspar; Crigler, William E.	King, Henry Haight	500	Minor	14 May 1883	D	190-191
1314	Wilsey, Sarah M.	Haney, Frank; Wilsey, H.	Wilsey, Frankie Jane	200	Minor	17 May 1883	D	193-194
1314	Wilsey, Sarah M.	Haney, Frank; Wilsey, H.	Wilsey, Henry Martin	200	Minor	17 May 1883	D	194-196
1314	Wilsey, Sarah M.	Haney, Frank; Wilsey, H.	Wilsey, Hayes	200	Minor	17 May 1883	D	196-197
1314	Wilsey, Sarah M.	Haney, Frank; Wilsey, H.	Wilsey, Mary Elizabeth	200	Minor	17 May 1883	D	197-199
1315	Marshall, Sarah A.	Pimm, Jacob; Curtiss, J. H.	Marshall, Marian A.	1,000	Minor	9 May 1883	D	200-202
1315	Marshall, Sarah A.	Pimm, Jacob; Curtiss, J. H.	Marshall, Annabell	1,000	Minor	9 May 1883	D	199-200
1321	Groff, Maria	Roney, J. M.; Noonan, George P.	Groff, Caroline	800	Minor	21 May 1883	D	209-211
1321	Groff, Maria	Roney, J. M.; Noonan, George P.	Groff, Sarah E.	800	[Minor]	21 May 1883	D	208-209
1321	Groff, Maria	Roney, J. M.; Noonan, George P.	Groff, William S.	800	[Minor]	21 May 1883	D	206-208
1321	Groff, Maria	Roney, J. M.; Noonan, George P.	Groff, Louis W.	800	[Minor]	21 May 1883	D	205-206
1324	Dolan, Peter	Kelly, James W.; McDonald, John	Dolan, Martha Rose	200	Minor	29 May 1883	D	217-218
1324	Dolan, Peter	Kelly, James W.; McDonald, John	Dolan, Katie	200	Minor	29 May 1883	D	220-221
1324	Dolan, Peter	Kelly, James W.; McDonald, John	Dolan, Maggie Alice	200	Minor	29 May 1883	D	218-219
1324	Dolan, Peter	Kelly, James W.; McDonald, John	Dolan, Annie	200	Minor	29 May 1883	D	215-217
1324	Dolan, Peter	Kelly, James W.; McDonald, John	Dolan, Charles	200	Minor	29 May 1883	D	214-215
1329	Coolidge, Jane	Morrison, John; Wisecarver, Joseph R.	Coolidge, Nellie	10,000	Minor	22 Jun 1883	D	222-224
1344	Leiding, C. F.	Aguillon, C.; Poppe, Catherine	Bahr, Albert F.	500	Minor	18 Sep 1883	D	234-235
1344	Leiding, C. F.	Aguillon, C.; Poppe, Catherine	Oettl, Frank	500	Minor	18 Sep 1883	D	236-237
1344	Leiding, C. F.	Aguillon, C.; Poppe, Catherine	Oettl, Bertha	500	Minor	18 Sep 1883	D	237-238
1344	Oettl, Maria M.	Gould, W. H.; Bowman, Henry	Oettl, Bertha	500	Minor	22 Sep 1891	1	161
1345	Underhill, Milley	Underhill, W. H.; Underhill, Charles	Underhill, Neva	900	[Minor]	17 Sep 1883	D	240-241
1345	Underhill, Milley	Underhill, W. H.; Underhill, Charles	Underhill, John Lee	900	[Minor]	17 Sep 1883	D	238-240
1348	Drees, Johanne H. L.	Tempel, C.; Meyerholtz, H.	Drees, William Elimar	2,000	Minor	27 Nov 1883	D	264-265
1348	Drees, Johanne H. L.	Hess, Fred; Schmitt, George	Drees, Johanna Elizabeth	2,000	Minor	26 Nov 1883	D	262-263
1348	Drees, Johanne H. L.	Hess, Fred; Schmitt, George	Drees, Ernest Emil	2,000	Minor	26 Nov 1883	D	261-262
1348	Drees, Johanne H. L.	Tempel, C.; Meyerholtz, H.	Drees, Herman Adolph	2,000	Minor	17 Nov 1883	D	265-266

Case #	Principals	Sureties	Bound to	Amount ($)	Type	Date	Book	Page(s)
1349	Starr, A. D.	Rideout, N. D.; Greely, Justus; Starr, William M.; Prescott, George W.	Bowman, Robert B.	12,800	Minor	8 Oct 1883	D	246-248
1349	Starr, A. D.	Rideout, N. D.; Greely, Justus; Starr, William M.; Prescott, George W.	Bowman, John P.	12,800	Minor	8 Oct 1883	D	244-246
1349	Starr, A. D.	Rideout, N. D.; Greely, Justus; Starr, William M.; Prescott, George W.	Bowman, Hattie P.	12,800	Minor	8 Oct 1883	D	242-244
1349	Bowman, F. J.	Prescott, George W.; Holloway, J. C.	Bowman, Robert B.	10,500	Minor	29 Mar 1887	1	45, 46
1349*	Teegarden, F. Josephine (formerly Bowman, F. Josephine)	Bowman, Hattie P.; Bowman, John Percy	Bowman, Robert B.	7,000	Minor	5 Feb 1896	D	482-485
1349	Bowman, F. Josephine	Cooley, Charles H.; Chalfant, J. E.	Bowman, John P.	10,500	Minor	29 Mar 1887	1	45
1354	Sargent, Joshua C.	Forsythe, Charles; Graves, J. Q.	Sargent, Ruth	100	[Minor]	29 Oct 1883	D	252-254
1354	Sargent, Joshua C.	Forsythe, Charles; Graves, J. Q.	Sargent, Alvin Z.	100	[Minor]	29 Oct 1883	D	251-252
1354	Sargent, Joshua C.	Forsythe, Charles; Graves, J. Q.	Sargent, Nanie E.	100	[Minor]	29 Oct 1883	D	250-251
1355	Skinner, W. G.	Williams, W. H.; Skinner, L. T.	Skinner, Ada	200	Minor	29 Oct 1883	D	254-255
1355	Skinner, W. G.	Williams, W. H.; Harris, Jacob	Skinner, Ada	200	Minor	4 Nov 1889	1	119
1360	Peugh, Jennie	Hood, T. B.; Burnett, A. G.	State of California; The Superior Court of Sonoma County appointed Jennie Peugh the guardian of Ida Mabel Haggard, a minor, on 12 Nov 1883 upon her executing this bond.	500	Minor	14 Jun 1890	1	130
1365	Clark, George W.	Craig, O. W.; Carriger, Nicholas	Clark, Howard	1,360	Incompetent person	26 Dec 1883	1	1
1369	Johnson, Henry	Dinwiddie, J. L.; Scudder, N. W.	Dickson, Joshua Bates	500	Minor	10 Dec 1883	D	270-271
1375	Harmon, F. V.	Mills, George W.; Cook, John	Harmon, Owen	350	Minor	31 Dec 1883	1	1
1376	Cochron, A. E.	Barnes, E. H.; Warfield, R. H.	Marshall, Marion A.	1,000	Minor	7 Jan 1884	1	2
1378	Matthies, Lina	Schmitt, George; Dortmund, H.	Matthies, Henry	2,500	Minor	28 Feb 1884	1	2
1381	Hill, William	Doyle, M.; Kennelly, J.	Bean, Mary F.	1,000	Minor	22 Jan 1884	1	3, 6
1381	Hill, William	Doyle, M.; Kennelly, J.	Bean, Joseph M.	1,000	Minor	22 Jan 1884	1	3
1390	Shuster, Sarah E.	Shuster, James E.; Shuster, Jacob F.	Shuster, Marvin	300	Minor	10 Mar 1884	1	4, 7
1390	Shuster, Sarah E.	Purrine, A. S.; Shuster, James E.	Shuster, Josie	300	Minor	10 Mar 1884	1	4, 6
1397	Austin, Herbert W.	Allen, Samuel I.; Austin, James	Austin, James Howard	5,000	Minor	6 May 1884	1	5, 7
1398	Pimm, Jacob	Alexander, Charles; Curtiss, J. H.	Marshall, Annabell	1,000	Minor	8 May 1884	1	5, 8
1400	Pierce, Mary J.	Fritsch, John; Purvine, T. B.	Pierce, William S.	10,000	Minor	21 May 1884	1	8

Case #	Principals	Sureties	Bound to	Amount ($)	Type	Date	Book	Page(s)
1402	Longmore, Thomas	Hudspeth, J. M.; Lawrence, H. E.	Longmore, Alexander	1,000	Incompetent person	2 Jun 1884	1	9
1405	Drahms, A.	Ewell, P. D. F.; Shaw, S. H.	Moore, Myrta	5,500	[Minor]	5 Jul 1884	1	9
1411	Brooks, Emma S.	Mardon, Henry; Hutchinson, F. A.	Brooks, Earnest K.	200	Minor	27 Aug 1884	1	15
1411*	Brooks, Emma S.	Mardon, Henry; Hutchinson, F. A.	Brooks, Frederick A.	200	Minor	27 Aug 1884	1	10
1419	Chapman, Mary C.	Chapman, Edwin A.; Chapman, Harry E.	Chapman, Phoebe M.	1,000	[Minor]	25 Sep 1884	1	10
1419	Chapman, Mary C.	Chapman, Edwin A.; Chapman, Harry E.	Chapman, Elliott C.	1,000	[Minor]	25 Sep 1884	1	11
1419	Chapman, Mary C.	Chapman, Edwin A.; Chapman, Harry E.	Chapman, Mary L.	1,000	[Minor]	25 Sep 1884	1	11
1420	Christie, Frances A.	Christie, Alfred; Percival, W. C.	Christie, John	400	Minor	10 Oct 1884		
1420	Christie, Frances A.	Christie, Alfred; Percival, W. C.	Christie, Georgie	400	Minor	9 Oct 1884		
1420	Christie, Frances A.	Christie, Alfred; Percival, W. C.	Christie, Nellie	400	Minor	10 Oct 1884	1	12
1422	Blair, Thomas N.	Holmes, H. P.; Warner, James	Blair, Frank P.	500	Minor	1 Oct 1884	1	13
1437*	Meyerholtz, Henry	Denman, E.; Hill, William	Williges, Elize	5,000	Incompetent person	20 Dec 1884	1	13
1439	O'Hara, John	Pearce, George; Willy, J. W.	Neil, Katie	100	Minor	[?] Dec 1884	1	14
1440	Alexander, Carrie	McConnell, William E.; Rutledge, Thomas	Pechaco, George	100	Minor	15 Dec 1884	1	14
1451	Hoffstetter, Albertine	Hoffstetter, B. (Dr.); Scheibel, Theobald	Hoffstetter, Eleanora	1,350	Minor	9 Feb 1885	1	16
1451*	Dietrich, Albertine	Scheibel, Theobald; Dietrich, Gottlieb	Hoffstetter, Eleanora	1,350	[Minor]	6 May 1895	D	449-450
1451	Hoffstetter, Albertine	Hoffstetter, B. (Dr.); Scheibel, Theobald	Hoffstetter, Jeanne	1,350	Minor	9 Feb 1885	1	17
1451*	Dietrich, Albertine	Scheibel, Theobald; Dietrich, Gottlieb	Hoffstetter, Jeanne	1,350	[Minor]	6 May 1895	D	451-452
1455	Hunter, Nathaniel	Muther, Frank; Hall, J. E.	Duck, Ah	300	Minor	9 Mar 1885	1	18
1465	Carithers, D. N.	Taylor, John S.; Gray, J. W.	Hendley, William G.	6,000	Minor	23 Apr 1885	1	19
1465	Carithers, D. N.	Taylor, John S.; Gray, J. W.	Hendley, Frank P.	5,000	Minor	23 Apr 1885	1	18
1472	Mee, Ava C.	Vance, James M.; Klotz, C. G.	Mee, Belle	1,240	Minor	1 Jun 1885	1	21
1472	Mee, Ava C.	Vance, James M.; Klotz, C. G.	Mee, Thomas	1,240	Minor	1 Jun 1885	1	21
1473	Powell, R.	Nalley, A. B.; Barnes, E. H.	Powell, Nettie	5,000	Minor	23 May 1885	1	20
1473	Powell, R.	Nalley, A. B.; Barnes, E. H.	Powell, Jesse	5,000	Minor	23 May 1885	1	20
1474	McNear, George P.	Haskell, William B.; McNear, John A.	McNear, Clara	300	Minor	6 Jun 1885	1	22
1477	Harbine, L.	Solomon, Charles; Lindemood, Israel	Scott, Edna Bell	1,500	Minor	15 Jun 1885	1	22, 77
1477	Scott, H. W.	Sawyer, E. A.; Melendy, Henry	Scott, Edna Belle	1,200	Minor	11 Apr 1889	1	107
1479	Hardin, James A.	Frost, C. W.; Coughran, W.	Hardin, George W.	200	Minor	16 Jul 1885	1	24

Case #	Principals	Sureties	Bound to	Amount ($)	Type	Date	Book	Page(s)
1479	Hardin, James A.	Frost, C. W.; Coughran, W.	Hardin, Henry	200	Minor	16 Jul 1885	1	24
1480	Grove, C. C.	Smith, Henry W.; Roney, J. M.	Walker, Rudolphus	800	Incompetent person	6 Jul 1885	1	23
1490	Schweitzer, William	Hagmayer, Gottlob; Haehl, Henry	Schweitzer, Albert	2,500	Incompetent person	17 Aug 1885	1	25
1492	Congrove, Lucy A.	Falkner, M. H.; Arnold, W. J.	Crow, William W.	4,000	Minor	26 Aug 1885	1	25
1499	Proctor, T. J.	Gray, J. W.; Carithers, D. N.	Arnold, George W.	4,300	Insane person	5 Oct 1885	1	26
1501	Leffingwell, Margaret	Cowen, Philip; Morse, A.	Leffingwell, William Charles	250	Minor	15 Oct 1885	1	27
1501	Leffingwell, Margaret	Cowen, Philip; Morse, A.	Leffingwell, John Henry	250	[Minor]	15 Oct 1885	1	27
1507	Rodgers, J. P.	Phillips, Jacob; Lawrence, J. A.	Woods, Mary Alice	1,500	[Minor]	13 Mar 1886	1	32
1507	Ballard, Carrie H.	Ames, C. G.; Hardin, James A.	Woods, Mary Alice	2,000	Minor	4 Sep 1889	1	118
1512	Swett, Frank H.	Mailer, James C.; Allen, Samuel I.	Sargent, Ruth I.	9[00]	Minor	[4 Jan 1886]	1	28
1512	Swett, Frank H.	Mailer, James C., Allen, Samuel I.	Sargent, Alvin Z.	900	Minor	[4 Jan 1886]	1	28
1512	Swett, Frank H.	Mailer, James C.; Allen, Samuel I.	Sargent, Nynie E.	900	Minor	[4 Jan 1886]	1	29
1517	Warfield, R. H.	Powell, R.; Barnes, E. H.	Peck, Mabel E.	3,000	Minor	18 Jan 1886	1	29
1517	Kimball, C. L.	Slocum, George; Rosenberg, W.	Peck, Mabel	500	Minor	1 May 1891	1	148
1520	Dinwiddie, J. L.; Fairbanks, H. T.; Weston, H. L.	Brainerd, H. P.; Denman, E.	Lane, Lincoln	4,000	Minor	11 Mar 1886	1	33
1523	Kauffmann, Phillipe L.	Meyer, Lorentz; Bower, Louis	Meyer, Carolina Louisa	1,500	Minor	8 Feb 1886	1	30
1523	Kauffmann, Phillipe L.	Meyer, Lorentz; Bower, Louis	Meyer, William Jacob	1,500	Minor	8 Feb 1886	1	30
1523	Kauffmann, Phillipe L.	Meyer, Lorentz; Bower, Louis	Meyer, Catharina Bertha	1,500	Minor	8 Feb 1886	1	32
1523	Kauffmann, Phillipe L.	Bushnell, Amasa; Maddocks, Winthrop	Meyer, Margaretha Salome	1,500	Minor	8 Feb 1886	1	31
1523	Kauffmann, Phillipe L.	Bushnell, Amasa; Maddocks, Winthrop	Meyer, Lawrence	1,500	Minor	8 Feb 1886	1	31
1532	Patten, Hugh	Gum, Isaac; Ragan, Joel	Patten, Nettie	500	Incompetent person	23 Mar 1886	1	33
1532	Patten, Hugh	Gum, Isaac; Cameron, G.	Patten, Nettie	500	Insane person	9 May 1887	1	47
1533	Baylis, Theo. H. T.	Skiffington, John; Cronin, P.	Connolly, Arthur Henry	2,000	Minor	23 Mar 1886	1	34
1535	Miser, Hannah	Mead, James A.; Cohn, S.	Miser, Mary E.	1,000	Minor	3 Apr 1886	1	34
1535	Miser, Hannah	Mead, James A.; Cohn, S.	Miser, Frank S.	1,000	Minor	3 Apr 1886	1	35
1535	Miser, Hannah	Mead, James A.; Cohn, S.	Miser, Ross N.	1,000	Minor	3 Apr 1886	1	35

Case #	Principals	Sureties	Bound to	Amount ($)	Type	Date	Book	Page(s)
1535	Frampton, Hannah (formerly Miser, Hannah)	Mead, James A.; Rosenberg, W.	Miser, Mary E.	1,000	Minor	28 May 1888	1	78
1535	Frampton, Hannah (formerly Miser, Hannah)	Mead, James A.; Rosenberg, W.	Miser, Frank S.	1,000	Minor	28 May 1888	1	78
1535	Frampton, Hannah (formerly Miser, Hannah)	Mead, James A.; Rosenberg, W.	Miser, Ross N.	1,000	Minor	28 May 1888	1	79
1540	Cadwell, Jacob A.	Van Doren, John S.; Dougherty, S. K.	Shedd, Charles; Shedd, Clarence	1,000	Minors	22 Apr 1886	1	37
1543	Redmond, Mary Jane	Noonan, Patrick H.; Hyde, Patrick	Redmond, Francis M.	300	[Minor]	3 May 1886	1	37
1543	Redmond, Mary Jane	Noonan, Patrick H.; Hyde, Patrick	Redmond, Philip J.	2,200	[Minor]	3 May 1886	1	38
1555	McGee, James H.	Overton, A. P.; Noonan, George P.	Clark, Estelle	2,500	Minor	22 Jun 1886	1	39
1555	McGee, James H.	Overton, A. P.; Noonan, George P.	Clark, Gertrude L.	2,500	Minor	22 Jun 1886	1	38
1555	McGee, James H.	Overton, A. P.; Noonan, George P.	Clark, Frederick W.	2,500	Minor	22 Jun 1886	1	39
1555	Clark, Margaret E.	Clark, F. W.; Clark, Estelle	Clark, Gertrude L.	2,600	Minor	27 Dec 1887	1	56
1557	Luce, Milton Y.	Monmonier, William B.; Luce, Jirah	Litton, Ida Blanche	2,600	Minor	13 Jul 1886	1	40
1557	Luce, Milton Y.	Monmonier, William B.; Luce, Jirah	Litton, Thomas G.	2,600	Minor	13 Jul 1886	1	40
1561	Hoskins, T. D.	Harris, Jacob; Hoag, O. H.	Rien, George E.	1,700	Minor	23 Aug 1886	1	41
1561	Hoskins, T. D.	Harris, Jacob; Hoag, O. H.	Rien, Nellie J.	1,700	Minor	23 Aug 1886	1	41
1567	Clanton, D. C.	Brown, Harry C.; Laughlin, Lee; Hotchkiss, W. J.	Clanton, Samuel T.	6,500	Incompetent person	8 Sep 1886	D	290-291, 301-302
1586	Gannon, James	Walker, John; Morris, Joseph H. P.	Seeley, David	1,000	Incompetent person	19 Oct 1886	1	75
1598	Alexander, Joseph	Alexander, Thomas; Alexander, Caroline; Alexander, Henry	Alexander, George Cyrus	20,000	Minor	15 Jan 1887	1	42
1602	Kearns, Bernard	Kaen, Thomas L.; Carroll, Thomas	Kearns, James	4,000	Incompetent person	25 Jan 1887	1	42
1603	Starke, Fred J.	Bryant, C. G.; Buckins, William L.	Starke, Francis	1,000	Incompetent person	8 Feb 1887	1	43
1609	Thompson, Charles H.	Warboys, J. W.; Savage, C. W.	Thompson, Carrie A.	500	Minor	25 Jul 1887	1	50
1611	Jones, John H.; Jones, Martha	Booth, Jesse; Boswell, J. H.	Kraft, Violet	500	Minor	28 Feb 1887	1	43
1625	Keyes, M. M.	Tupper, G. A.; Breitenbach, Louis	Barnes, Jennett	100	Minor	4 Apr 1887	1	44
1626	Hale, William	Bates, George E.; Bendit, Samuel	Steel, Mabel	300	Minor	1 Apr 1887	1	44
1630	Clark, Fannie E.	Gibson, L. B. (Mrs.); Clark, Zoe	Clark, Maud E.	7,000	Minor	26 Apr 1887	1	46

142

Case #	Principals	Sureties	Bound to	Amount ($)	Type	Date	Book	Page(s)
1640	Appleton, Horatio	Cady, M. K.; Baxter, T. P.	Appleton, William G.	480	[Minor]	24 May 1887	1	47
1640	Appleton, Horatio	Cady, M. K.; Baxter, T. P.	Appleton, Eliza G.	180	[Minor]	24 May 1887	1	48
1641	Staedler, Elizabeth	Morse, Amasa; Haney, Frank	Staedler, Harry	600	Minor	4 Aug 1887	1	52
1641	Staedler, Elizabeth	Cavanagh, John; Scott, J. C.	Staedler, Harry	600	Minor	13 Oct 1888	1	87
1644	Givens, R. R.	McDonald, Mark L.; Phillips, D. D.	Givens, Ada	200	Minor	6 Jun 1887	1	49
1644	Givens, R. R.	McDonald, Mark L.; Phillips, D. D.	Givens, David G.	200	Minor	6 Jun 1887	1	48
1644	Givens, R. R.	McDonald, Mark L.; Phillips, D. D.	Givens, Anna J.	200	Minor	6 Jun 1887	1	49
1644	Givens, R. R.	McDonald, Mark L.; Phillips, D. D.	Givens, Grace M.	200	Minor	6 Jun 1887	1	50
1647	Clarke, Charlotte F.	Perrin, Robert; Craig, William; Meredith, J. H.	Clarke, Jeremiah	40,000	Incompetent person	21 Jun 1887	D	308-310
1654	Sawyer, Lucy H.	Haight, Robert; Kohlman, Solomon	Sawyer, Charles H.	400	Minor	26 Jul 1887	1	53
1654	Sawyer, Lucy H.	Haight, Robert; Kohlman, Solomon	Sawyer, Florence	400	Minor	26 Jul 1887	1	53
1657	Murphy, William	Hopper, J. W.; Walker, J. L.	Murphy, Armidale	100	Minor	1 Aug 1887	1	51
1661	Singley, Charles E.	Kahn, Moise; Cox, B. F.	Martin, Fannie	1,000	Minor	8 Aug 1887	1	51
1661	Singley, Charles E.	Kahn, Moise; Cox, B. F.	Martin, James	1,000	Minor	8 Aug 1887	1	52
1663	Delafield, Robert H.	Hopper, J. W.; Roney, J. M.	Sensibaugh, Johnson	100	Minor	24 Sep 1887	1	55
1663	Delafield, Robert H.	Hopper, J. W.; Roney, J. M.	Sensibaugh, Alzirus	100	Minor	24 Sep 1887	1	54
1664	Hopper, Thomas	Taylor, John S.; McConnell, William E.	Scoville, Benjamin	2,000	Minor	22 Aug 1887	1	54
1666	Lavell, John	Hassett, Aaron; Neely, T. L.; Mead, James A.; Cohn, S.	Lambert, George Lee	8,000	Minor	27 Oct 1887	1	57
1666	Lavell, John	Cohn, S.; Mead, James A.; Hassett, Aaron; Hall, L. J.	Lambert, George Lee	8,000	Minor	19 Sep 1887	D	318-319
1666	Lavell, John	Hassett, Aaron; Neely, T. L.; Bishop, Tennessee C.	Lambert, George Lee	8,000	Minor	16 Oct 1888	1	88
1670	Robertson, William A.	Barry, Thomas F.; Anderson, James W.	Robertson, Sarah Jessie	100	Minor	14 Sep 1887	1	58
1670	Robertson, William A.	Barry, Thomas F.; Anderson, James W.	Robertson, James Calhoun	100	Minor	14 Sep 1887	1	59
1676	Bradshaw, Emma (Mrs.)	Clark, David; Carithers, D. N.	Bradshaw, Arthur	200	Minor	26 Sep 1887	1	60
1682	Ricksecker, L. E.	Sheldon, D. B.; Walker, John	Ricksecker, Helen Pearson	200	Minor	17 Oct 1887	1	58
1690	McGee, James H.	Overton, A. P.; Noonan, George P.	Richardson, Holena E.	1,500	Incompetent person	31 Oct 1887	1	57
1693	Blume, Julius	Cereghino, A.; Tempel, C.	Hinrichs, Carl	300	Insane person	23 Nov 1887	1	74
1697	Gossage, Rachel A.	Gossage, Joseph; Stratton, F. W.	Gossage, Winfield S.	3,000	Minor	31 Dec 1887	1	55
1697	Gossage, Rachel A.	Gossage, Joseph; Wickersham, I. G.	Gossage, Harry S.	3,000	Minor	31 Dec 1887	1	61

Case #	Principals	Sureties	Bound to	Amount ($)	Type	Date	Book	Page(s)
1697*	Gossage, Rachel A.	Gossage, Joseph; Haskell, William B.	Gossage, Jerome B.	3,000	Minor	31 Dec 1887	1	56
1713	Overholser, W. R.	Collins, F. M.; Phillips, Jacob	State of California; The Superior Court of Sonoma County appointed W. R. Overholser the guardian of the person and the estate of Barton E. Overholser, a minor, on 20 Feb 1888 upon his executing this bond.	500	Minor	25 Feb 1888	1	62
1717	Murdock, L. A.	Tupper, G. A.; Harris, Jacob	Hawkins, Maud	1,200	Minor	14 Mar 1888	1	65
1717	Murdock, L. A.	Tupper, G. A.; Harris, Jacob	Hawkins, Mamie	1,200	Minor	14 Mar 1888	1	66
1717	Murdock, L. A.	Tupper, G. A.; Harris, Jacob	Hawkins, Mark	1,200	Minor	14 Mar 1888	1	66
1725	Winder, Mary A.	Harris, W. F.; Winder, Joseph	Winder, Edward C.	200	Minor	12 May 1888	1	75
1725	Winder, Mary A.	Harris, W. F.; Winder, Joseph	Winder, Robert J.	200	Minor	12 May 1888	1	76
1729	Charles, Vernetta	Hill, William; White, Harrison	Charles, Nellie Gertrude	1,000	Minor	24 Mar 1888	1	68
1729	Charles, Vernetta	Hill, William; White, Harrison	Charles, Leon Lester	1,000	Minor	24 Mar 1888	1	69
1730	Read, Minnie I.	Decker, Peter; Jewett, John H.	Read, Mary	1,500	Minor	9 Apr 1888	1	70
1730	Read, Minnie I.	Decker, Peter; Jewett, John H.	Read, Bertha A.	1,500	Minor	9 Apr 1888	1	70
1730	Read, Minnie I.	Decker, Peter; Jewett, John H.	Read, Decker Jewett	1,500	Minor	9 Apr 1888	1	71
1736	Kendall, John	Crane, R.; Mitchener, J.	Kendall, Homer	200	Minor	5 May 1888	1	73
1736	Kendall, John	Crane, R.; Mitchener, J.	Kendall, Arthur	200	Minor	5 May 1888	1	73
1739	Letold, J. G.	Geick, Leo; Fehrmann, Johann	Jose, Sophia	440	Minor	23 Apr 1888	1	71
1739	Letold, J. G.	Geick, Leo; Fehrmann, Johann	Jose, Louisa	440	Minor	23 Apr 1888	1	72
1739	Letold, J. G.	Geick, Leo; Fehrmann, Johann	Jose, Paul Henry	440	Minor	23 Apr 1888	1	72
1739	Jose, Emanuel	Sanborn, W. B.; Nye, B. M.	State of California; The Superior Court of Sonoma County appointed Emanuel Jose the guardian of the estate of Louisa Jose, a minor, on 19 Jan 1891 upon his executing this bond.	350	Minor	20 Jan 1891	1	144
1739	Jose, Emanuel	Sanborn, W. B.; Nye, B. M.	State of California; The Superior Court of Sonoma County appointed Emanuel Jose the guardian of the estate of Sophia Jose, a minor, on 19 Jan 1891 upon his executing this bond.	350	Minor	20 Jan 1891	1	145
1739	Jose, Emanuel	Sanborn, W. B.; Nye, B. M.	State of California; The Superior Court of Sonoma County appointed Emanuel Jose the guardian of the estate of Paul Henry Jose, a minor, on 19 Jan 1891 upon his executing this bond.	350	Minor	20 Jan 1891	1	145
1739	Jose, Emanuel	Geick, Leo; Pipher, Philip	Jose, Sophia	350	Minor	4 Sep 1893	1	202
1739	Jose, Emanuel	Geick, Leo; Pipher, Philip	Jose, Paul Henry	350	Minor	4 Sep 1893	1	202

Case #	Principals	Sureties	Bound to	Amount ($)	Type	Date	Book	Page(s)
1744	Gale, Demus	Gale, Otis; Nickels, Thomas A.	McGrew, James C.	4,000	Insane person	21 May 1888	1	76
1745	Huntley, Will	Coffman, N. B.; Raabe, M.	Huntley, John Stanley	200	[Minor]	23 May 1888	1	77
1746	Rafael, M. E.	Peters, Manuel; Vitaes, F. Perera	Machado, Mary	2,600	Minor	14 May 1888	1	74
1747	Rathcke, Fred	Pedigo, E. M.; Harris, Jacob	Aiken, Della	1,600	[Minor]	16 Jun 1888	1	83
1749	Haskell, William B.	Fritsch, John; Poehlmann, Conrad	Haskell, Euna G.	2,000	Minor	7 Jun 1888	1	79
1751	Brown, Catherine	Brown, Robert S.; Brown, Alice J.	Brown, Genevieve	7,000	[Minor]	16 Jun 1888	1	80
1751	Brown, Catherine	Brown, Robert S.; Brown, Mary	Brown, Edith	7,000	Minor	16 Jun 1888	1	80
1751	Brown, Catherine	Brown, Robert S.; Brown, Alice J.	Brown, Ada E.	7,000	[Minor]	16 Jun 1888	1	81
1751	Brown, Catherine	Brown, Robert S.; Brown, Mary	Brown, John McAllen, Jr.	7,000	[Minor]	16 Jun 1888	1	81
1751	Brown, Catherine	Brown, Robert S.; Brown, John McA.	Brown, Genevieve	2,000	Minor	20 May 1892		
1759*	Tivnen, John	Roney, J. M.; Fisher, A. L.; Lewis, George W.	Ewell, Mary M.	7,000	Incompetent person	21 Jul 1888	1	83
1759	Ewell, Fred F.	Granice, H. H.; Fochetti, Julius	Ewell, Mary M.	3,000	Incompetent person	23 Dec 1890	1	143
1759	Ewell, E. C.	Granice, H. H.; Peers, Alexander	Ewell, Mary M.	2,060	Incompetent person	13 Dec 1892	1	190
1763	Fordyce, Emma	Whitaker, G. N.; Whitaker, J. P.	Fordyce, Grace	2,000	Minor	15 Aug 1888	1	84
1763	Fordyce, Emma	Whitaker, G. N.; Whitaker, J. P.	Fordyce, Mabel	2,000	Minor	15 Aug 1888	1	84
1772	Jewell, Grace A.	Bishop, T. C.; McKinley, D. E.	Jewell, Ida M.	200	Minor	5 Oct 1888	1	85
1772	Jewell, Grace A.	Bishop, T. C.; McKinley, D. E.	Jewell, George W.	200	Minor	5 Oct 1888	1	86
1772	Jewell, Grace A.	Bishop, T. C.; McKinley, D. E.	Jewell, Ruby Grace	200	Minor	5 Oct 1888	1	86
1780	Andrews, W. E.	Howell, O.; Hillis, John A.	Edsall, Juana B.	500	Insane person	25 Oct 1888	1	89
1780	Andrews, W. E.	Reynolds, W. D.; Andrews, J. F. W.	Edsall, Juana B.	500	Insane person	20 Mar 1906	2	130
1782	Fix, J. K.	Sullivan, J. W.; Gregson, James	Sterling, Carrie	200	Minor	22 Oct 1888	1	87
1782	Fix, J. K.	Sullivan, J. W.; Gregson, James	Sterling, James F.	200	Minor	22 Oct 1888	1	88
1782	Markwell, S.	Hassett, Aaron; Powell, R.	Sterling, Carrie	300	Minor	15 Jul 1889	1	113
1782	Markwell, S.	Hassett, Aaron; Powell, R.	Sterling, James F.	300	Minor	15 Jul 1889	1	113
1782	Cramer, D. R.	Davis, G. V.; Brooks, Elmont	Sterling, Carrie	300	Minor	16 Mar 1891	1	147
1782	Cramer, D. R.	Davis, G. V.; Brooks, Elmont	Sterling, James F.	300	Minor	16 Mar 1891	1	148
1794	Fick, Margarette F.	Schroder, John; Seegelken, E. A.	Fick, Henry William	50	Minor	4 Dec 1888	1	91

Case #	Principals	Sureties	Bound to	Amount ($)	Type	Date	Book	Page(s)
1794	Fick, Margarette F.	Schroder, John; Seegelken, E. A.	Fick, John Frederick	50	Minor	4 Dec 1888	1	91
1794	Fick, Margarette F.	Schroder, John; Seegelken, E. A.	Fick, Hermine Dorethe	50	Minor	4 Dec 1888	1	90
1796	Gregory, Mattie M.	Wickersham, I. G.; Maynard, F. T.	Gregory, Lulu	600	Minor	11 Dec 1888	1	90
1796	Gregory, Annie E. (Mrs.)	Wickersham, I. G.; Maynard, F. T.	Gregory, Lulu	300	Minor	3 Feb 1890	1	120
1797	Tarrant, H. F.	Drummond, I. H.; Weise, C.	Tarrant, Joseph Henry	600	Minor	29 Dec 1888	1	92
1797	Tarrant, H. F.	Drummond, I. H.; Weise, C.	Tarrant, Emily Augusta	600	Minor	29 Dec 1888	1	93
1797	Tarrant, H. F.	Drummond, I. H.; Weise, C.	Tarrant, Rosalie	600	Minor	29 Dec 1888	1	93
1797	Tarrant, H. F.	Drummond, I. H.; Weise, C.	Tarrant, Sophie A.	600	Minor	29 Dec 1888	1	94
1807	Brooke, T. J.	Burris, L. W.; Harris, Jacob	Lucas, Nellie B.	1,000	Minor	24 Dec 1888	1	92
1808	Wendt, Fred	Downs, Vernon; Pfister, C.	Demetz, Edward	1,000	[Minor]	2 Feb 1889	1	95
1808	Wendt, Fred	Downs, Vernon; Pfister, C.	Demetz, Anna	1,000	[Minor]	2 Feb 1889	1	95
1808	Wendt, Fred	Downs, Vernon; Pfister, C.	Demetz, Louisa	1,000	[Minor]	2 Feb 1889	1	96
1815	Hayes, Emma	Shea, C.; Harris, Jacob	Hayes, Rosa	800	Minor	7 Jan 1889	1	94
1820	McCumiskey, Rose	Deveraux, E. W.; Shea, Con	McCumiskey, Raymond J.	100	Minor	9 Feb 1889	1	97
1820	McCumiskey, Rose	Deveraux, E. W.; Shea, Con	McCumiskey, David J.	100	Minor	9 Feb 1889	1	97
1820	McCumiskey, Rose	Deveraux, E. W.; Shea, Con	McCumiskey, Levi	100	Minor	9 Feb 1889	1	98
1820	McCumiskey, Rose	Deveraux, E. W.; Shea, Con	McCumiskey, Florence I.	100	Minor	9 Feb 1889	1	98
1820	McCumiskey, Rose	Deveraux, E. W.; Shea, Con	McCumiskey, James	100	Minor	9 Feb 1889	1	99
1820	McCumiskey, Rose	Deveraux, E. W.; Shea, Con	McCumiskey, Dasie E.	100	Minor	9 Feb 1889	1	99
1824	Bailey, B. H.	Swisher, J. R.; Daly, John	Carver, Rolla E.	4,000	Minor	7 Feb 1889	1	100
1824	Bailey, B. H.	Osborn, S. L.; Mulgrew, J. F.	Carver, Dora C.	4,000	Minor	7 Feb 1889	1	100
1824	Swisher, J. R.	Whitney, William B.; Fox, Henry	Carver, Rolla E.	1,600	Minor	24 Apr 1896	1	242
1827	Jose, Emanuel	Wolf, Charles; Geick, F.	Feltz, Louise	100	Minor	12 Feb 1889		
1828	Fulkerson, S. T.	Taylor, John S.; Maddux, J. P.	Fulkerson, Richard	200	Minor	4 Feb 1889	1	96
1829	Perry, C. A.	Frost, C. W.; Kirkpatrick, T. F.	Steel, James Henry	225	Minor	20 Feb 1889	1	101
1833	Oates, James W.	Rule, C. H. S.; Noonan, George P.	West, Fred	1,000	Minor	8 Apr 1889	1	105
1833	Oates, James W.	Rule, C. H. S.; Noonan, George P.	West, Henry	400	Minor	8 Apr 1889	1	106
1833	Oates, James W.	Rule, C. H. S.; Noonan, George P.	West, Charles	1,000	Minor	8 Apr 1889	1	106
1834	Stewart, Ann	Fairbanks, H. T.; Poehlmann, Conrad	Stewart, John A.	2,000	[Minor]	19 Mar 1889	1	103
1836	Ronsheimer, Katy	Muther, Frank; Jud, Christian	Ronsheimer, Lizzie	1,200	Minor	18 Mar 1889	1	101
1836	Ronsheimer, Katy	Muther, Frank; Jud, Christian	Ronsheimer, Tony	1,200	Minor	18 Mar 1889	1	102

146

Case #	Principals	Sureties	Bound to	Amount ($)	Type	Date	Book	Page(s)
1836	Ronsheimer, Katy	Dunbar, John; Seegelken, E. A.	Ronsheimer, Mary	1,200	Minor	18 Mar 1889	1	102
1836	Ronsheimer, Katy	Dunbar, John; Seegelken, E. A.	Ronsheimer, Peter	1,200	Minor	18 Mar 1889	1	103
1837	Tomasini, Louis	Garzoli, William; Tomasini, Matteo	Tomasini, Lila	7,000	Minor	18 Mar 1889	1	104
1837	Tomasini, Louis	Piezzi, Victor; Tomasini, Matteo	Tomasini, Waldo A.	7,000	Minor	18 Mar 1889	1	104
1837	Tomasini, Louis	Piezzi, Victor; Tomasini, Matteo	Tomasini, Juliet	7,000	Minor	18 Mar 1889	1	105
1837	Tomasini, Louis	Berri, Vittore; Tomasini, Matteo	Tomasini, Juliet	2,000	Minor	30 Nov 1897	1	274
1837	Tomasini, Louis	Berri, Vittore; Tomasini, Matteo	Tomasini, Lila	1,700	Minor	30 Nov 1897	1	275
1837	Tomasini, Louis	Tomasini, Matteo; Piezzi, Victor	Tomasini, Waldo	1,700	Minor	30 Nov 1897	1	275
1844	Monahan, Thomas F.	Barbarin, G.; Monahan, Mary	Monahan, Catherine T.	2,500	Minor	20 Apr 1889	1	107
1850	Reynolds, W. D.	Young, Mary R.; Prindle, William	Young, Lena C.	4,000	Minor	7 May 1889	1	108
1850	Reynolds, W. D.	Young, Mary R.; Prindle, William	Young, Clement C.	4,000	Minor	7 May 1889	1	108
1853	Churchill, H. H.	Mulgrew, John F.; Crawford, R. F.	Wright, Myrtle J.	200	Minor	15 May 1889	1	109
1853	Churchill, H. H.	Mulgrew, John F.; Crawford, R. F.	Wright, Daisy A.	200	Minor	15 May 1889	1	109
1867	Tate, Alice	Davis, G. V.; Hodgson, W. H.	Tate, Hazel D.	7,000	Minor	1 Jul 1889	1	110
1867	Tate, Alice	Tate, A. F.; Hodgson, W. H.	Tate, Minnie Ann	7,000	Minor	1 Jul 1889	1	110
1867*	Tate, Alice	Fisher, A. L.; Hodgson, W. H.	Tate, Robert J.	7,000	Minor	1 Jul 1889	1	111
1868	Katen, John	Rafael, M. E.; Lopes, Manuel	Rodgers, J. P.	50	Minor	31 Jul 1889	1	114
1870	Smith, A. H.	Taylor, John S.; Carithers, D. N.	Johnson, Mary	300	Incompetent person	17 Jul 1889	1	111
1871	Drees, Gustave A.	Drees, E. E.; Drees, J. E.	Drees, W. E.	3,200	Minor	17 Jul 1889	1	112
1871	Drees, Gustave A.	Drees, E. E.; Drees, L. H.	Drees, H. A.	3,200	Minor	17 Jul 1889	1	112
1874	Kuchler, Carolina	Agnew, Samuel J.; Champlin, Charles C.	Kuchler, Josephine	200	Minor	10 Aug 1889	1	114
1874	Kuchler, Carolina	Agnew, Samuel J.; Champlin, Charles C.	Kuchler, Blaseus	200	Minor	10 Aug 1889	1	115
1874	Kuchler, Carolina	Agnew, Samuel J.; Champlin, Charles C.	Kuchler, Joseph	200	Minor	10 Aug 1889	1	115
1874	Kuchler, Carolina	Agnew, Samuel J.; Champlin, Charles C.	Kuchler, Rosalie	200	Minor	10 Aug 1889	1	116
1877	Grieves, William	Gray, J. W.; Maddux, J. P.	Grieves, Samuel H.	100	Incompetent person	19 Aug 1889	1	117
1878	Gibson, Silas W.	Whitney, W. B.; Brown, H. K.	Lambert, Ellen A.	1,000	Minor	20 Aug 1889	1	116
1878	Gibson, Silas W.	Hassett, Aaron; Mead, James A.	Lambert, George F.	1,000	Minor	20 Aug 1889	1	117
1894	Ellsworth, Clara	Jones, William; Jones, Walter	Ellsworth, Leonard F.	1,000	Minor	30 Oct 1889	1	118
1896	King, Elnora C.	Pollard, Thomas; Blair, Samuel	King, William F.	100	Minor	29 Oct 1889	1	119

147

Case #	Principals	Sureties	Bound to	Amount ($)	Type	Date	Book	Page(s)
1930	Robinson, George	Bryant, Allen; Roney, J. M.	Agnew, Richard Arthur	65	[Minor]	11 Mar 1890	1	121
1930	Robinson, George	Bryant, Allen; Roney, J. M.	Agnew, Clairisse Adele	65	[Minor]	11 Mar 1890	1	121
1933	Kelsey, Mary	Kelsey, R. J.; Kelsey, Mary H.	Kelsey, Alice F.	600	Minor	8 Apr 1890	1	122
1933	Kelsey, Mary	Meyer, Anton; Meyer, F. A.	Kelsey, Thomas H.	600	Minor	12 Apr 1890	1	122
1933	Kelsey, Mary	Kelsey, R. J.; Kelsey, Mary H.	Kelsey, Annie R.	600	Minor	8 Apr 1890	1	123
1933	Kelsey, Mary	Meyer, Anton; Haskell, William B.	Kelsey, Daniel M.	600	Minor	12 Apr 1890	1	123
1933	Kelsey, Mary	Kelsey, R. J.; Kelsey, Mary H.	Kelsey, Edwin J.	600	Minor	8 Apr 1890	1	124
1951	Anderson, Catharine V.	Petersen, Hans P.; Boyson, C. C.	Anderson, Jennie P.	200	Minor	26 Apr 1890	1	127
1951	Anderson, Catharine V.	Petersen, Hans Peter; Boyson, C. C.	Anderson, John A.	200	Minor	26 Apr 1890	1	128
1951	Anderson, Catharine V.	Petersen, Hans Peter; Boyson, C. C.	Anderson, Paul J.	200	Minor	26 Apr 1890	1	128
1951	Anderson, Catharine V.	Petersen, Hans P.; Boyson, C. C.	Anderson, Emma J.	200	Minor	26 Apr 1890	1	129
1960	Springer, Christopf	Kroeger, F.; Weisshand, August	Springer, Lena	350	Minor	10 May 1890	1	125
1960	Springer, Christopf	Kroeger, F.; Weisshand, August	Springer, Maria E.	350	Minor	10 May 1890	1	124
1960	Springer, Christopf	Kroeger, F.; Weisshand, August	Springer, Frank	350	Minor	10 May 1890	1	125
1962	Marshall, Hugh A.	Marshall, James; Weeks, Frank P.	Wright, Arthur Gordon	100	Minor	5 May 1890	1	126
1962	Marshall, Hugh A.	Marshall, James; Weeks, Frank P.	Wright, Ernest Walter	100	Minor	5 May 1890	1	126
1962	Marshall, Hugh A.	Marshall, James; Weeks, Frank P.	Wright, Ethel Audrey	100	Minor	5 May 1890	1	127
1966	Towey, Peter	Heisel, Ellen; Cumming, John	Heisel, John	2,000	Minor	24 May 1890	QUAL	146
1966	Towey, Peter	Prindle, William; Noonan, P. H.	Heisel, Caroline	2,000	Minor	24 May 1890	1	129
1966	Towey, Peter	Heisel, Ellen; Cumming, John	Heisel, Nellie	2,000	Minor	24 May 1890	QUAL	146
1966	Towey, Peter	Prindle, William; Noonan, P. H.	Heisel, Paul	2,000	Minor	24 May 1890	QUAL	147
1970	Thompson, Robert A.	Noonan, George P.; Thompson, Thomas L.	Thompson, Wilmer	1,000	Minor	21 May 1890	QUAL	145
1976	Wagele, Dorris	Pries, George; Grater, J. F.	Wagele, Charles	3,200	Minor	20 Jun 1890	1	131
1976	Wagele, Dorris	Grater, J. F.; Schnittger, C. H.	Wagele, Charles	3,200	Minor	8 Aug 1893	1	197
1976*	Wagele, Doris	Claussen, August A.; Fricke, John F.	Wagele, Charles	3,200	Minor	31 Jan 1896	QUAL	257
1978	Nagle, William L.	Dunbar, John; Collins, C. N.	State of California; The Superior Court of Sonoma County appointed William L. Nagle the guardian of the estate of Carrie Mabel Deems, a minor, on 23 Jun 1890 upon his executing this bond.	50	Minor	[23] Jun 1890	1	131

148

Case #	Principals	Sureties	Bound to	Amount ($)	Type	Date	Book	Page(s)
1981	Wilcox, Sidney B.	Milam, M. S.; Milam, Thomas	Milam, Benjamin L.	300	Incompetent person	28 Jul 1890	1	135
1983	Faudre, Stewart W.	Lee, William H.; Carter, E. D.	State of California; The Superior Court of Sonoma County appointed Stewart W. Faudre the guardian of the estate of Martha E. Ashley, a minor, on 20 Jun 1890 upon his executing this bond.	600	Minor	20 Jun 1890	1	130
1984	McGee, Cerro Gordo (Mrs.)	Ragsdale, J. W.; McGee, William M.	McGee, Irene	100	Minor	30 Jun 1890	1	132
1989	Miller, John	Seibt, Gustav; Seibt, Mary	Miller, Andrew	300	[Minor]	17 Jul 1890	1	132
1989	Miller, John	Seibt, Gustav; Seibt, Mary	Miller, Jeanie M.	300	[Minor]	17 Jul 1890	1	133
1989	Miller, John	Seibt, Gustav; Seibt, Mary	Miller, Lucy P.	300	[Minor]	17 Jul 1890	1	133
1989	Miller, John	Seibt, Gustav; Seibt, Mary	Miller, Charles A.	300	[Minor]	17 Jul 1890	1	134
1989	Miller, John	Seibt, Gustav; Seibt, Mary	Miller, John O.	300	Minor	17 Jul 1890	1	134
1989	Miller, John	Seibt, Gustav; Seibt, Mary	Miller, Bertha J.	300	[Minor]	17 Jul 1890	1	135
1990	Young, George C.	Cereghino, A.; Matzenbach, W. B.	McKinney, Katie	5,000	Incompetent person	13 Sep 1890	1	136
1996	Fay, J. P.	Swain, R. M.; Prindle, William	Brannan, Margaret	50	Minor	31 Jul 1890	1 / QUAL	136 / 156
1996	Fay, J. P.	Swain, R. M.; Prindle, William	Brannan, Joseph	50	Minor	31 Jul 1890	QUAL	157
1996	Fay, J. P.	Swain, R. M.; Prindle, William	Brannan, Peter	50	Minor	31 Jul 1890	QUAL	157
1996	Fay, J. P.	Swain, R. M.; Prindle, William	Brannan, James	50	Minor	31 Jul 1890	QUAL	158
1996	Fay, J. P.	Swain, R. M.; Prindle, William	Brannan, Anthony	50	Minor	31 Jul 1890	QUAL	158
1996	Fay, J. P.	Swain, R. M.; Prindle, William	Brannan, Gertrude	50	Minor	31 Jul 1890	QUAL	159
2002	Adamson, Mary E.	Grainger, W. C.; Liter, W.	Adamson, James T.	100	Minor	16 Sep 1890	1	137
2002	Adamson, Mary E.	Grainger, W. C.; Liter, W.	Adamson, Bertha	100	Minor	16 Sep 1890	1	137
2010	Mountjoy, Mary L. P.	Healey, W. E.; Carter, Dan P.	Vance, Stewart	100	Minor	17 Nov 1890	1	138
2010	Mountjoy, Mary L. P.	Healey, W. E.; Carter, Dan P.	Vance, Robbin	100	Minor	17 Nov 1890	1	138
2011	McCabe, S. H.	Haehl, Jacob; Howell, Orrin	Haehl, Amy Mary	1,200	Minor	12 Nov 1890	1	142
2011	McCabe, S. H.	Haehl, Jacob; Howell, Orrin	Haehl, Harry L.	1,200	Minor	12 Nov 1890	1	142
2013	Drees, Marie A. C.	Lohrmann, John; Meyerholtz, Henry	Drees, Carson F.	200	Minor	28 Nov 1890	1	141
2013	Drees, Marie A. C.	Lohrmann, John; Meyerholtz, Henry	Drees, C. F. A.	200	Minor	28 Nov 1890	1	111
2013	Drees, Marie A. C.	Lohrmann, John; Meyerholtz, Henry	Drees, John R. A.	200	Minor	28 Nov 1890	1	140

Case #	Principals	Sureties	Bound to	Amount ($)	Type	Date	Book	Page(s)
2014	McConathy, F. A. (Mrs.)	Seitz, Calvin; Brush, William T.	State of California; The Superior Court of Sonoma County appointed Mrs. F. A. McConathy the guardian of the person and estate of Emma McConathy, a minor, on 10 Nov 1890 upon her executing this bond.	300	Minor	11 Nov 1890	1	139
2020	Beall, Susan E.	Rose, J. E. B.; Gardner, D. P.	Beall, Mary F.	400	Minor	24 Nov 1890	1	139
2021	Mead, James A.	Weaver, C. W.; Norton, L. A.	Walker, E. S.	5,000	Insane person	25 Nov 1890	1	140
2029	Appleton, Horatio	Weyl, Henry; Craig, Oliver W.	Appleton, Caroline Spring	5,000	Minor	16 Dec 1890	1	143
2044	Blaney, Andrew J.	Owens, James; Swygert, Isaac	Chapman, Charles L.	50	Minor	2 Feb 1891	1	146
2044	Blaney, Andrew J.	Owens, James; Swygert, Isaac	Chapman, Maria	50	Minor	2 Feb 1891	1	146
2045	Swygert, Isaac	Robertson, John; Swygert, John	Swygert, Sarah A.	1,000	Insane person	2 Feb 1891	1	144
2054	Graeter, Ida S.	Lewis, G. W.; Roney, J. M.	Thompson, Gertrude	1,200	Minor	6 Mar 1891	1	147
2071	Schieffer, C. H.	Einhorn, J. H.; Healey, W. E.	Schieffer, Frances C.	400	Minor	4 May 1891	1	149
2071	Schieffer, C. H.	Einhorn, J. H.; Healey, W. E.	Schieffer, Frederick H.	400	Minor	4 May 1891	1	149
2071	Schieffer, C. H.	Einhorn, J. H.; Healey, W. E.	Schieffer, Clara H.	400	Minor	4 May 1891	1	150
2071	Schieffer, C. H.	Einhorn, J. H.; Healey, W. E.	Schieffer, Robert A.	400	Minor	4 May 1891	1	150
2071	Schieffer, C. H.	Einhorn, J. H.; Healey, W. E.	Schieffer, Louis E.	400	Minor	4 May 1891	1	151
2071	Schieffer, C. H.	Einhorn, J. H.; Healey, W. E.	Schieffer, Albert A.	400	Minor	4 May 1891	1	151
2071	Schieffer, C. H.	Einhorn, J. H.; Healey, W. E.	Schieffer, Joseph C.	400	Minor	4 May 1891	1	152
2071	Schieffer, C. H.	Einhorn, J. H.; Healey, W. E.	Schieffer, Millie I.	400	Minor	4 May 1891	1	152
2071	Schieffer, C. H.	Einhorn, J. H.; Healey, W. E.	Schieffer, William H.	400	Minor	4 May 1891	1	153
2071	Schieffer, C. H.	Einhorn, J. H.; Healey, W. E.	Schieffer, Emma H.	400	Minor	4 May 1891	1	153
2073	McClish, John N.	McClendon, William J.; Laughlin, J. H.	Bice, Frank S.	10,000	Minor	13 May 1891	1	154
2081	Graves, Luella B.	Noonan, George P.; Overton, A. P.	Graves, Hill B.	4,000	Minor	1 Jun 1891	1	155
2081	Graves, Luella B.	Noonan, George P.; Overton, A. P.	Graves, Georgie	4,000	Minor	1 Jun 1891	1	154
2085	Perry, Jeanette V.	Lawrence, H. E.; Mitchener, J.	Parker, George J.	1,200	Minor	24 Jun 1891	1	155
2087	Rafael, A. J.	Rafael, M. E.; Francisco, Joseph	Marshall, Mary	200	Minor	25 Jul 1891	1	156
2087	Rafael, A. J.	Rafael, M. E.; Francisco, Joseph	Marshall, Manuel	200	Minor	25 Jul 1891	1	156
2087	Rafael, A. J.	Rafael, M. E.; Francisco, Joseph	Marshall, Rosa	200	Minor	25 Jul 1891	1	157
2087	Rafael, A. J.	Rafael, M. E.; Francisco, Joseph	Marshall, John	200	Minor	25 Jul 1891	1	157
2087	Rafael, A. J.	Rafael, M. E.; Francisco, Joseph	Marshall, Domingo	200	Minor	25 Jul 1891	1	158

Case #	Principals	Sureties	Bound to	Amount ($)	Type	Date	Book	Page(s)
2087	Rafael, A. J.	Rafael, M. E.; Francisco, Joseph	Marshall, Joseph	200	Minor	25 Jul 1891	1	158
2087	Rafael, A. J.	Rafael, M. E.; Francisco, Joseph	Marshall, Frank	200	Minor	25 Jul 1891	1	159
2102	Haskins, Robert	Lawler, John; Veale, W. R.	Stacey, William	500	Incompetent person	3 Sep 1891	1	159
2103	Wilson, Thomas B.	Granice, H. H.; Wegner, Ed	Wilson, Daydawn	1,000	Minor	16 Sep 1891	1	160
2103	Wilson, Thomas B.	Modini, Lorenzo; Marti, M.	Wilson, Joseph Percy	1,000	Minor	16 Sep 1891	1	160
2103	Wilson, Thomas B.	Schocken, S.; Laux, H.	Wilson, Robert J.	1,000	Minor	16 Sep 1891	1	161
2106	Forsyth, Robert A.	Mailer, J. C.; Taylor, John S.	Epperly, Levi O.	2,800	Minor	7 Oct 1891	1	162
2111	Rafael, M. E.	Rafael, J. E.; Lopes, Manuel	Rogers, Frank	50	Minor	20 Oct 1891	1	162
2111	Rafael, M. E.	Rafael, J. E.; Lopes, Manuel	Katen, Annie	50	Minor	20 Oct 1891	1	163
2111	Rafael, M. E.	Rafael, J. E.; Lopes, Manuel	Rogers, William	50	Minor	20 Oct 1891	1	163
2115	Patty, L. H.	Towne, Lester B.; Towne, Walter	Towne, Beverly M.	2,500	Minor	29 Oct 1891	1	164
2116	Warner, Alma	Starr, Mary L.; Kaler, George	Warner, Henrietta	275	Minor	11 Dec 1891	1	173
2116	Warner, Alma	Starr, Mary E.; Kaler, George	Warner, William E.	275	Minor	11 Dec 1891	1	173
2117	Oates, James W.	Noonan, George P.; Walker, J. M.	St. Clair, Mary Ellen	200	Minor	9 Nov 1891	1	165
2117	Oates, James W.	Noonan, George P.; Walker, J. M.	St. Clair, Frank C.	200	Minor	9 Nov 1891	1	166
2117	Oates, James W.	Noonan, George P.; Walker, J. M.	St. Clair, Freddie	200	Minor	9 Nov 1891	1	166
2117	Oates, James W.	Noonan, George P.; Walker, J. M.	St. Clair, Estelle	200	Minor	9 Nov 1891	1	167
2117	Oates, James W.	Noonan, George P.; Walker, J. M.	St. Clair, Richardson	200	Minor	9 Nov 1891	1	167
2117	Patteson, William	Patteson, Addie; St. Clair, Mary E.	St. Clair, Richardson	700	Minor	15 Sep 1893	1	203
2117	Patteson, William	Patteson, Addie; St. Clair, Mary E.	St. Clair, Estelle	700	Minor	14 Sep 1893	1	203
2117	Patteson, William	Patteson, Addie; St. Clair, Mary E.	St. Clair, Freddie	700	Minor	15 Sep 1893	1	204
2121	Hoadley, Harriet	Doyle, M.; Davis, G. V.	Hoadley, George H.	2,600	Minor	9 Nov 1891	1	165
2122	Mulvehill, Margaret	Keegan, J. W.; Keegan, Thomas P.	Mulvehill, Ellen G.	3,000	Minor	9 Nov 1891	1	164
2129	Smith, L. M.	Knowles, D. C.; Blaney, Andrew J.	Knowles, Clarence E.	1,000	Incompetent person	23 Nov 1891	1	168
2132*	McCleave, H. P.	Hill, William; Zartman, William	Harvey, Elmer R.; Harvey, Calvin A.	2,500	Minors	14 Dec 1891	1	168
2165	Chauvet, Joshua	Wegener, Julius; Burris, Jesse; Litzius, Louis; Weyl, Henry	Barbarin, Gratien	7,500	Incompetent person	26 Jan 1892	D	359-362
2169	Silzle, George	Sioli, Victor; Phillips, S. E.	Silzle, Minnie	100	Minor	6 Feb 1892	1	169
2169	Silzle, George	Sioli, Victor; Phillips, S. E.	Silzle, Kate A.	100	Minor	6 Feb 1892	1	169
2169	Silzle, George	Sioli, Victor; Phillips, S. E.	Silzle, Lena A.	100	Minor	6 Feb 1892	1	170

Case #	Principals	Sureties	Bound to	Amount ($)	Type	Date	Book	Page(s)
2169	Silzle, George	Sioli, Victor; Phillips, S. E.	Silzle, William H.	100	Minor	6 Feb 1892	1	170
2169	Silzle, George	Sioli, Victor; Phillips, S. E.	Silzle, Roy J.	100	Minor	6 Feb 1892	1	171
2169	Silzle, George	Sioli, Victor; Phillips, S. E.	Silzle, Benjamin C.	100	Minor	6 Feb 1892	1	171
2176	Warfield, R. H.	Barnes, E. H.; Miller, G. T.	Brown, Carrie	6,200	Minor	15 Feb 1892	1	172, 174
2180	Farmer, C. C.	Hopper, Thomas; Taylor, John S.	Young, Mariah E.	1,600	Incompetent person	11 Feb 1892	1	172
2181	Kreuz, Frank P.	Noonan, Patrick H.; Trembley, A.	Kreuz, Katharina	5,000	Insane person	6 Apr 1892	1	179
2192	Minoggio, Mary	Filippini, Charles; Pezzaglia, Filippo	Minoggio, Louis; Minoggio, Ambrogio	200	Minors	9 Mar 1892	1	178
2198	Dana, Alfred W.	Brooke, T. J.; Good, W. C.	Dana, Alfred H.	100	Minor	14 Mar 1892	1	174
2198	Dana, Alfred W.	Brooke, T. J.; Good, W. C.	Dana, W. S. B.	100	Minor	14 Mar 1892	1	175
2198	Dana, Alfred W.	Brooke, T. J.; Good, W. C.	Dana, Charles B.	100	Minor	14 Mar 1892	1	175
2198	Dana, Alfred W.	Brooke, T. J.; Good, W. C.	Dana, John A.	100	Minor	14 Mar 1892	1	176
2198	Dana, Alfred W.	Brooke, T. J.; Good, W. C.	Dana, Harold B.	100	Minor	14 Mar 1892	1	176
2198	Dana, Alfred W.	Brooke, T. J.; Good, W. C.	Dana, E. Mabel	100	Minor	14 Mar 1892	1	177
2198	Dana, Alfred W.	Brooke, T. J.; Good, W. C.	Dana, Frank	100	Minor	14 Mar 1892	1	177
2198	Dana, Alfred W.	Brooke, T. J.; Good, W. C.	Dana, Ruth	100	Minor	14 Mar 1892	1	178
2202	Rogers, Louisa M.	Warboys, J. W.; Barnett, J. D.	Rogers, Hattie D.	500	Minor	19 Apr 1892	1	179
2202	Rogers, Louisa M.	Warboys, J. W.; Barnett, J. D.	Rogers, Howard D.	500	Minor	19 Apr 1892	1	180
2217	Caldwell, William	Burrough, James; Brush, William T.	Matthews, George Jones	5,500	Incompetent person	22 Aug 1892	1	187
2231	Fairbanks, D. B.	Fairbanks, H. T.; Fairbanks, J. F.	Corrick, Louisa	1,150	Incompetent person	20 Jul 1892	1	186
2232	Shafer, Sarah C.	Cooley, John B.; Burnett, Albert G.	Shafer, Ignitz	500	Incompetent person	27 Mar 1894	1	211
2233	Adams, Mary M.	Hiatt, E. M.; Ink, W. P.	Adams, Bertha Porthenia	1,300	Minor	15 Aug 1892	1	180
2233	Adams, Mary M.	Hiatt, E. M.; Ink, W. P.	Adams, Mary Edith	1,300	Minor	15 Aug 1892	1	181
2256	Fairbanks, D. B.	Fairbanks, H. T.; Maynard, F. T.	Hatch, Chester P.	8,000	Incompetent person	14 Oct 1892	1	181
2257	Chandler, George W.	Weeks, Braddock; Chandler, Lafayette	Chandler, Noah	26,000	Incompetent person	1 Nov 1892	D	396-399
2258	Cereghino, Mary	Adams, R. S.; Cereghino, A.	Cereghino, Antonio D.	636	Minor	4 Nov 1892	1	182
2258	Cereghino, Mary	Adams, R. S.; Cereghino, A.	Cereghino, Joseph	636	Minor	4 Nov 1892	1	183

Case #	Principals	Sureties	Bound to	Amount ($)	Type	Date	Book	Page(s)
2258	Cereghino, Mary	Adams, R. S.; Cereghino, A.	Cereghino, Verna M.	636	Minor	4 Nov 1892	1	183
2258	Cereghino, Mary	Adams, R. S.; Cereghino, A.	Cereghino, Francis	636	Minor	4 Nov 1892	1	184
2258	Cereghino, Mary	Adams, R. S.; Cereghino, A.	Cereghino, Frederick	636	Minor	4 Nov 1892	1	184
2258	Cereghino, Mary	Adams, R. S.; Cereghino, A.	Cereghino, Attillio	636	Minor	4 Nov 1892	1	185, 186
2266	Winters, Dennis	Loughnane, James; Roberts, Hugh	Winters, Joseph	300	Incompetent person	14 Nov 1892	1	185
2267	Atkinson, Percy Herbert	Morris, Joseph H. P.; Baxter, George P.	Plunket, John	1,000	Minor	28 Nov 1892	1	187
2270	Pitt, J. W.	Mailer, J. C.; Fine, W.	Pitt, Ida	200	Minor	15 Dec 1892	1	188
2270	Pitt, J. W.	Mailer, J. C.; Fine, W.	Pitt, Charles W.	200	Minor	15 Dec 1892	1	188
2270	Pitt, J. W.	Mailer, J. C.; Fine, W.	Pitt, Ralph	200	Minor	15 Dec 1892	1	189
2270	Pitt, J. W.	Mailer, J. C.; Fine, W.	Pitt, Maud	200	Minor	15 Dec 1892	1	189
2282	Callaway, David	Wegner, Ed; Weyl, H.	Tivnen, Mary Clara	500	Minor	17 Jan 1893	1	190
2283*	Hassett, Ora T.	Mead, James A.; Koenig, F.	Hassett, Carrie Josephine	3,000	Minor	7 Jan 1893	1	191
2283*	Hassett, Ora T.	Haigh, Edwin; Koenig, F.	Hassett, Carrie Josephine	3,000	Minor	9 Jan 1895	1	230
2290	Barnes, E. H.	Norton, E. M.; Ferguson, H. O.	France, Waldo E.	2,400	Minor	9 Feb 1893	1	191
2290	Barnes, E. H.	Norton, E. M.; Ferguson, H. O.	France, Frank D.	2,400	Minor	9 Feb 1893	1	192
2290	Barnes, E. H.	Norton, E. M.; Ferguson, H. O.	France, Mabel A.	2,400	Minor	9 Feb 1893	1	192
2290	Weaver, C. W.	Grater, J. F.; Norton, Lew A.	France, Waldo E.	2,400	Minor	9 Feb 1893	1	193
2290	Weaver, C. W.	Grater, J. F.; Norton, Lew A.	France, Frank D.	2,400	Minor	9 Feb 1893	1	193
2290	Weaver, C. W.	Grater, J. F.; Norton, Lew A.	France, Mabel A.	2,400	Minor	9 Feb 1893	1	194
2295	Wilson, Matthew Alexander	Grace, F. P.; Bledsoe, Linn	Byrn, George M.	800	Minor	20 Feb 1893	1	194
2305	Laughlin, Cordelia G.	McConnell, William E.; Overton, John P.	Knight, George W.	1,300	Minor	18 Apr 1893	1	195
2308	Dunn, Philip H.	Merritt, John; Murphy, John	Moan, Catherine	3,000	Minor	24 Apr 1893	1	195
2316	Peterson, Pelina A.	Swank, J. W.; Talmadge, Samuel	Peterson, Lillie	300	Minor	8 May 1893	1	196
2327	Abendroth, F.	Keegan, Thomas P.; Einhorn, J. H.	Short, O. B.	1,500	Incompetent person	26 Jun 1893	D	411-412
2334	Dana, Mary B.	Good, W. C.; Overton, A. P.	Dana, Frank	1,000	Minor	17 Jul 1893	1	198
2334	Dana, Mary B.	Good, W. C.; Overton, A. P.	Dana, E. Mabel	1,000	Minor	17 Jul 1893	1	198
2334	Dana, Mary B.	Good, W. C.; Overton, A. P.	Dana, Ruth	1,000	Minor	17 Jul 1893	1	199
2334	Dana, Mary B.	Good, W. C.; Overton, A. P.	Dana, Harold B.	1,000	Minor	17 Jul 1893	1	199

Case #	Principals	Sureties	Bound to	Amount ($)	Type	Date	Book	Page(s)
2334	Dana, Mary B.	Good, W. C.; Overton, A. P.	Dana, William S.	1,000	Minor	17 Jul 1893	1	200
2334	Dana, Mary B.	Good, W. C.; Overton, A. P.	Dana, John A.	1,000	Minor	17 Jul 1893	1	200
2334	Dana, Mary B.	Good, W. C.; Overton, A. P.	Dana, Charles B.	1,000	Minor	17 Jul 1893	1	201
2334	Dana, Mary B.	Good, W. C.; Overton, A. P.	Dana, Alfred H.	1,000	Minor	17 Jul 1893	1	201
2337	Ronsheimer, John A.	Hagedohm, Johanna; Hagedohm, Herman	Hagedohm, William	150	Minor	5 Aug 1893	1	196
2342	Sartori, Giuseppe	Piezzi, S.; Pozzi, M. C.	Sartori, Charles	250	Incompetent person	28 Aug 1893	1	197
							QUAL	259
2346	Lichau, Henry Philip, Sr.	Atwater, F. H.; McNear, George P.	Lichau, Elmer C.	20	Minor	23 Sep 1893	1	204
2346	Lichau, Henry Philip, Sr.	Atwater, F. H.; McNear, George P.	Lichau, Arthur L.	20	Minor	23 Sep 1893	1	205
2346	Lichau, Henry Philip, Sr.	Atwater, F. H.; McNear, George P.	Lichau, Albert E.	20	Minor	23 Sep 1893	1	205
2346	Lichau, Henry Philip, Sr.	Atwater, F. H.; McNear, George P.	Lichau, Edward P.	20	Minor	23 Sep 1893	1	206
2346	Lichau, Henry Philip, Sr.	Atwater, F. H.; McNear, George P.	Lichau, Archie C.	20	Minor	23 Sep 1893	1	206
2346	Lichau, Henry Philip, Sr.	Atwater, F. H.; McNear, George P.	Lichau, Henry Phillip, Jr.	20	Minor	23 Sep 1893	1	207
2346	Lichau, Henry Philip, Sr.	Atwater, F. H.; McNear, George P.	Lichau, Charles F.	20	Minor	23 Sep 1893	1	207
2354	Carvey, James	Carroll, P.; Hinshaw, E. C.	Carvey, Kate	3,000	Incompetent person	30 Oct 1893	1	208
2358	Vanderhoof, M. V.	Barnett, J. D.; Woodward, E. F.	Burg, Ferdinand	500	Incompetent person	6 Nov 1893	1	208
2360	Fisher, Mary L. V.	Fisher, B. O.; Brainard, L. E.	Fisher, Clare V.	1,500	Minor	20 Nov 1893	1	209
2377	Campbell, Joseph	Brainerd, H. P.; Fritsch, John	Fernald, Orlando Johnson	2,500	Minor	2 Feb 1895	1	232
2383	Cereghino, A.	Zimmerman, George H.; Maddalena, Charles	Ferrari, Angelica	500	[Minor]	2 Apr 1894	1	210
2383	Cereghino, A.	Zimmerman, George H.; Maddalena, Charles	Ferrari, Carlo	500	[Minor]	2 Apr 1894	1	210
2385	Cunningham, Samuel	Kee, James; Doran, W. M.	Delahanty, May	200	Minor	5 Mar 1894	1	209
2390	Hartsock, Florence A.	Hendricks, J. M.; Schnittger, C. H.	Hartsock, Bonnie	400	Minor	28 Mar 1894	1	212
2390	Hartsock, Florence A.	Hendricks, J. M.; Schnittger, C. H.	Hartsock, Freedom	400	Minor	28 Mar 1894	1	212
2395	Cameron, Jennie	Baer, Reuben E.; Cameron, Gordon	Cameron, Russell L.	100	Minor	[30] Mar 1894	1	211
2398	Conniff, Sadie F.	Meyer, F. A.; Haskell, William B.	Conniff, Bridget	400	Insane person	14 Apr 1894	QUAL	275
2400	Goodman, L. S.	Kee, James; Overton, J. P.	Goodman, S. F.	500	Minor	14 Jun 1894	1	215
2400	Goodman, L. S.	Kee, James; Overton, J. P.	Goodman, David	500	Minor	14 Jun 1894	1	216
2402	Grant, Anita F.	Rose, J. W.; Prince, J. B.	Grant, Frederick T.	700	Minor	1 May 1894	1	213

154

Case #	Principals	Sureties	Bound to	Amount ($)	Type	Date	Book	Page(s)
2408	Purvine, John C.	Purvine, T. B.; Purvine, William B.	Purvine, Mary Jane	4,000	Incompetent person	26 May 1894	1	213
2416	Noonan, George P.	McDonald, M. L.; Markham, Andrew	Noonan, Paul M.	1,000	Minor	5 Jun 1894	1	214
2421	Lindsay, Esther A.	Lindsay, Walter C.; Clark, Benjamin	Lindsay, Adin A.	2,145	Minor	25 Jun 1894	1	217
2421	Lindsay, Esther A.	Lindsay, Walter C.; Clark, Benjamin	Lindsay, Maggie F.	2,145	Minor	25 Jun 1894	1	216
2427	Cassin, J. M.	Grace, Frank P.; Keegan, J. W.	Norton, John Lewis	100	Minor	11 Jun 1894	1	214
2427	Cassin, J. M.	Grace, Frank P.; Keegan, J. W.	Norton, Elizabeth Jane	100	Minor	11 Jun 1894	1	215
2434	Coffey, Ellen A.	Coffey, H.; Coffey, J. H.	Lemay, Elva; Lemay, Edna	50	Minors	16 Jul 1894	1	217
2434	Coffey, Ellen A.	Coffey, H.; Coffey, J. H.	Lemay, Elva; Lemay, Edna	50	Minors	16 Jul 1894	1	218
2435	Poehlmann, Conrad	Poehlmann, Henry J.; Holm, Jacob F.	Seavy, Laura V.	900	Minor	13 Jul 1894	1	218
2435	Poehlmann, Conrad	Poehlmann, Henry J.; Holm, Jacob F.	Seavy, Robert T.	900	Minor	13 Jul 1894	1	219
2435	Dinwiddie, J. L.	Hill, William; Brainerd, H. P.	Seavy, Robert T.	900	Minor	26 Jun 1896	1	246
2435	Dinwiddie, J. L.	Hill, William; Brainerd, H. P.	Seavy, Laura V.	900	Minor	26 Jun 1896	1	246
2450	Bentley, Harriet A.	Casey, Julia L.; Cooley, John B.	Casey, Elbert Hiram	500	Minor	13 Sep 1894	1	219
2450	Bentley, Harriet A.	Casey, Julia L.; Cooley, John B.	Casey, David Earl	500	Minor	13 Sep 1894	1	220
2457	Jackson, Maye D.	Jackson, L. W.; Rickett, J. W.	Jackson, Ward Sutliff	100	Minor	27 Sep 1894	1	220
2457	Jackson, Maye D.	Jackson, L. W.; Rickett, J. W.	Jackson, Beatrice Anna	100	Minor	27 Sep 1894	1	221
2459	Hicklin, George T.	Rice, J. H.; Garnett, W. H.	Hicklin, Georgia	60	Minor	2 Oct 1894	1	221
2459	Hicklin, George T.	Rice, J. H.; Garnett, W. H.	Hicklin, Mabel E.	60	Minor	2 Oct 1894	1	222
2461	Barbarin, Jean Baptiste	Chauvet, Joshua; Modini, Lorenzo	Barbarin, Augustina	1,200	Minor	12 Oct 1894	1	222
2463*	Kruse, F. A.	Voss, Claus; Kruse, Louise J. (Mrs.)	State of California; The Superior Court of Sonoma County appointed F. A. Kruse the guardian of the person and the estate of August Kruse, a minor, on 22 Oct 1894 upon his executing this bond.	6,000	Minor	29 Oct 1894	1	223
2469	Joost, Jacob	Seegelken, J. W.; Hoskins, William	Moland, John	2,160	Insane person	19 Nov 1894	1	224
2470	Dinwiddie, J. L.	Haskell, William B.; Veale, W. R.	Polk, Ella Josephine	50	Minor	6 Dec 1894	1	227
2470	Dinwiddie, J. L.	Haskell, William B.; Veale, W. R.	Polk, Edward Hubbard	50	Minor	6 Dec 1894	1	227
2470	Dinwiddie, J. L.	Haskell, William B.; Veale, W. R.	Polk, Charles Ephraim	50	Minor	6 Dec 1894	1	228
2470	Dinwiddie, J. L.	Haskell, William B.; Veale, W. R.	Polk, William Clement	50	Minor	6 Dec 1894	1	228

155

Case #	Principals	Sureties	Bound to	Amount ($)	Type	Date	Book	Page(s)
2471	Kearney, Francis P.	Grothaus, F.; Harris, G. S.	State of California; The Superior Court of Sonoma County appointed Francis P. Kearney the guardian of the person and the estate of Alice Kearney, a minor, on 26 Nov 1894 upon his executing this bond.	200	Minor	27 Nov 1894	1	226
2471	Kearney, Francis P.	Grothaus, F.; Harris, G. S.	State of California; The Superior Court of Sonoma County appointed Francis P. Kearney the guardian of the person and the estate of Louis Phillip Kearney, a minor, on 26 Nov 1894 upon his executing this bond.	200	Minor	27 Nov 1894	1	226
2473	Moyer, John A.	Dudley, W. S.; Ingalls, J. C.	Beal, Kirk S.	50	Minor	16 Nov 1894	1	223
2480	Lauteren, Antoinette M.	Cnopius, Johan; Cnopius, J., Jr.	Lauteren, Gertrude C.	150	Minor	30 Nov 1894	1	224
2480	Lauteren, Antoinette M.	Cnopius, Johan; Cnopius, J., Jr.	Lauteren, Edgar F.	150	Minor	30 Nov 1894	1	225
2480	Lauteren, Antoinette M.	Cnopius, Johan; Cnopius, J., Jr.	Lauteren, Anton J.	150	Minor	30 Nov 1894	1	225
2484*	Wisecarver, Elizabeth	Smith, H. W.; Davis, B. J.	Gill, Charles	100	Minor	17 Dec 1894	1	230
2485	Huhn, Fritz	Schnittger, Friedericke (Mrs.); Leppo, D.	Schnittger, Claus H.	600	Insane and incompetent person	17 Dec 1894	1	229
2488	Gum, Clara	Bush, Eli; Clack, J. W.	Gum, Nellie Hazel	1,040	Minor	12 Jan 1895	D	440-442
2488	Gum, Schuyler Colfax	Weaver, C. W.; Passalacqua, A. D.	Gum, Nellie Hazel	1,040	Minor	12 Jan 1895	1	231
2498	Feehan, John P.	Scoggan, John M.; Roberts, Alonzo	Feehan, Edward M.; Feehan, Mary G.; Feehan, Ursula E.	600	Minors	11 Mar 1895	1	234
2504	Doyle, Frank P.	Shelton, A. C.; Doyle, M.	Loranger, Frank; Loranger, Willie; Loranger, Hattie	4,500	Minors	4 Mar 1895	1	232
2504	Loranger, Lillian E.	Grace, Frank P.; Hall, Gil P.	Loranger, Frank; Loranger, William; Loranger, Hattie	300	Minors	4 Mar 1895	1	233
2507	Atherton, Joseph N.	Jones, H. M.; Frain, Thomas	Wyman, William Henry	1,000	Incompetent person	7 Mar 1895	1	233
2507	Atherton, Joseph N.	Pullen, Granville; Frain, Thomas	Wyman, William Henry	1,000	Incompetent person	14 Mar 1896	1	240
2516	Ungewitter, H. W.	Hockin, William; Orr, W. J. T.	Sicotte, Fred	200	Minor	18 Mar 1895	1	234
2537	Austin, Rosa	Howard, George; Bloch, George; Barnes, E. H.; Norton, E. M.; Norton, L. A.	Austin, Emile W.	25,000	Minor	8 Jun 1895	D	453-455
2537	Austin, Rosa	Howard, George; Bloch, George; Barnes, E. H.; Norton, E. M.; Norton, L. A.	Austin, Charles A.	25,000	Minor	8 Jun 1895	D	455-457
2543	Geiger, Anna	Magnes, R.; Gieske, Henry C.	DeMetz, Edward	1,000	Minor	17 Jun 1895	1	235
2569	Litton, H. B.	Litton, A. P.; Porter, H. J.	Hill, Emily	1,200	Incompetent person	21 Oct 1895	1	235

Case #	Principals	Sureties	Bound to	Amount ($)	Type	Date	Book	Page(s)
2569	Yarbrough, R. Lee	Litton, A. P.; Porter, H. J.	Hill, Emily	1,200	Incompetent person	21 Oct 1895	1	236
2588	Mothorn, David H.	McClish, John; Warner, A. L.	Mothorn, Emily Dessie	1,000	Minor	2 Jan 1896	1	237
2588	Mothorn, David H.	McClish, John; Miller, George T.	Mothorn, Emily Dessie	1,000	Minor	13 Mar 1897	1	271
2588	Mothorn, Lydia	Donahue, T. P.; Rosenquest, Hans	State of California; The Superior Court of Sonoma County appointed Lydia Mothorn the guardian of the estate of Emily Dessie Mothorn, a minor, on 2 May 1898 upon her executing this bond.	1,000	Minor	9 May 1898	AD 2	32
2589	Overton, John P.	Overton, A. P.; Hoffer, C. A.	Shoemake, Charley D.	600	Minor	16 Dec 1895	1	236
2589	Overton, John P.	Overton, A. P.; Hoffer, C. A.	Shoemake, Ella C.	600	Minor	16 Dec 1895	1	237
2601*	Brandon, Elvus	Brandon, Kate; Allen, Mary	State of California; The Superior Court of Sonoma County appointed Elvus Brandon the guardian of the estate of James Emmet Brandon, a minor, on 27 Jan 1896 upon his executing this bond.	700	Minor	28 Jan 1896	1	238
2610*	Sutton, Hannah	Haskell, William B.; Veale, William R.	Edwards, Frank G.; Edwards, Bessie H.; Edwards, Leland S.; Edwards, Joseph L.; Edwards, Lulu A.; Edwards, Benjamin; Edwards, Mary	100	Minors	21 Feb 1896	1	239
2611*	Meriwether, H. D.	Weaver, C. W.; Miller, J. R.	Meriwether, Randolph M.	2,000	Minor	14 Apr 1896	1	244
2611*	Meriwether, H. D.	Merchant, T. S.; McDonough, John	Meriwether, Herbert F.	2,000	Minor	14 Apr 1896	1	244
2613	Brush, Frank A.	Brush, J. H.; Hood, John	Brown, Viola (formerly Bunnell, Viola)	1,350	Incompetent person	26 Feb 1896	1	239
2616	Dudley, Annie	Dudley, W. S.; Norton, Lew A.	Tombs, Ann P.	250	Incompetent person	19 Mar 1896	1	240
2619	Benton, L. J.	Hoar, B. F.; Blackburn, John S.	State of California; The Superior Court of Sonoma County appointed L. J. Benton the guardian of the person and the estate of Eliza Salter, an incompetent person, on 23 Mar 1896 upon his executing this bond.	1,500	Incompetent person	30 Mar 1896	1	241
2625	Pyne, Henry H.	Whitney, William B.; Weaver, C. W.	Pyne, Willie H.	400	Minor	25 Apr 1896	1	241
2626	Swisher, J. R.	Burr, Frank; Byington, Charles T.	Bartlett, Clara Theresa	150	Minor	25 Apr 1896	1	242
2626	Swisher, J. R.	Burr, Frank; Byington, Charles T.	Bartlett, Ella	150	Minor	25 Apr 1896	1	243
2626	Swisher, J. R.	Burr, Frank; Byington, Charles T.	Bartlett, George R.	150	Minor	25 Apr 1896	1	243
2677	Holman, E. Josephine	Maher, M.; Holman, J. H.	Vance, Robbin; Vance, Stewart	100	Minors	6 Apr 1896	1	276
2631	Walker, J. L	Markham, Andrew; Overton, John P.	Walker, John Cecil	500	Minor	29 Jun 1896	1	247
2631	Walker, J. L.	Markham, Andrew; Overton, John P.	Walker, Water Lawrence	500	Minor	29 Jun 1896	1	248

157

Case #	Principals	Sureties	Bound to	Amount ($)	Type	Date	Book	Page(s)
2631	Hassett, Sarah E.	Moore, Robert Drake; Clack, J. W.	Walker, Nellena	1,000	Minor	3 Jul 1896	1	250
2636	Farmer, George	Passalacqua, A. D.; Upson, William A.	Prows, D. W.	1,200	Incompetent person	27 May 1896	1	245
2638	Truett, M. K.	Shores, Leander; Bryan, William J.	Madden, Adelia	1,000	Insane person	27 May 1896	1	245
2638	Truett, A. D.	Locke, Albert; Mac, M. B.	State of California; The Superior Court of Sonoma County appointed A. D. Truett the guardian of the estate of Adelia Madden, an insane person, on 17 Apr 1899 upon his executing this bond.	125	Insane person	17 Apr 1899	AD 2	72
2642*	Brown, Henry W.	Nisson, J.; Harris, R. J.	Brown, Edward S.	500	Minor	27 Jun 1896	1	247
2651*	Thomas, W. E.	Tupper, G. A.; Healey, W. E.	Thomas, Oscar	700	[Minor]	4 Aug 1896	1	248
2651*	Thomas, W. E.	Tupper, G. A.; Healey, W. E.	Thomas, Sylvia	700	[Minor]	4 Aug 1896	1	249
2651*	Thomas, W. E.	Tupper, G. A.; Healey, W. E.	Thomas, Bertha	700	[Minor]	4 Aug 1896	1	249
2654	Wescoatt, O. K.	Wescoatt, Effie E.; Wescoatt, Nelson	Wescoatt, Glenn	1,240	Minor	17 Aug 1896	1	251
2655*	Parsons, Mary F.	Markham, Andrew; Overton, J. P.	Fahrion, Wallace G.	620	Minor	17 Aug 1896	1	250
2655*	Parsons, Mary F.	Markham, Andrew; Overton, J. P.	Fahrion, Harold C.	620	Minor	17 Aug 1896	1	251
2657*	Anderson, John	Stenzel, C.; Luttringer, J.	Board of Directors of Mendocino State Insane Asylum at Ukiah; The Superior Court of Sonoma County appointed John Anderson the guardian of the estate of John Ingmansen, an insane person, on 31 Aug 1896 upon his executing this bond.	1,000	Insane person	12 Sep 1896	QUAL	339
2665*	Filippini, Achille	Filippini, Leonard R.; Maggetti, P.	Bolla, Oliva	600	Minor	17 Oct 1896	1	252
2665*	Filippini, Achille	Filippini, Leonard R.; Maggetti, P.	Bolla, Ida	600	Minor	17 Oct 1896	1	252
2665*	Filippini, Achille	Filippini, Leonard R.; Maggetti, P.	Bolla, Olympio	600	Minor	17 Oct 1896	1	253
2665*	Filippini, Achille	Filippini, Leonard R.; Maggetti, P.	Bolla, Elvezio	600	Minor	17 Oct 1896	1	253
2666	Ingalls, Timothy A.	McDonnell, Henry; Warren, W. P.	Ingalls, Chester A.	2,000	Minor	3 Dec 1896	D	519-520
2675*	Lewis, Lena May	Mothorn, F. C.; Mothorn, P. D.; Mothorn, Sarah A.; Mothorn, Cashia S.	Lewis, Prudie Mabel	8,800	Minor	9 Nov 1896	D	504-506
2681	Sherman, Allie A.	Coffman, J. T.; Swisher, J. R.	Sherman, Ellen	40	Minor	31 Dec 1896	1	277
2681	Sherman, Allie A.	Coffman, J. T.; Swisher, J. R.	Sherman, Sarah	40	Minor	31 Dec 1896	1	278
2681	Sherman, Allie A.	Coffman, J. T.; Swisher, J. R.	Sherman, Dell	40	Minor	31 Dec 1896	1	278
2681	Sherman, Allie A.	Coffman, J. T.; Swisher, J. R.	Sherman, James G.	40	Minor	31 Dec 1896	1	279
2684	Walliser, Carl	Walliser, Lucie deB.; Duhring, Frederick T.	Walliser, Emily Constance	1,525	Minor	30 Nov 1896	1	269
2684	Walliser, Carl	Walliser, Lucie deB.; Duhring, Frederick T.	Walliser, Carl Alfred	1,525	Minor	30 Nov 1896	1	269

Case #	Principals	Sureties	Bound to	Amount ($)	Type	Date	Book	Page(s)
2689	Beaver, William J.	Mosely, A. P.; Carr, Charles F.	Beaver, Henry	4,000	Incompetent person	22 Dec 1896	1	268
2712	Hoffer, C. A.	Overton, J. P.; Markham, Andrew	Muller, Mary Barbet	200	Minor	8 Mar 1897	D	525-526
2712	Hoffer, C. A.	Overton, J. P.; Markham, Andrew	Muller, Francis Leon	1,200	Minor	8 Mar 1897	D	521-522
2712	Hoffer, C. A.	Overton, J. P.; Markham, Andrew	Muller, Amanda Louise	1,200	Minor	8 Mar 1897	D	523-524
2712	Foerstler, Mary	Doggett, William J.; Barham, H. W.	Muller, Mary B.	250	Minor	2 Sep 1905	2	113
2715	Cunningham, John F.	Terschuren, G. F.; Cunningham, Joseph H.	Hosking, Mary Jane Elizabeth	6,000	Insane person	30 Apr 1897	1	272
2721	Lowe, Celia K.	Jacobsen, C. A.; Roberts, Hugh	Herges, Mary Elizabeth	700	Minor	27 Mar 1897	1	271
2732	Knapp, Alice B.	Hamilton, G. W.; Doran, W. M.	Knapp, Hope Irene	400	Minor	29 Mar 1897	1	270
2732	Knapp, Alice B.	Hamilton, G. W.; Doran, W. M.	Knapp, Ida Lulu	400	Minor	29 Mar 1897	1	270
2732	Knapp, Alice B.	Hamilton, G. W.; Fisher, A. L.	Knapp, Ida Lulu	400	Minor	11 Nov 1897	1	276
2732	Knapp, Alice B.	Hamilton, G. W.; Fisher, A. L.	Knapp, Hope Irene	400	Minor	11 Nov 1897	1	277
2740	Henrichsen, Henry Richard	Breckwoldt, Joe; Fredericks, M. H.	Henrichsen, Nicolaus	50	Minor	12 May 1897	1	254
2740	Henrichsen, Henry Richard	Breckwoldt, Joe; Fredericks, M. H.	Henrichsen, Henry	50	Minor	12 May 1897	QUAL	360
							1	254
							QUAL	360
2741	Fairbanks, D. B.	Fairbanks, J. F.; Fairbanks, H. T.	Ellsworth, Percy L.	480	Minor	28 Apr 1897	1	272
2763	Norton, Eliza J.	Norton, Charles; Brewer, Harry	Richards, Ethel M.	50	[Minor]	12 Jul 1897	AD 2	4
2763	Norton, Eliza J.	Norton, Charles; Brewer, Harry	Richards, Harrison A.	50	[Minor]	12 Jul 1897	AD 2	4
2763	Norton, Eliza J.	Norton, Charles; Brewer, Harry	Richards, Curtis H.	50	[Minor]	12 Jul 1897	AD 2	5
2763	Norton, Eliza J.	Norton, Charles; Brewer, Harry	Richards, Jennie J.	50	[Minor]	12 Jul 1897	AD 2	5
2767	Martin, F. McG.	Stuart, A. McG.; Juilliard, L. W.	York, Louis	1,000	Incompetent person	20 Jul 1897	AD 2	7
2775	Cummings, Harry W.	Cummings, Frank; McDonough, John	Madeira, Harry W.	1,350	Minor	31 Aug 1897	1	255
2777	Neeley, William	Mothorn, Sarah Adaline; Mothorn, Cashia Sylvania (Mrs.); Nichols, Martha Augusta (Mrs.); Young, Lena May (Mrs.); Martin, Rebecca Ann; King, Mary E. (Mrs.)	Neeley, William Harten	1,000	[Minor]	14 Sep 1897	D	531-532
2777	Neeley, William	Mothorn, Sarah Adaline; Mothorn, Cashia Sylvania (Mrs.); Nichols, Martha Augusta (Mrs.); Young, Lena May (Mrs.); Martin, Rebecca Ann; King, Mary E. (Mrs.)	Neeley, Rachel Susan	1,000	Minor	14 Sep 1897	D	529-530
2777	Neeley, William						1	255

Case #	Principals	Sureties	Bound to	Amount ($)	Type	Date	Book	Page(s)
2777	Neeley, William	Mothorn, Sarah Adaline; Mothorn, Cashia Sylvania (Mrs.); Nichols, Martha Augusta (Mrs.); Young, Lena May (Mrs.); Martin, Rebecca Ann; King, Mary E. (Mrs.)	Neeley, Keith Jacob	1,000	Minor	14 Sep 1897	D	535–536
2777	Neeley, William						1	255
2777	Neeley, William	Mothorn, Sarah Adaline; Mothorn, Cashia Sylvania (Mrs.); Nichols, Martha Augusta (Mrs.); Young, Lena May (Mrs.); Martin, Rebecca Ann; King, Mary E. (Mrs.)	Neeley, Lena May	1,000	Minor	14 Sep 1897	D	533–534
2777	Neeley, William						1	255
2777	Neeley, William	Mothorn, Sarah Adaline; Mothorn, Cashia Sylvania (Mrs.); Nichols, Martha Augusta (Mrs.); Young, Lena May (Mrs.); Martin, Rebecca Ann; King, Mary E. (Mrs.)	Neeley, Edith Mabel	1,000	Minor	14 Sep 1897	D	527–528
2777	Neeley, William						1	255
2779	Hopkins, M. D.	Walls, David; Hall, A. S.	Hopkins, Willott	100	Minor	24 Dec 1897	1	265
2779	Hopkins, M. D.	Walls, David; Hall, A. S.	Hopkins, Lottie	100	Minor	24 Dec 1897	1	266
2779	Hopkins, M. D.	Walls, David; Hall, A. S.	Hopkins, Hiram	100	Minor	24 Dec 1897	1	266
2780	Kiser, Josephine	Lord, Edwin; McMackin, James	Kiser, Anton; Kiser, Joseph; Kiser, Theodore	1,500	Minors	25 Oct 1897	1	256
2788	Williams, John A.	Overton, A. P.; Markham, Andrew	Davis, Calvin P.	16,000	Incompetent person	1 Nov 1897	1	256
2788	Davis, Henry Clay	Fidelity and Deposit Company of Maryland	Davis, Calvin P.	15,000	Incompetent person	19 Jun 1899	1	295
2790	Keegan, Maggie A.	Hinshaw, E. C.; Keegan, Dennis	Keegan, James	800	Minor	13 Nov 1897	1	267
2790	Keegan, Maggie A.	Keegan, Mary E.; Keegan, Dennis	Keegan, Daisy I.	800	Minor	13 Nov 1897	1	267
2790	Keegan, Maggie A.	Keegan, Mary E.; Keegan, Dennis	Keegan, Lilly A.	800	Minor	13 Nov 1897	1	268
2792	Skaggs, Julia	Gryff, John A.; Stamer, Julius	Skaggs, Edward W.	1,800	Minor	30 Nov 1897	1	280
2792	Skaggs, Julia	Gryff, John A.; Stamer, Julius	Skaggs, Alex, Jr.	1,800	Minor	30 Nov 1897	1	280
2796	Baer, George B.	Mowbray, Mary J.; Wambold, Daniel M.	Larrison, Samuel	800	Incompetent person	2 Dec 1897	1	279
2797*	Hart, B. F.	Lewis, Jere; Bell, W. M.	Hart, Charles E.	400	[Minor]	26 Jan 1898	AD 2	21
2804	Hopper, J. W.	Hopper, Thomas; Finley, H.	Hickson, Clarence	500	Minor	6 Dec 1897	1	273
2804	Hopper, J. W.	Hopper, Thomas; Finley, H.	Hickson, Mabel	500	Minor	6 Dec 1897	1	273
2804	Hopper, J. W.	Hopper, Thomas; Finley, H.	Hickson, Willie	500	Minor	6 Dec 1897	1	274
2817	Behrens, Henry	Caltoft, John; Nisson, C.	Behrens, Dora	50	Minor	13 Jan 1898	1	264
2817	Behrens, Henry	Caltoft, John; Nisson, C.	Behrens, Carl	50	Minor	13 Jan 1898	1	264
2817	Behrens, Henry	Caltoft, John; Nisson, C.	Behrens, Albert	50	Minor	13 Jan 1898	1	265
2827	Bell, R. W.	Prindle, William; Dennett, Edward P.	Bell, Rosa E.	50	Minor	2 Feb 1898	1	281

Case #	Principals	Sureties	Bound to	Amount ($)	Type	Date	Book	Page(s)
2829	Warner, Augusta L.	Rosenberg/Rosenburg, W.; Bush, Eli	Warner, Frederick A.	700	Minor	5 Feb 1898	1	285
2829	Warner, Augusta L.	Rosenberg, W.; Bush, Eli	Warner, Oscar E.	700	Minor	5 Feb 1898	AD 2	23
2844	Griggs, W. B.	Forsyth, Robert A.; Forsyth, B.	Tuttle, Charles L.	500	Minor	24 Feb 1898	1	281
2849	Harris, A. L.	Burris, L. W.; Reynolds, W. D.	Langley, Eliza	600	Insane person	8 Mar 1898	1	282
2850	Violetti, Angolina	Bacigalupi, N.; Grace, J. T.	Violetti, Joseph	1,300	Incompetent person	14 Mar 1898	1	283
2855*	Pursell, John	Ricksecker, L. E.; Vanderhoof, M. V.	Ford, Lydia E.	450	Minor	28 Mar 1898	AD 2	28
2868	Yarbrough, R. L.	Hockin, William; Orr, W. J. T.	Yarbrough, Frederic C.	50	Minor	25 Apr 1898	1	283
2892	Decoe, T. C.	Craig, D. N.; Cannon, L. L.	Wilkinson, Bertha	250	Minor	2 Jul 1898	D	540-541
2897	Phillips, A. A.; Phillips, M. E.	Mead, James A.; Clack, J. W.	Phillips, George D.	5,000	Minor	20 Jul 1898	D	542-543
2897	Phillips, A. A.; Phillips, M. E.	Barnes, E. H.; Weaver, C. W.	Phillips, Maud R.	5,000	Minor	20 Jul 1898	D	544-545
2897	Bell, Amelia Ann; Somes, Mary Ellen	Somes, G. R.; Bell, G. S.	Phillips, George D.	5,000	Minor	28 Mar 1905	2	108
2901	Freeman, Mary E.	Fidelity and Deposit Company of Maryland	Barnes, Etta Ellen; Barnes, Dora Harlan	1,000	[Minors]	25 Jul 1898	1	257
2902	Runyon, Ella	Talmadge, Samuel; Hood, John	Runyon, Raleigh B.	7,000	Minor	21 Jul 1898	1	284
2902	Runyon, Ella	Talmadge, Samuel; Hood, John	Runyon, Charles D.	7,000	Minor	21 Jul 1898	1	284
2903	Beattie, Susan C.	Beattie, Anthony; Savage, C. W.	Meyer, Gladys F.	100	Minor	25 Jul 1898	AD 2	41
2903	Beattie, Susan C.	Beattie, Anthony; Savage, C. W.	Meyer, Linda Z.	100	Minor	25 Jul 1898	AD 2	41
2903	Goeppert, George	Dittmann, Adolph; Schultz, Otto	Meyer, Gladys F.	100	Minor	19 Oct 1900	2	18
2903	Goeppert, George	Dittmann, Adolph; Schultz, Otto	Meyer, Linda Z.	100	Minor	19 Oct 1900	2	19
2909	Wilson, Ellen P.	Ferrin, Cornelia L.; Parsons, John I.	Mitchell, Evelyn D.; Mitchell, Armor W.; Mitchell, Merle E.	300	Minors	16 Aug 1898	AD 2	43
2914	Hinkston, Annie	Blackburn, J. S.; Collins, F. M.	Timms, Ann	2,000	Incompetent person	17 Sep 1898	1	229
2921	Wilkinson, Mattie V.	Barnes, Henry; Decoe, T. C.	Wilkinson, Alfred	250	Minor	28 Sep 1898	1	260
2921	Wilkinson, Mattie V.	Barnes, Henry; Decoe, T. C.	Wilkinson, Henry Dean	250	Minor	28 Sep 1898	1	260
2923	Scott, Sarah A.	Bell, Henry; Adamson, Edward F.	Weber, Alma P.	150	Minor	16 Sep 1898	1	257
2923	Scott, Sarah A.	Bell, Henry; Adamson, Edward F.	Weber, Franklin B.	150	Minor	16 Sep 1898	1	258
2923	Scott, Sarah A.	Bell, Henry; Adamson, Edward F.	Weber, Richard B. F.	150	Minor	16 Sep 1898	1	258
2923	Scott, Sarah A.	Bell, Henry; Adamson, Edward F.	Weber, Mary E.	150	Minor	16 Sep 1898	1	259

Case #	Principals	Sureties	Bound to	Amount ($)	Type	Date	Book	Page(s)
2923	Scott, Sarah A.	Bell, Henry; Adamson, Edward F.	Weber, Clara A. B.	150	Minor	16 Sep 1898	1	259
2925	Clark, Minnie L.	Clark, Samuel B.; Cabel, E. H.	Clark, David S. F.	200	Minor	3 Oct 1898	1	261
2925	Clark, Minnie L.	Clark, Samuel B.; Cabel, E. H.	Clark, Lettie Ann	200	Minor	3 Oct 1898	1	261
2927	White, William	Potter, Joseph; Dawson, Rebecca	Sloan, John R.	600	Minor	20 Oct 1898	1	262
2927	White, William	Potter, Joseph; Dawson, Rebecca	Sloan, Maggie E.	600	Minor	20 Oct 1898	1	262
2927	White, William	Potter, Joseph; Dawson, Rebecca	Sloan, Elizabeth R.	600	Minor	20 Oct 1898	1	263
2931	Wines, W. F.	Doyle, Frank P.; Hutchinson, T. J.	State of California; The Superior Court of Sonoma County appointed W. F. Wines the guardian of the estate of Daisy Kidd, a minor, on 24 Oct 1898 upon his executing this bond.	700	Minor	24 Oct 1898	AD 2	51
2931*	Wines, W. F.	Doyle, F. P.; Hutchinson, T. J.	State of California; The Superior Court of Sonoma County appointed W. F. Wines the guardian of the estate of [Daisy Kidd], a minor, on 28 Nov 1898 upon his executing this bond.	500	Minor	30 Nov 1898	1	263
2931	Kidd, F. A. (Mrs.)	Knapp, W. D.; Scoggan, John	Kidd, Daisy	275	Minor	6 May 1901	2	27
2941	Barbarin, Louissa	Lounibos, John; Weyl, Henry; Pinelli, A.; Filippini, Charles; Fochetti, Julius; Granice, H. H.	Barbarin, Augustina	10,000	Minor	3 Jan 1899	D	548-550
2941	Barbarin, Louissa	Harris, Granville S.; Fochetti, Julius; Modini, Lorenzo; Granice, H. H.	State of California; The Superior Court of Sonoma County appointed Louissa Barbarin the guardian of the person and the estate of Augustina Barbarin, a minor, and letters of guardianship were issued to her on 16 Jan 1899.	4,000	Minor	31 Dec 1901	MISC	21-22
2953	Ortman, George E.	American Surety Company of New York	Ortman, Thomas	13,500	Incompetent person	11 Feb 1899	D	583-585
2954	Soldate, M. A.	Cereghino, A.; Soldati, Alex	Soldate, Albert	2,500	Incompetent person	14 Jan 1899	1	286
2954	Giacomini, M.	Wickersham, F. A.; Collins, F. M.	Soldate, Albert	1,500	Incompetent person	9 Mar 1900		
2954	Giacomini, M.	Brown, Robert S.; Collins, F. M.	Soldate, Albert	1,500	Incompetent person	24 Oct 1903	2	76
2954	Soldate, John	National Surety Company of New York	Soldate, Albert	7,690	Incompetent person	3 Jan 1905	2	104
2954	Soldate, John	McNear, George P.; Denman, Frank H.	Soldate, Albert	7,015	Incompetent person	3 Feb 1906	2	126
2957	Coffman, N. B.	Raabe, M.; Hazen, Frank	Coffman, Henry W.	200	Minor	1 Feb 1899	1	287
2957	Coffman, N. B.	Raabe, M.; Hazen, Frank	Coffman, Mary Gertrude	200	Minor	1 Feb 1899	1	287

162

Case #	Principals	Sureties	Bound to	Amount ($)	Type	Date	Book	Page(s)
2959	McGrew, James G.	Gale, M. C.; McGrew, Sophia	McGrew, James C.	2,000	Insane person	25 Jan 1899	1	286
2964	Ducker, Andrew	Markham, Andrew; Overton, J. P.	Ducker, Sarah	8,000	Incompetent person	26 Jan 1899	1	285
2971	DeBernardi, Giovanni	Pinelli, A.; Ciucci, S.	DeBernardi, Pietro	50	Minor	17 Feb 1899	1	288
2971	DeBernardi, Giovanni	Pinelli, A.; Ciucci, S.	Minoggio, Louis	50	Minor	17 Feb 1899	1	288
2971	DeBernardi, Giovanni	Pinelli, A.; Ciucci, S.	Minoggio, Ambrogio	50	Minor	17 Feb 1899	1	289
2982	Crist, Katie M.	Campion, Tom; Crist, A. B.	Brown, Walter T.	1,000	Minor	31 Mar 1899	1	290
2987	Yates, Amy	Eardley, W. J.; Bower, M. J.	Yates, Florence	1,200	Minor	10 Apr 1899	1	291
2989	Young, Amelia	Ferguson, H. O.; Young, George E.	Young, Clarence Henry	500	Minor	16 Mar 1899	1	289
2989	Young, Amelia	Gird, H. S.; Swisher, J. R.	Young, Clarence Henry	1,000	Minor	16 Jun 1899		
2989	Young, George E.	Ferguson, John N.; Swisher, James R.	Young, Clarence Henry	4,000	Minor	4 May 1901	2	25
2989	Hinshaw, William Pettis	Fidelity and Deposit Company of Maryland	Young, Clarence	7,500	Minor	18 Jul 1903	2	66
2997	Allen, Harriet A.	Talmadge, Samuel; Overton, John P.	Allen, Mary C.	3,500	Minor	3 Apr 1899	1	290
2999	Ingalls, J. C.	Haigh, Edwin; Rickman, Mary E.	State of California; The Superior Court of Sonoma County appointed J. C. Ingalls the guardian of the person and the estate of Chester A. Ingalls, a minor, on 3 Apr 1899 upon his executing this bond.	1,800	Minor	22 Apr 1899	1	291
3003	Kirby, Sarah A.	Brainerd, H. P.; Winans, J. L.	Kirby, E. C.	200	Incompetent person	13 May 1899	1	293
3003	Kerbey, Sarah A.	Brainerd, H. P.; Winans, J. L.	Kerbey, Ebenezer W.	300	Incompetent person	17 Jun 1899	AD 2	83
3007	Lauritzen, Clara	Caltoft, John; King, James	Lauritzen, Augusta	800	Minor	29 Apr 1899	1	292
3007	Lauritzen, Clara	Caltoft, John; King, James	Lauritzen, Harold	800	Minor	29 Apr 1899	1	292
3012*	Matthias, Frances L.	Green, W. S.; Davis, W. S.	Matthias, Edna Antoinette	100	Minor	3 May 1899	1	293
3012*	Matthias, Frances L.	Green, W. S.; Davis, W. S.	Matthias, Frederick Leon	100	Minor	3 May 1899	1	294
3014	Clement, L. G.	Kimball, C. L.; Doane, L. W.	State of California; The Superior Court of Sonoma County appointed L. G. Clement the guardian of the estate of Archa Barton, a minor, on 22 May 1899 upon his executing this bond.	100	Minor	8 Jun 1899	1	295
3018	Hirth, Fred	Hadrich, C. F. Hugo; Kopf, C. L.	Hirth, Albrecht	1,000	Minor	29 May 1899	1	294
3032	Beedle, Louis S.	Drago, Nelson, Sr.; Astl, Joseph	Howard, John James	250	Minor	3 Jul 1899	1	296
3044	Steiner, John R.	Frei, A.; Jud, Christian	Huni, Otto	2,000	Insane person	7 Aug 1899	1	296

Case #	Principals	Sureties	Bound to	Amount ($)	Type	Date	Book	Page(s)
3050	Wiley, Maud C.	Markham, Andrew; Overton, John P.	Wiley, Edith	3,500	Minor	19 Aug 1899	2	1
3050	Wiley, Maud C.	The United States Fidelity and Guaranty Company		1,000	Minor	28 Jan 1902	MISC	23-24
3052	Barney, Anna E.	Pacific Surety Company of California	Mann, Adelia A.	400	Incompetent person	15 Sep 1899	D	590-591
3060	Coon, Hannah A.	Coon, John; Graham, W. F.	Norris, Alferetta	75	[Minor]	9 Oct 1899	2	2
3060	Coon, Hannah A.	Coon, John; Graham, W. F.	Norris, Basil S.	75	[Minor]	9 Oct 1899	2	2
3061	Lewis, I. S.	Wambold, D. M.; Pinschower, S.	Smith, Charles B.	1,500	Insane person	21 Sep 1899	2	1
3064	Martin, Susan	Striening, M. J.; Wheeler, Jacob	Martin, Mary L.	2,200	Minor	10 Oct 1899	2	3
3066	Tomasini, Matteo	Berri, V.; Traversi, Joseph	Tomasini, Waldo A.	4,000	Minor	17 Oct 1899	2	3
3066	Tomasini, Matteo	Berri, V.; Traversi, Joseph	Tomasini, Lila	4,000	Minor	17 Oct 1899	2	4
3066	Tomasini, Americo F.	Tomasini, Sabina; Tomasini, Marino	Tomasini, Waldo A.	2,850	Minor	2 Jan 1905	2	103
3078	Shelford, P. L.	Orr, Thomas D.; McCowen, Hale	Shelford, Lorena L.	100	Minor	17 Nov 1899	2	4
3078	Shelford, P. L.	Orr, Thomas D.; McCowen, Hale	Shelford, Mabel W.	100	Minor	17 Nov 1899	2	5
3079	Jewett, L. L.	Starrett, Robert; King, Thomas	Coburn, Walter	50	Minor	24 Nov 1899	2	5
3079	Jewett, L. L.	Starrett, Robert; King, Thomas	Coburn, George	50	Minor	24 Nov 1899	2	6
3081	Hamilton, Georgia H.	Fidelity and Deposit Company of Maryland	Hamilton, Alethia Blanche	600	Minor	27 Nov 1899	2	6
3083	Lastufka, John C.	Korbel, F.; Korbel, A.	Urban, Joseph; Urban, Frank; Urban, Martha	350	Minors	8 Dec 1899	2	7
3094	Zimmerman, William W.	The American Surety Company	King, Mathew Wallace, Jr.	400	Minor	21 Dec 1899	D	601-602
3099	Fritch, J. Homer	Kruse, Emil T.; Kruse, Edward P. E.	State of California; The Superior Court of Sonoma County appointed J. Homer Fritch the guardian of the person and the estate of William H. Kruse, an incompetent person, on 15 Jan 1900 upon his executing this bond.	500	Incompetent person	15 Jan 1900	D	599-600
3104	Blackburn, John S.	Hopkins, S. J.; Fairbanks, D. B.	Schultz, Frederick O.	1,500	Incompetent person	12 Feb 1900	2	7
3104	Bell, W. S.	Fairbanks, D. B.; Hill, A. B.	Schulze, Frederick O.	4,000	Incompetent person	23 Jul 1903	2	67
3104	Turner, R. W.	Fairbanks, D. B.; Lawler, John	Schulze, Frederick O.	1,200	Incompetent person	4 Dec 1907	2	163
3127*	Prows, Elizabeth	Bond, J. W.; Daly, John	Prows, Sylvester W.	100	Minor	10 Apr 1900	2	8
3127*	Prows, Elizabeth	Bond, J. W.; Daly, John	Prows, James F.	100	Minor	10 Apr 1900	2	8
3131	McNear, George P.	Murphy, George B.; Denman, Frank H.	Holland, Annie F.	200	Minor	20 Apr 1900	2	9

Case #	Principals	Sureties	Bound to	Amount ($)	Type	Date	Book	Page(s)
3131	McNear, George P.	Murphy, George B.; Denman, Frank H.	Holland, Michael H.	200	Minor	20 Apr 1900	2	9
3131	McNear, George P.	Murphy, George B.; Denman, Frank H.	Holland, Maggie M.	200	Minor	20 Apr 1900	2	10
3147	Butcher, Squire	Skaggs, W. W.; Smith, C. J.	Butcher, Charles Walter	1,000	Minor	23 Apr 1900	2	10
3147*	Skaggs, E. W.	Cook, E. D.; Skaggs, Julia (Mrs.)	Butcher, Charles Walter	300	Minor	30 Jul 1901	2	31
3165	Howe, Robert	Dowd, F. E.; Grace, Frank P.	Harper, Maggie Ann	300	Minor	25 Jun 1900	2	11
3173	Corbin, Ruth G.	Corbin, George H.; Cline, J. W.	Corbin, George Benjamin	4,000	Minor	2 Jul 1900	2	11
3180	Riewerts, Mathilda (Mrs.)	Blackburn, John S.; Frohlking, William	Riewerts, Ocke M; Riewerts, Christian C.; Riewerts, Minnie H.; Riewerts, Martha C.	500	Minors	26 Jul 1900	2	12
3188	Connolly, Minnie A.	Connolly, Adele G.; Connolly, Frank B.	Connolly, Clarence; Connolly, Leo V.; Connolly, Paul A.	100	Minors	10 Aug 1900	2	13
3188	Connolly, Minnie A.	Healey, D. J.; Blackburn, J. S.	Connolly, Arthur H.	1,500	Minor	10 Aug 1900	2	13
3189	Brown, Daniel	Overton, John P.; Shea, Con	Rochford, Josephine Morrow	2,000	Minor	7 Aug 1900	2	12
3198	Reynolds, W. D.	Mather, J.; Taylor, John S.	Doyle, Winifred; Doyle, John Charles	50	Minors	4 Sep 1900	2	14
3202	Bruner, Edith T.	Stanley, J. F.; Bruner, C. M.	State of California; The Superior Court of Sonoma County appointed Edith T. Bruner the guardian of the estate of Arthur C. McWilliams, a minor, on 17 Sep 1900 upon her executing this bond.	600	Minor	17 Sep 1900	2	14
3202	Bruner, Edith T.	Bruner, C. M.; Parks, S. L.	McWilliams, Arthur	600	Minor	26 Sep 1901	AD 2	173
3214	Slusser, S. Effie	Young, James M.; Young, James N.	Lingenfelter, Charley H.	100	Minor	1 Oct 1900	2	15
3214	Slusser, S. Effie	Young, James M.; Young, James N.	Lingenfelter, Jesse A.	100	Minor	1 Oct 1900	2	15
3214	Slusser, S. Effie	Young, J. N.; Young, J. M.; Chamberlain, A. F.	Lingenfelter, Charley H.	900	Minor	4 Feb 1901	2	20
3214	Slusser, S. Effie	Young, J. N.; Young, J. M.; Chamberlain, A. F.	Lingenfelter, Jesse A.	900	Minor	4 Feb 1901	2	20
3226	Woodworth, Abby H.	Pacific Surety Company	Matthews, Sarah H.	44,000	Incompetent person	20 Oct 1900		
3228	Hemenway, Alice T.	Hemenway, D. D.; Blackburn, J. S.	Ward, Franklin Arthur	2,000	Minor	28 Nov 1900	2	17
3229	Grove, William H.	King, Fred; Jacobson, J. H.	Haubrick, Peter	1,500	Incompetent person	22 Nov 1900	2	16
3237	Burns, J. F.	Fairbanks, J. F.; Burns, Ellen	Kelly, Francis Peter	2,100	Minor	21 Nov 1900	2	16
3240	Watson, Alexander	Brush, William T.; Baer, R. E.	Leitch, Margaret G.	200	Incompetent person	13 Dec 1900	2	17
3245	Fisher, Rebecca A.	Arnold, A. W.; Doyle, F. P.; Kinslow, J. F.; Loomis, F. C.	Fisher, Augustus L.	10,000	Insane person	26 Dec 1900	2	18
3250	Tuttle, Grace C.	Merritt, E. C.; Griggs, W. B.	Tuttle, Charles L.	100	Minor	4 Feb 1901	2	22

Case #	Principals	Sureties	Bound to	Amount ($)	Type	Date	Book	Page(s)
3251	Joost, Martin	Joost, Jacob; Seegelken, J. W.	State of California; The Superior Court of Sonoma County appointed Martin Joost the guardian of the person and the estate of Carl Joost, a minor, on 4 Jan 1901 upon his executing this bond.	1,600	Minor	4 Jan 1901	2	19
3251	Joost, Martin	Joost, Jacob; Seegelken, J. W.	State of California; The Superior Court of Sonoma County appointed Martin Joost the guardian of the person and the estate of Nettie Joost, a minor, on 4 Jan 1901 upon his executing this bond.	1,600	Minor	4 Jan 1901	AD 2	144
3251	Joost, Martin	Joost, Jacob; Seegelken, J. W.	State of California; The Superior Court of Sonoma County appointed Martin Joost the guardian of the person and the estate of Anna Joost, a minor, on 4 Jan 1901 upon his executing this bond.	1,600	Minor	4 Jan 1901	AD 2	144
3251	Joost, Martin	Joost, Jacob; Seegelken, J. W.	State of California; The Superior Court of Sonoma County appointed Martin Joost the guardian of the person and the estate of Rudolph Joost, a minor, on 4 Jan 1901 upon his executing this bond.	1,600	Minor	4 Jan 1901	AD 2	145
3251	Joost, Martin	Joost, Jacob; Seegelken, J. W.	State of California; The Superior Court of Sonoma County appointed Martin Joost the guardian of the person and the estate of Harry Joost, a minor, on 4 Jan 1901 upon his executing this bond.	1,600	Minor	4 Jan 1901	AD 2	145
3253	Logan, Samuel	Houche, C. H., Sr.; McDuffie, J. H.	Logan, Phebe H.	100	Incompetent person	22 Jan 1901	2	21
3259	Clary, Agnes	Keegan, Thomas P.; Mulvehill, M. (Mrs.)	Clary, Paul D.; Clary, Thomas P.; Clary, Mary K.; Clary Abigail E.; Clary, Ida M.	1,000	Minors	4 Feb 1901	2	21
3266*	Merritt, Edson C.	The United States Fidelity and Guaranty Company	Merritt, Clifford E.	12,000	Minor	27 Feb 1901	D	617-619
3276	Collins, F. M.	Palmer, William J.; Hill, A. B.	McNamara, Elizabeth	2,000	Incompetent person	23 Mar 1901	2	23
3276	Green, Lyman	Palmer, William J.; Hill, A. B.	McNamara, Elizabeth	2,000	Incompetent person	20 May 1902	2	39
3277	Collins, F. M.	Palmer, William J.; Hill, A. B.	McNamara, Loretta	2,000	Minor	23 Mar 1901	2	23
3277	Green, Lyman	Palmer, William J.; Hill, A. B.	McNamara, Loretta	2,000	Minor	20 May 1902	2	40
3281	Rathcke, Fred C.	Joost, Jacob; Bayer, Herman	Rathcke, Walter Linton	333.33	Minor	11 Mar 1901	1	298
3281	Rathcke, Fred C.	Joost, Jacob; Bayer, Herman	Rathcke, Henrietta	333.33	Minor	11 Mar 1901	1	298
3281	Rathcke, Fred C.	Joost, Jacob; Bayer, Herman	Rathcke, Floyd Cecil	333.33	Minor	11 Mar 1901	1	299
3281	Rathcke, Fred C.	Joost, Jacob; Bayer, Herman	Rathcke, Lewis Carl	333.33	Minor	11 Mar 1901	1	299
3283	Necker, Mary E.	Overton, John P.; Edwards, James R.	Necker, Bryant Taylor Earl	4,000	Minor	27 Mar 1901	2	24

166

Case #	Principals	Sureties	Bound to	Amount ($)	Type	Date	Book	Page(s)
3288	McClish, John N.	Bice, Frank S.; Mothorn, F. C.	Martin, Nellie	300	Minor	7 May 1901	2	26
3289	Mothorn, F. C.	McClish, John N.; Mothorn, Sarah A.	Martin, Joseph L.	300	Minor	7 May 1901	2	26
3293	Grewell, Lottie B.	Marshall, William; Gilliam, Emily; Maddocks, Irene	State of California; The Superior Court of Sonoma County appointed Lottie B. Grewell the guardian of the estate of Howard Marshall Grewell, a minor, on 10 Apr 1901 upon her executing this bond.	4,400	Minor	10 Apr 1901	2	24
3295	Sommers, Mary	Sommers, Louisa; Heinrich, John A.	Sommers, Minnie	100	Minor	12 Apr 1901	2	25
3297	Thilo, Anna; Kerth, J. G.	Pacific Surety Company	Thilo, C. A.	25,000	Incompetent person	2 May 1901	D	627-629
3298	Armstrong, E. J.	Pacific Surety Company	Armstrong, Lewis A.; Armstrong, Albert; Armstrong, Frank L.; Armstrong, Earl N.; Armstrong, Ruby A.; Armstrong, Roy V.; Armstrong, Hazel	7,000	Minors	8 May 1901	MISC	1-3
3298	Todd, Calvin	Pacific Surety Company	Armstrong, Lewis A.; Armstrong, Albert; Armstrong, Frank L.; Armstrong, Earl N.; Armstrong, Ruby A.; Armstrong, Roy V.; Armstrong, Hazel	6,300	Minors	8 Jan 1902	MISC	17-18
3315*	Atkinson, Minnie J.	Atkinson, J.; Davidson, Adam	Higgins, Percy Clarence	500	Minor	11 Jun 1901	2	27
3326*	Harmes, Catherine D.	Bundesen, Martin; Bundesen, Charles	Harmes, Frederick K.	250	Minor	13 Jul 1901	2	29
3326*	Harmes, Catherine D.	Bundesen, Martin; Bundesen, Charles	Harmes, Leland	250	Minor	13 Jul 1901	2	29
3326*	Harmes, Catherine D.	Bundesen, Martin; Bundesen, Charles	Harmes, Charles M.	250	Minor	13 Jul 1901	2	30
3326*	Harmes, Catherine D.	Bundesen, Martin; Bundesen, Charles	Harmes, Clarence	250	Minor	13 Jul 1901	2	30
3333*	Yordi, A. H.	Appleton, W.; Hubbard, Henry	Yordi, Alice C.	500	Minor	1 Jun 1901	2	28
3333*	Yordi, A. H.	Appleton, W.; Hubbard, Henry	Yordi, Nellie E.	500	Minor	1 Jul 1901	2	28
3339*	Gallagher, John P.; Connolly, Louisa A.	Grass, Peter; Lynch, John	Gallagher, John	2,400	Incompetent person	17 Aug 1901	2	31
3340*	Hyde, M. D.	Hyde, F. A.	Hand, Ella N.	100	Incompetent person	20 Aug 1901	1	300
3342*	Jones, Patrick Carroll	Roach, Patrick; Jones, William J.	State of California; The Superior Court of Sonoma County appointed Patrick Carroll Jones the guardian of the person of Guadalupe Ignacio Carroll Bostwick, a minor, on 12 Aug 1901 upon his executing this bond.	200	Minor	12 Aug 1901	2	32
3351*	Meyer, Kate	Kahn, A.; Riedi, V.	State of California; The Superior Court of Sonoma County appointed Kate Meyer the guardian of the estate of Fridolin Durst, an incompetent person, on 26 Aug 1901 upon her executing this bond.	500	Incompetent person	29 Aug 1901	2	32

Case #	Principals	Sureties	Bound to	Amount ($)	Type	Date	Book	Page(s)
3364*	Stearns, Martha T.	Duhring, Frederick T.; Ryland, Caius T.	State of California; The Superior Court of Sonoma County appointed Martha T. Stearns the guardian of the person and the estate of John P. Stearns, an incompetent person, on 23 Sep 1901 upon her executing this bond.	10,000	Incompetent person	25 Sep 1901	AD 2	182
3365*	Church, Carrie	Church, Herman H.; Turner, O. W.	Church, Edith	2,500	Minor	23 Sep 1901	2	33
3372*	Jones, Mary J.	Blackburn, John S.; Cereghino, Antonio	Jones, Robert R.	1,600	Minor	19 Oct 1901	2	34
3373*	Cox, A. E. (Mrs.)	Hardin, James A.; Eardley, W. J.	State of California; The Superior Court of Sonoma County appointed Mrs. A. E. Cox the guardian of the person of Henrietta A. Cox, a minor, on 14 Oct 1901 upon her executing this bond.	200	Minor	14 Oct 1901	AD 2	180
3373*	Cox, A. E. (Mrs.)	Hardin, James A.; Eardley, W. J.	State of California; The Superior Court of Sonoma County appointed Mrs. A. E. Cox the guardian of the person of Jessie I. Cox, a minor, on 14 Oct 1901 upon her executing this bond.	200	Minor	14 Oct 1901	AD 2	181
3375*	Bagley, H. F.	Wescoatt, O.; Carr, W. M.	Berry, Joseph	2,800	[Insane person]	30 Oct 1901	2	34
3385*	Brown, Charlotte M.	Harrison, George; Kennedy, B. D.	Brown, Edwin M.	1,200	Incompetent person	[11 Nov 1901]	AD 2	180
3385*	Brown, Charlotte	Otis, Charles W.; Harrison, George	State of California; The Superior Court of Sonoma County appointed Charlotte Brown the guardian of the person and the estate of Edwin M. Brown, an incompetent person, heretofore.	800	Incompetent person	21 May 1902	AD 2	201
3396*	Einhorn, Mary A.	Einhorn, Joseph H.; Rohrer, Charles F.	Weber, Clara A. B.	300	Minor	23 Dec 1901	2	35
3396*	Einhorn, Mary A.	Einhorn, Joseph H.; Rohrer, Charles F.	Weber, Alma P.	300	Minor	23 Dec 1901	2	35
3397*	Heitmann, Frederick	Schillingman, J. William; Hill, A. B.	State of California; The Superior Court of Sonoma County appointed Frederick Heitmann the guardian of the estate of William Heitmann, a minor, on 17 Dec 1901 upon his executing this bond.	800	Minor	16 Dec 1901	AD 2	179
3408*	Mobley, John Elmer	The United States Fidelity and Guaranty Company	Burger, Elmer Ross	5,000	Minor	15 Jan 1902	AD 2	184
3408*	Mobley, John Elmer	The United States Fidelity and Guaranty Company	Burger, Lillian	700	Minor	20 Jan 1902	AD 2	185
3409*	Wines, W. F.	Grace, Frank P.; Gist, John L.	Blish, Bessie	700	Incompetent person	13 Jan 1902	AD 2	184
3425*	McKeadney, Katie	Fidelity and Deposit Company of Maryland	McKeadney, Hugh	1,500	Incompetent person	15 Mar 1902	MISC	43
3427*	Scott, Mary (widow)	Van Buren, E.; Thompson, J. J.	Scott, George W.; Scott, Lloyd A.; Scott, Pearl	150	Minors	1 Feb 1902	MISC	31-32

168

Case #	Principals	Sureties	Bound to	Amount ($)	Type	Date	Book	Page(s)
3440*	Shaw, Mary H.	Hodge, Robert; Hahman, Henrietta A.	Hood, William	100	Incompetent person	17 Mar 1902	AD 2	193
3440*	Shaw, Mary H.	The United States Fidelity and Guaranty Company	Hood, William	2,000	Incompetent person	31 Jul 1902	MISC	68-69
3441*	Burns, Edward	Duhring, Frederick T.; Harris, Granville S.	Burns, Joseph	100	Minor	24 Mar 1902	MISC	37-38
3442*	Howe, Robert	Ford, John W.; Dowd, Frank E.	Harper, Sarah	90	Minor	10 Mar 1902	AD 2	192
3448*	Kinne, Seeley D.	Stuart, A. McG.; Doggett, W. J.	Kinne, Ethel S.; Kinne, Mary F.; Kinne, G. Newton	3,000	Minors	2 Apr 1902	2	36
3452*	Darby, Jasper	Walters, Solomon; McClish, J. N.	Darby, Floyd Donald	100	Minor	19 Apr 1902	MISC	50-51
3452*	Darby, Jasper	Walters, Solomon; McClish, J. N.	Darby, Jasper Basil	100	Minor	19 Apr 1902	2	37
3456*	Hoyle, G. W.	Crigler, W. E.; Marshall, A. S.	Carico, J. W.	3,500	Incompetent person	22 Apr 1902	2	36
3458*	Holmes, Emma M.	The United States Fidelity and Guaranty Company	Holmes, Carrie Edna	1,000	Minor	28 Apr 1902	MISC	52-53
3460*	McCown, George M.	LeBaron, H. M.; LeBaron, H. W.	McCown, Ethel I.	450	Minor	12 May 1902	2	37
3460*	McCown, George M.	LeBaron, H. M.; LeBaron, H. W.	McCown, George R.	450	Minor	12 May 1902	2	38
3460*	McCown, George M.	LeBaron, H. M.; LeBaron, H. W.	McCown, Chester B.	450	Minor	12 May 1902	2	38
3460*	McCown, George M.	LeBaron, H. M.; LeBaron, H. W.	McCown, Elizabeth	450	Minor	12 May 1902	2	39
3469*	Goncalves, Antonio F.	Nunes, M. S.; Lawrence, Manuel B.	Baptista, Lena	100	[Minor]	1 Jul 1902	MISC	57-58
3469*	Goncalves, Antonio F.	Nunes, M. S.; Lawrence, Manuel B.	Baptista, Mary	100	Minor	1 Jul 1902	MISC	59-60
3469*	Goncalves, Antonio F.	Nunes, M. S.; Lawrence, Manuel B.	Baptista, Rosie	100	Minor	1 Jul 1902	2	40
3482½*	Woolsey, E. W.; Woolsey, W. E.	Brush, J. H.; Merritt, E. C.	Woolsey, Martha A.	12,000	Incompetent person	28 Jul 1902	2	41
3484*	Smith, Edmund	Pacific Surety Company	Smith, Roy E.; Smith, Marion	1,350	Minors	11 Aug 1902	MISC	62-63
3488*	Burdell, James B.	Burdell, Galen; Sweetser, John A.	Burdell, James B., Jr.	2,000	Minor	30 Aug 1902	2	45
3496*	Morrow, John	McCarthy, D.; Stephenson, John N.	Rochford, Josephine M.	1,400	Minor	30 Sep 1902	2	43
3502*	Meyer, F. A.	Poehlmann, Henry J.; Neuburger, Morris	Mayr, Johanna	350	Minor	5 Sep 1902	2	41
3502*	Meyer, F. A.	Poehlmann, Henry J.; Neuburger, Morris	Mayr, Theresa	350	Minor	5 Sep 1902	2	42
3502*	Meyer, F. A.	Poehlmann, Henry J.; Neuburger, Morris	Jorg, Crescenz	350	Minor	6 Sep 1902	2	42
3509*	Sales, W. L.	Sales, John; Roberts, Hugh	Santos, Gussie	800	Minor	1 Oct 1902	2	43
3514*	Kearney, William J.	Graham, A. D.; Dowdall, R. J.	Walsh, Thomas E.	550	Minor	16 Oct 1902	2	44
3514*	Kearney, William J.	Graham, A. D.; Dowdall, R. J.	Walsh, Mary E.	550	Minor	16 Oct 1902	2	44
3516*	Weaver, C. W.	Barnes, E. H.; Moore, R. D.	Cook, Israel	10,000	Incompetent person	15 Oct 1902	2	46

169

Case #	Principals	Sureties	Bound to	Amount ($)	Type	Date	Book	Page(s)
3519*	Daly, Mary	Schwab, F. J.; Daly, John	State of California; The Superior Court of Sonoma County appointed Mary Daly the guardian of the person and the estate of James Golden, a minor, on 3 Nov 1902 upon her executing this bond.	600	Minor	10 Nov 1902	MISC	72-73
3526*	Boyce, Annie V.	Shea, Con; Bertolani, P. A.	Boyce, Ruth A.	200	Minor	17 Nov 1902	2	46
3526*	Boyce, Annie V.	Shea, Con; Bertolani, P. A.	Boyce, John E.	200	Minor	17 Nov 1902	2	47
3528*	Weigand, Christina	Fairbanks, D. B.; Bell, W. S.	State of California; The Superior Court of Sonoma County appointed Christina Weigand the guardian of the estate of Charles Weigand, a minor, on 24 Nov 1902 upon her executing this bond.	300	Minor	29 Nov 1902	AD 2	217
3528*	Wohlers, Winifred	Fairbanks, D. B.; Bell, W. S.	State of California; The Superior Court of Sonoma County appointed Winifred Wohlers the guardian of the person and the estate of Charles Weigand, a minor, on 12 Oct 1903 upon her executing this bond.	375	Minor	16 Oct 1903	2	75
3528*	Weigand, Christina	Fairbanks, D. B.; Bell, W. S.	State of California; The Superior Court of Sonoma County appointed Christina Weigand the guardian of the estate of George Washington Weigand, a minor, on 24 Nov 1902 upon her executing this bond.	300	Minor	29 Nov 1902	AD 2	218
3528*	Wohlers, Winifred	Fairbanks, D. B.; Bell, W. S.	State of California; The Superior Court of Sonoma County appointed Winifred Wohlers the guardian of the person and the estate of George Washington Weigand, a minor, on 12 Oct 1903 upon her executing this bond.	375	Minor	16 Oct 1903	2	76
3530*	Hubbell, Phoebe	Hubbell, Orton B.; Hubbell, Orton	State of California; The Superior Court of Sonoma County appointed Phoebe Hubbell the guardian of the person and the estate of John Marshall, an incompetent person, on 1 Dec 1902 upon her executing this bond.	10,000	Incompetent person	8 Dec 1902	2	48
3531*	Abshire, Dorlesca	Cooper, F. M.; Seibel, C. J.	Abshire, James H.	1,500	Insane person	4 Dec 1902	2	47
3532*	Clary, Agnes E.	Keegan, Thomas P.; Towey, Peter	Clary, Dennis G.	4,000	Incompetent person	9 Dec 1902	AD 2	218
3532*	Clary, Agnes E.	The United States Fidelity and Guaranty Company	Clary, Dennis G.	2,800	Incompetent person	16 Jan 1907	2	145
3535*	Ayers, W. D.	Doss, John W.; Gray, James	Seavy, Robert T.	800	Minor	9 Dec 1902	2	49
3550*	Thomas, Henry R.	Thomas, Alfred R.; Maddocks, L. A.	Rambo, Mary E.	500	Incompetent person	28 Feb 1903	2	53
3562*	Nye, B. M.	Warboys, J. W.; Hadrich, Charles F. H.	Nye, Elsa H.; Nye, Frances A.; Nye, Helen; Nye, Pauline P.; Nye, B. Max	650	Minors	28 Jan 1903	2	49

170

Case #	Principals	Sureties	Bound to	Amount ($)	Type	Date	Book	Page(s)
3562*	Nye, B. M.	Boyd, R. S.; Light, E. H.	Nye, Frances A.; Nye, Helen; Nye, Pauline P.; Nye, B. Max; Nye, Elsa H.	300	Minors	17 Jun 1904	2	89
3564*	American Home Finding Association	Reading, George J.; Irwin, S. P.	Gordon, Rhoda	10	Minor	2 Feb 1903	2	50
3581*	Respini, Mariana	Respini, Americo; Respini, Leodina	Respini, Henry	500	Minor	7 Mar 1903	2	54
3584*	Dixon, Jennie (Mrs.)	Dixon, C. H.; Brush, J. H.	Dixon, Leona	582	[Minor]	[25 Feb 1903]	2	50
3584*	Dixon, Jennie (Mrs.)	Dixon, C. H.; Brush, J. H.	Carson, Mabel Alma	740	[Minor]	[25 Feb 1903]	2	51
3584*	Dixon, Jennie (Mrs.)	Dixon, C. H.; Brush, J. H.	Dixon, Walter Church	582	[Minor]	[25 Feb 1903]	2	51
3584*	Dixon, Jennie (Mrs.)	Dixon, C. H.; Brush, J. H.	Dixon, George Harold	582	[Minor]	[25 Feb 1903]	2	52
3584*	Dixon, Jennie (Mrs.)	Dixon, C. H.; Brush, J. H.	Dixon, Winona	582	[Minor]	[25 Feb 1903]	2	52
3584*	Dixon, Jennie (Mrs.)	Dixon, C. H.; Brush, J. H.	Carson, Jennie Blanche	740	[Minor]	[25 Feb 1903]	2	53
3588*	Phillips, Lulu J.	Swisher, J. R.; Ingalls, J. C.	Phillips, Fannie P.	1,520	Minor	20 Mar 1903	2	54
3596*	Faio, Frances B.	Paula, John A.; Mendonca, J. J.	Faio, Maria; Faio, Mariana; Faio, Amelia; Faio, Ida	30	Minors	8 Apr 1903	2	57
3597*	Focha, Anna M.	Vitoes, F. P.; Focha, C. J.; Silva, Mary A.	Maderas, Leopolinda	3,000	Incompetent person	8 Apr 1903	2	58
3599*	Taylor, T. F.	Markley, John; Taylor, Nannie S.	Taylor, John S.	106	Minor	2 Apr 1903	2	55
3599*	Taylor, T. F.	Markley, John; Taylor, Nannie S.	Taylor, Thomas Flint	106	[Minor]	2 Apr 1903	2	56
3599*	Taylor, T. F.	Markley, John; Taylor, Nannie S.	Taylor, Brown S.	106	[Minor]	2 Apr 1903	2	56
3605*	Lyttaker, F. E.	Smithers, George E.; Lowrey, Robert L.; Shudy, John	Lytakker, Rowland G.	800	Insane person	26 Jun 1903	2	65
3610*	Smith, C. P.	Shelton, A. C.; Doyle, F. P.	State of California; The Superior Court of Sonoma County appointed C. P. Smith the guardian of the persons and the estates of Russell Smith, Sidney Smith, Wayne Smith, and Salome Smith, minors, on 14 Apr 1903 upon his executing this bond.	3,200	Minors	14 Apr 1903	2	57
3613*	Modini, Lorenzo	Schocken, S.; Pinelli, A.	Maionchi, Leopold	3,500	Incompetent person	3 Jun 1903	2	64
3614*	Wells, Ellen S.	Bryant, Allen; Bryant, Arthur S.	McReynolds, Mary Frances	10	Minor	20 Apr 1903	2	58
3616*	Harrington, Huldah N.	Newell, J. H.; Roach, P.	Harrington, John O.; Harrington, William B.; Harrington, Alfred B.; Harrington, Florence E.; Harrington, Ralph I.; Harrington, Mabel E.	3,000	Minors	27 Apr 1903	2	69
3619*	Pitkin, David W.	Pitkin, Sarah; Dibble, N. P.	Pitkin, Alpha A.; Pitkin, Zelda	400	Minors	27 May 1903	2	64

Case #	Principals	Sureties	Bound to	Amount ($)	Type	Date	Book	Page(s)
3625*	Nobles, Harmon	Haupt, Charles W.; Hayden, S. R.	Marshall, Sadie	350	Minor	1 Jun 1903	2	61
3625*	Nobles, Harmon	Haupt, Charles W.; Hayden, S. R.	Marshall, Robert	350	Minor	1 Jun 1903	2	61
3625*	Nobles, Harmon	Haupt, Charles W.; Hayden, S. R.	Marshall, Charles	350	Minor	1 Jun 1903	2	62
3626*	Hayden, S. R.	Miller, George; Nobles, Harmon	Hayden, Richard	500	Minor	1 Jun 1903	2	62
3626*	Hayden, S. R.	Miller, George; Nobles, Harmon	Hayden, Rodney	500	Minor	1 Jun 1903	2	63
3626*	Hayden, S. R.	Miller, George; Nobles, Harmon	Hayden, Birdie	500	Minor	1 Jun 1903	2	63
3630*	Weston, George	Bentley, A.; Bridges, I. N.	State of California; The Superior Court of Sonoma County appointed George Weston the guardian of the persons and the estates of Robert W. Weston and Elizabeth P. Weston, minors, on 25 May 1903 upon his executing this bond.	300	Minors	25 May 1903	2	59
3633*	Petray, C. B.	Petray, R. A.; Barnes, E. H.	Strode, Charles	180	Minor	10 Jun 1903	2	59
3633*	Petray, C. B.	Petray, R. A.; Barnes, E. H.	Strode, James	180	Minor	10 Jun 1903	2	60
3633*	Petray, C. B.	Petray, R. A.; Barnes, E. H.	Strode, George	180	Minor	10 Jun 1903	2	60
3641*	Strong, John	Forsyth, Robert A.; Fowler, John H.	Davis, William Boyd	5,000	Minor	30 Mar 1903	2	55
3642*	Brown, Carrie P.	Lee, W. H.; Moore, P.	Wightman, Lulu	50	Minor	30 Jun 1903	2	66
3643*	Hendricks, George L.	Barnes, E. H.; Bush, Eli	State of California; The Superior Court of Sonoma County appointed George L. Hendricks the guardian of the person and the estate of Leon Hendricks, a minor, on 13 Jul 1903 upon his executing this bond.	2,800	Minor	15 Jul 1903	2	65
3651*	Butts, Florence	Pacific Surety Company	Butts, Nellie	2,000	Minor	22 Jul 1903	2	67
3655*	McReynolds, Emma	The United States Fidelity and Guaranty Company	McReynolds, Samuel Floyd; McReynolds, Frank Cleveland; McReynolds, Mary Frances; McReynolds, Marion Ralph; McReynolds, Vernon Clifford	400	Minors	6 Jan 1904	2	81
3655*	McReynolds, Emma	The United States Fidelity and Guaranty Company	McReynolds, Mary Frances	450	Minor	21 Dec 1905	2	123
3655*	McReynolds, Emma	The United States Fidelity and Guaranty Company	McReynolds, Marion Ralph	450	Minor	21 Dec 1905	2	123
3655*	McReynolds, Emma	The United States Fidelity and Guaranty Company	McReynolds, Frank Cleveland	450	Minor	21 Dec 1905	2	124
3655*	McReynolds, Emma	The United States Fidelity and Guaranty Company	McReynolds, Vernon Clifford	450	Minor	21 Dec 1905	2	124
3655*	McReynolds, Emma	The United States Fidelity and Guaranty Company	McReynolds, Samuel Floyd	450	Minor	21 Dec 1905	2	125
3660*	Ottolini, Maria	Codoni, G. A.; Grandi, S.	Ottolini, Eda	5,666.66	Minor	3 Sep 1903	2	70
3660*	Ottolini, Maria	Codoni, G. A.; Grandi, S.	Ottolini, Henry	5,666.66	Minor	3 Sep 1903	2	71

Case #	Principals	Sureties	Bound to	Amount ($)	Type	Date	Book	Page(s)
3660*	Ottolini, Maria	Codoni, G. A.; Genazzi, John	Ottolini, Lily	5,666.66	Minor	3 Sep 1903	2	71
3662*	Ross, Benjamin F.	Ross, Losson; Rayner, Aaron	Webber, L. Ross	4,000	Minor	24 Aug 1903	2	70
3666*	Oates, James W.	Paxton, B. W.; Reynolds, W. D.	Hamill, John	3,000	Minor	25 Aug 1903	2	68
3666*	Oates, James W.	Paxton, B. W.; Reynolds, W. D.	Gill, Charles	3,000	Minor	25 Aug 1903	2	69
3668*	Fredricks, J. W.	Stridde, Charles; Fredricks, Francisca	Barnes, Arthur	800	Minor	13 Oct 1903	2	75
3671*	Mordecai, Eva T.	Houx, W. D.; Denman, Frank H.	Mordecai, William	2,000	Minor	14 Sep 1903	2	72
3673*	Rambo, Ardon	Behmer, Daniel; Rambo, William	Rambo, Ruby	780	Minor	12 Oct 1903	2	74
3673*	Rambo, Arden M.	Behmer, Daniel; Rainsbury, Caroline	Rambo, Ruby	1,000	Minor	1 Oct 1906	2	141
3675*	Brown, Sarah E.	Whitney, W. B.; Bush, Eli	Brown, Harry O.	300	Minor	24 Sep 1903	2	73
3678*	Sherwood, Ruby A.	The United States Fidelity and Guaranty Company	Sherwood, Glen Milton	2,000	[Minor]	21 Sep 1903	2	72
3678*	Sherwood, Ruby A	The United States Fidelity and Guaranty Company	Sherwood, Effie	2,000	Minor	21 Sep 1903	2	73
3679*	Steiger, Edward	Lounibos, John; Weber, Henry	Steiger, George; Steiger, Fritz; Steiger, Emma; Steiger, William; Steiger, Herman	20	Minors	31 Oct 1903	2	78
3682*	Fredricks, J. W.	Stridde, Charles; Fredricks, Francisca	Barnes, Ivan Aaron	100	Minor	13 Oct 1903	2	77
3684*	Carmichael, Emily	Freeman, C. J.; Canevascini, S. J.	Carmichael, Leona	400	Minor	12 Oct 1903	2	74
3686*	Guidotti, G.	Fidelity and Deposit Company of Maryland	Guidotti, Celestine	1,100	Incompetent person	17 Oct 1903	AD 2	260
3686*	Quartaroli, L.	Bacigalupi, N.; Grace, Frank P.	Guidotti, C.	1,200	Incompetent and insane person	31 Oct 1904	2	99
3694*	Buck, Carl	King, George F.; Koenig, Frank	Cleaveland, Robert Fuller; Cleaveland, Harry James	200	Minors	6 Nov 1903	2	77
3694*	Tarwater, Edward Lewis	Rayner, A.; Sharp, Albert	Cleaveland, Harry James	1,800	Minor	[8 May 1907]	2	152
3694*	Tarwater, Edward Lewis	Rayner, A.; Sharp, Albert	Cleaveland, Robert Fuller	1,800	Minor	[8 May 1907]	2	153
3708*	Sherman, A.	Sherman, C. J.; Sherman, Franklin	Messersmith, Mabel C.; Messersmith, Gertrude M.	100	Minors	21 Dec 1903	2	79
3710*	Tomasi, Fedela	Tomasi, Americo L.; Tomasi, Alfonso M.	Tomasi, Linda O.	1,600	Minor	4 Jan 1904	2	80
3714*	Meriwether, Elizabeth B.	McDonough, John; Silberstein, J.	Meriwether, Herbert Francis; Meriwether, Randolph	6,400	Minors	22 Dec 1903	2	79
3717*	Warren, Mary L.	Newberry, C. R.; Kahn, A.	Warren, John R	3,000	Incompetent person	4 Jan 1904	2	80
3733*	Coburn, James	Burke, J. H.; Stump, J. A.	Coburn, Joseph; Coburn, Mabel	600	[Minors]	1 Feb 1904	2	81

173

Case #	Principals	Sureties	Bound to	Amount ($)	Type	Date	Book	Page(s)
3742*	Minetti, Jeanne Montalon	Minetti; G. Perelli; Saare, Louis	State of California; The Superior Court of Sonoma County appointed Jeanne Montalon Minetti the guardian of the persons of Flavien Mars Berton and Germain Mais Just Berton, [minors], on 15 Feb 1904 upon her executing this bond.	50	[Minors]	15 Feb 1904	2	82
3756*	Wright, Sampson B.	Taylor, John S.; Burris, L. W.	Wright, Girault S.; Wright, Winfield R.; Wright, Olive B.	1,600	Minors	3 Mar 1904	2	83
3757*	Cassin, J. M.	Dowd, Frank E.; Paddock, D. J.	Kelley, Willie; Kelley, Gertie; Kelley, Eddie; Kelley, Maud	10	Minors	24 Feb 1904	2	82
3767*	Amesbury, Mary	Weaver, C. W.; Snook, E. B.	Amesbury, Herbert	2,500	Minor	22 Mar 1904	2	83
3767*	Amesbury, Mary	Weaver, C. W.; Snook, E. B.	Amesbury, Carl	2,500	Minor	22 Mar 1904	2	84
3776*	Madeira, F. A.	Cook, F. W.; Wills, J. P.	Shinn, Paul; Shinn, Shirley	20	Minors	2 Apr 1904	2	84
3779*	Witbro, Kate B.	Hendricks, J. M.; Wagele, Charles	Witbro, Ernest H.; Witbro, Henry	1,000	Minors	20 Apr 1904	2	85
3784*	Rodehaver, George W.	Houx, W. D.; Brainerd, H. P.	Polk, Ella Josephine	240	Minor	25 Apr 1904	2	86
3786*	Williams, Sarah J.	Winkler, Arthur S.; Winkler, Oliver M.	Winkler, Walter S.	150	Minor	25 Apr 1904	2	85
3786*	Williams, Sarah J.	Winkler, Arthur S.; Winkler, Oliver M.	Winkler, Florence E.	150	Minor	25 Apr 1904	2	86
3790*	Woods, George E.	Belden, C. C.; Hehir, T. L.	Woods, Lillie B.; Woods, James A.	212	Minors	9 May 1904	2	87
3796*	Schaupp, Katherine	Kurtz, Fredericka; Kurtz, Lina	State of California; The Superior Court of Sonoma County appointed Katherine Schaupp the guardian of the person and the estate of Tille Flier, a minor, on 9 May 1904 upon her executing this bond.	500	Minor	10 May 1904	2	88
3801*	Wright, Sampson B.	Overton, J. P.; Taylor, John S.	Wright, Girault S.; Wright, Winfield R.; Wright, Olive B.; Wright, Esther	1,600	Minors	18 May 1904	2	87
3805*	Veale, W. R.	Brainerd, H. P.; Houx, W. D.	Rowlson, Eliza A.	1,720	Incompetent person	31 May 1904	2	88
3813*	Vanderleith, Elise	Lobenstein, Sol; Welling, Charles	Vanderleith, Violet	25	Minor	13 Jun 1904	2	90
3815*	Ungewitter, Mary	Ungewitter, H. W.; Overton, J. P.	Griffin, Catherine	2,550	Incompetent person	18 Jun 1904	2	89
3818*	Simpson, Willie B.	Keegan, Thomas P.; Trembley, A.	Simpson, William B.; Simpson, Philip A.; Simpson, Alice M.	3,000	Minors	20 Jun 1904	2	90
3821*	Johnson, David Q.	Johnson, Margaret J.; Kopf, C. L.	Ballou, Eunice	400	Incompetent person	27 Jun 1904	2	91
3822*	Wailes, J. A.	Forsyth, H. M.; Davis, H. S.	Wailes, Jessie L.; Wailes, Lulu M.; Wailes, Eugene A.; Wailes, Elbert S.	2,100	Minors	7 Jul 1904	2	91
3823*	McReynolds, Dennis H.	Walker, John L.; Peterson, John L.	McReynolds, Roy M.	100	Minor	5 Jul 1904	2	92
3827*	Darr, Flora E.	Hart, V. E.; Scott, Eli	Young, Hazel L.	240	Minor	4 Feb 1905	2	105

174

Case #	Principals	Sureties	Bound to	Amount ($)	Type	Date	Book	Page(s)
3834*	Clark, Sarah J.	Clark, James W.; Jamison, Sarah J.	Jamison, Rachel	1,000	Incompetent person	16 Aug 1904	2	94
3835*	Smith, Bertha E.	Remmel, George E.; Taylor, T. F.	Smith, Everett R.; Smith, Verna M.; Smith, Clifford F.; Smith, Violet E.	150	Minors	[8] Aug 1904	2	93
3835*	Smith, W. T.	Remmel, George E.; Cook, E. D.	Smith, Everett R.; Smith, Verna M.; Smith, Clifford F.; Smith, Violet E.	200	Minors	19 Dec 1904	2	102
3836*	Clark, James W.	Clark, Sarah J.; Jamison, Sarah Jane	Jamison, James M.	1,000	[Minor]	16 Aug 1904	2	94
3838*	Pool, Frank J.	Michelson, George; Emery, F. A.	Robinson, Ethel L.; Robinson, Roy L.	200	Minors	8 Aug 1904	2	93
3839*	Walker, Mary E.	Walker, L. F.; Abbey, Alfred	Torrance, Sophia P.	500	[Minor]	16 Aug 1904	2	95
3840*	Hall, Annie W.	Hall, H. L.; Hall, J. W.	Richardson, Mildred	3,200	Minor	31 Aug 1904	2	95
3846*	Pfalzgraf, Lydia	Ferguson, W. W.; Weaver, C. W.	Pfalzgraf, Eva; Pfalzgraf, Justina L; Pfalzgraf, Oscar H.; Pfalzgraf, Ruth; Pfalzgraf, Elsie; Pfalzgraf, Theodore	2,360	Minors	[12 Sep 1904]	2	96
3852*	Simi, Isabella	Warfield, George H.; Barnes, E. H.; Simi, Louis	Simi, Alvira	10,000	Minor	22 Sep 1904	2	96
3857*	Frain, Alice	Shaw, Isaac E.; Smith, W. J.	Frain, Maria	1,100	Insane person	3 Oct 1904	2	97
3857*	Lewis, Isaac S.	National Surety Company of New York	Frain, Marie	500	Insane person	2 Mar 1907	2	147
3858*	Haven, Celina	Straub, Anna C.; Brackett, J. H.; Brackett, Johanna	Haven, Elsie	2,000	Minor	3 Oct 1904	2	100
3861*	Wiswell, Nelson	McNear, George P.; Meyer, F. A.	Craig, Sophia T.	48,200	Incompetent person	17 Nov 1904	2	100
3868*	Abbey, Alfred	The Title Guaranty and Trust Company of Scranton, Pennsylvania	Abbey, Alfred B.	2,810	Minor	13 Oct 1904	2	97
3872*	Stump, Minnie S.	Orr, W. J. T.; Haub, Conrad	Stump, Vera V. G.	2,800	Minor	24 Oct 1904	2	98
3872*	Stump, Minnie S.	Orr, W. J. T.; Haub, Conrad	Stump, John Conrad	440	[Minor]	24 Oct 1904	2	99
3873*	Culbertson, Maria	Cooper, F. M.; Finley, Harrison	Olson, Frederick Morris	2,600	Minor	24 Oct 1904	2	98
3876*	Cootes, Mary L.	Unwiller, William; Unwiller, Lavinia	Cootes, William F.	360	Incompetent person	14 Nov 1904	2	101
3877*	Bottini, Julia	Fopiano, John; Passalacqua, A. D.	Bottini, Louis	500	Minor	30 Nov 1904	2	101
3881*	Schumacher, Jessie M.	Potter, Joseph H.; Duhring, Frederick T.	Alleman, Arzola Lee	1,100	Minor	8 Dec 1904	2	102
3886*	Maclay, Thomas	Hopkins, S. J.; Collins, F. M.	Gibbs, Sophronia	2,080	Incompetent person	28 Dec 1904	2	103
3899*	Meyer, F. A.	McNear, George P.; Denman, Frank H.	Wyatt, Raymond	4,900	Minor	27 Jan 1905	2	104

Case #	Principals	Sureties	Bound to	Amount ($)	Type	Date	Book	Page(s)
3899*	Meyer, F. A.	McNear, George P.; Denman, Frank H.	Wyatt, Melvin J.	500	Minor	27 Jan 1905	2	105
3907*	Mothorn, F. C.	McClish, John N.; Mothorn, Sarah A.	Martin, Josiah Lewis	525	Minor	14 Feb 1905	2	106
3917*	McElwain, A. E.	Truitt, J. W.; Coy, W. B.	State of California; The Superior Court of Sonoma County appointed A. E. McElwain the guardian of the persons and the estates of George McElwain, Agnes McElwain, Augustus McElwain, and Carrie B. McElwain, minors, on 6 Mar 1905 upon his executing this bond.	1,400	Minors	6 Mar 1905	2	107
3919*	Revermann, Charles	Towey, Peter; Wright, S. B.	Marsezell, Frank; Marsezell, George; Marsezell, Thomas; Marsezell, Samuel; Marsezell, Mary	208	Minors	7 Mar 1905	2	106
3919*	Towey, Peter	Gilman, P. E.; Millar, J. W.	Marsezell, Frank; Marsezell, Thomas; Marsezell, Samuel; Marsezell, George; Marsezell, Mary	780	Minors	18 Sep 1905	2	115
3935*	Dixon, William H.	The United States Fidelity and Guaranty Company	Dixon, Charles H.	1,300	Minor	10 Apr 1905	2	107
3942*	Thomas, Elsie	Roberts, Frank; Green, W. S.	Thomas, Lorraine	100	Minor	18 Sep 1905	2	116
3942*	Thomas, Elsie	Roberts, Frank; Green, W. S.	Thomas, Mabel	100	Minor	18 Sep 1905	2	116
3945*	O'Connor, Mary T.	Healey, D. J.; O'Hara, John	O'Connor, Amy J.	700	Minor	20 Jul 1905	2	110
3945*	O'Connor, Mary T.	Healey, D. J.; O'Hara, John	O'Connor, Robert J.	700	Minor	20 Jul 1905	2	111
3945*	O'Connor, Mary T.	Healey, D. J.; O'Hara, John	O'Connor, Edward W.	700	Minor	20 Jul 1905	2	111
3945*	O'Connor, Mary T.	Healey, D. J.; O'Hara, John	O'Connor, Eleanor C.	700	Minor	20 Jul 1905	2	112
3957*	Gibbens, Margaret M.	The United States Fidelity and Guaranty Company	Gibbens, Rose Elliott	1,000	Minor	3 Jun 1905	2	108
3957*	Gibbens, Margaret M.	The United States Fidelity and Guaranty Company	Gibbens, Rose Elliot	8,560	Minor	12 Feb 1906	2	129
3962*	Lawson, Mattie I.	Barnes, E. H.; Swisher, James R.	Young, Herbert E.	10,000	Minor	[10 Jul 1905]	2	109
3965*	Zimmermann, F. W.	Clough, M. E.; McNear, George P.	Zimmermann, William	400	Minor	8 Jul 1905	2	109
3965*	Zimmermann, F. W.	Clough, M. E.; McNear, George P.	Zimmermann, Frederick	400	Minor	8 Jul 1905	2	110
3984*	Fritsch, W. S.	Kahn, M.; Husler, E. A.	Fritsch, Mabel Isabel; Fritsch, Walter Mecham	100	[Minors]	23 Aug 1905	2	112
3989*	Grant, C. N.	The United States Fidelity and Guaranty Company	Ward, Harry B.	630	[Minor]	7 Sep 1905	2	113
3989*	Grant, C. N.	The United States Fidelity and Guaranty Company	Ward, Phil Demill	630	Minor	7 Sep 1905	2	114
3992*	George, Daniel W.	Brush, Fred W.; Shaw, C. B.	George, Lilla E.	100	Incompetent person	19 Sep 1905	2	115
3999*	Watt, John	Hall, Robert; Campbell, George O.	Watt, Mary E. (aka Watt, May)	165	Minor	16 Sep 1905	2	114

176

Case #	Principals	Sureties	Bound to	Amount ($)	Type	Date	Book	Page(s)
4001*	Lowrey, Mary J.	Meneray, P. A.; Anderson, J. A.	Davidson, Smith E.	1,200	Incompetent person	16 Oct 1905	2	117
4007*	Phair, Sara	Healey, D. J.; Healey, Maggie	Phair, Lucinda	250	[Minor]	21 Oct 1905	2	117
4007*	Phair, Sara	Healey, D. J.; Healey, Maggie	Phair, Carter Niles	750	[Minor]	21 Oct 1905	2	118
4015*	Avilla, Anton	Cardoza, Anton; Silver, Joseph	Avilla, Anton, Jr.	200	Minor	27 Nov 1905	2	118
4015*	Avilla, Anton	Cardoza, Anton; Silver, Joseph	Avilla, Frank	200	Minor	27 Nov 1905	2	119
4025*	Santos, Antonio	Sousa, M. C.; Silva, Charles J.	Santos, Alfred	200	Minor	29 Nov 1905	2	119
4025*	Santos, Antonio	Sousa, M. C.; Silva, Charles J.	Santos, Jackson	200	Minor	29 Nov 1905	2	120
4025*	Santos, Antonio	Sousa, M. C.; Silva, Charles J.	Santos, Ellen	200	Minor	29 Nov 1905	2	120
4025*	Santos, Antonio	Sousa, M. C.; Silva, Charles J.	Santos, William	200	Minor	29 Nov 1905	2	121
4025*	Santos, Antonio	Sousa, M. C.; Silva, Charles J.	Santos, Antonio	200	Minor	29 Nov 1905	2	121
4025*	Santos, Antonio	Sousa, M. C.; Silva, Charles J.	Santos, Sam	200	Minor	29 Nov 1905	2	122
4025*	Santos, Antonio	Sousa, M. C.; Silva, Charles J.	Santos, Philomena	200	Minor	29 Nov 1905	2	122
4032*	Winder, Elizabeth	Baer, George; Markell, C. J. (Mrs.)	Winder, Edward C.	1,000	Insane person	5 Jan 1906	2	125
4041*	Dahlmann, Henry	McNear, George P.; Murphy, George B.	Dahlmann, Wadsworth H.; Dahlmann, Alba F.; Dahlmann, Wilma G.; Dahlmann, Eugene C.; Dahlmann, Eunice F.; Dahlmann, Gladys M.; Dahlmann, Merriam K.	25	Minors	22 Jan 1906	2	126
4047*	Drake, Emma	Cobb, O. O.; Carr, William	Drake, Harry D.	210	Minor	10 Feb 1906	2	127
4047*	Drake, Emma	Cobb, O. O.; Carr, William	Drake, Ben F.	210	Minor	10 Feb 1906	2	128
4047*	Drake, Emma	Cobb, O. O.; Carr, William	Drake, Louis G.	210	Minor	10 Feb 1906	2	128
4051*	Genazzi, Mary N.	Pedrotti, Luis; Piezzi, Victor	State of California; The Superior Court of Sonoma County appointed Mary N. Genazzi the guardian of the person and the estate of John Genazzi, an incompetent person, on 12 Feb 1906 upon her executing this bond.	16,100	Incompetent person	12 Feb 1906	2	127
4062*	Davis, Walter S.	Arnold, A. W.; Rohrer, C. F.	Davis, Alys Marie	350	Minor	5 Mar 1906	2	129
4072*	Patchett, Mary O.	Skiffington, John R.; Petersen, Claus	Patchett, Walter C.	25	Minor	6 Apr 1906	2	130
4072*	Patchett, Mary O.	Skiffington, John R.; Petersen, Claus	Patchett, John M.	25	Minor	6 Apr 1906	2	131
4072*	Patchett, Mary O.	Skiffington, John R.; Petersen, Claus	Patchett, Roy C.	25	Minor	6 Apr 1906	2	131
4072*	Patchett, Mary O.	Skiffington, John R.; Petersen, Claus	Patchett, Ulysses A.	25	Minor	6 Apr 1906	2	132
4072*	Patchett, Mary O.	Skiffington, John R.; Petersen, Claus	Patchett, Dosha I.	25	Minor	6 Apr 1906	2	132

177

Case #	Principals	Sureties	Bound to	Amount ($)	Type	Date	Book	Page(s)
4075*	Woolsey, Nellie C.	McFarlane, George; Weeks, Horace	Woolsey, C. F.	200	Incompetent person	4 Jun 1906	2	134
4080*	Riley, Elizabeth	Lincoln, G. F.; Lane, C. W.	Riley, B. H.; Riley, E. H.	1,300	Minors	11 Jun 1906	2	134
4085*	Luff, Eva C.	Hale, O. A.; Owen, George E.	Luff, Hale	15,000	Minor	15 May 1906	2	133
4085*	Luff, Eva C.	Hale, O. A.; Owen, George E.	Luff, Genevieve	15,000	Minor	15 May 1906	2	133
4108*	Shaw, Minerva M.	McCray, W. L.; Shaw, C. B.	Shaw, Gertrude M.	7,200	[Minor]	6 Aug 1906	2	141
4128*	Juilliard, L. W.	Bacigalupi, N.; Haven, C. E.	Samuels, Thomas M.	300	Minor	26 Feb 1907	2	146
4138*	Green, Stella M.	Green, I. L.; Bowers, H. A.	Green, Emily	100	Minor	27 Jul 1906	2	135
4138*	Green, P. H.	French, Milton; Boyd, James	Green, Emily	100	Minor	28 Jul 1906	2	135
4139*	Fiori, Henry E.	Fiori, Orazio; Fiori, Attilio	Maddalena, Charles	1,500	Minor	6 Aug 1906	2	136
4139*	Fiori, Henry E.	Fiori, Orazio; Fiori, Attilio	Maddalena, Albert	1,500	Minor	6 Aug 1906	2	136
4140*	Newcom, Gesina	Cook, E. D.; Silberstein, J.	Newcom, Edgar; Newcom, Gertrude	500	Minors	23 Aug 1906	2	137
4142*	Andrews, Walter J.	The Aetna Indemnity Company of Hartford, Connecticut	Maggetti, Robert H.	200	Minor	29 Aug 1906	2	140
4143*	Baccala, Joseph K.	The Aetna Indemnity Company of Hartford, Connecticut	Baccala, Peter, Jr.	400	Minor	29 Aug 1906	2	139
4143*	Baccala, Joseph K.	The Aetna Indemnity Company of Hartford, Connecticut	Baccala, Henry	300	Minor	29 Aug 1906	2	139
4143*	Baccala, Joseph K.	The Aetna Indemnity Company of Hartford, Connecticut	Baccala, Della	300	Minor	29 Aug 1906	2	140
4149*	Hansen, Peter; Hansen, Emma	National Surety Company of New York	Bremer, Elmira	300	Minor	20 Aug 1906	2	138
4149*	Hansen, Peter; Hansen, Emma	National Surety Company of New York	Bremer, Jeanette	300	Minor	20 Aug 1906	2	138
4150*	Steiner, John, Sr.	National Surety Company of New York	Steiner, John, Jr.	2,000	Minor	17 Aug 1906	2	137
4164*	Dayton, Carrie F.	Stengel, Christian; Dayton, W. A.	Dayton, John J.	1,200	[Insane person]	[8] Oct 1906	2	142
4173*	Stebbins, Lambert W.	Kidd, William H.; Nowell, John W.	State of California; The Superior Court of Sonoma County appointed Lambert W. Stebbins the guardian of the person and the estate of Mrs. Emma Stebbins, an incompetent person, on 15 Oct 1906 upon his executing this bond.	1,000	Incompetent person	15 Oct 1906	2	142
4179*	Larsen, Anne C.	Bassett, W. D.; Larsen, R.	Larsen, Myrtle Lee	5,500	Minor	14 Nov 1906	2	143
4196*	Pozzi, Rafael	Bonetti, Joseph; Piezzi, Victor	Pozzi, Phillip (aka Pozzi, Fillipo)	5,000	Incompetent person	28 Dec 1906	2	144

Case #	Principals	Sureties	Bound to	Amount ($)	Type	Date	Book	Page(s)
4203*	King, N.	Lawrence, H. E.; Meyer, F. A.	Reynolds, Margaret M.	1,920	Incompetent person	22 Dec 1906	2	143
4222*	Martinelli, Attilio C.	Griess, George; Griess, George J.	Ludy, Freda A.; Ludy, Selma E.; Ludy, Catherine E.; Ludy, G. H.	50	Minors	23 Feb 1907	2	145
4223*	Rodehaver, George W.	Hill, A. B.; Atkinson, P. H.	Miller, C. S.	15,000	Incompetent person	11 Feb 1907	2	144
4232*	Leppo, O. F.	Leppo, D.; Leppo, D. H.	Craig, James	3,000	Incompetent person	26 Feb 1907	2	146
4239*	Crowell, A.	Rose, Fred; Gibson, J. A.	Crowell, Roy Victor	50	Minor	27 Feb 1907	2	147
4242*	Kinsell, Dudley	The United States Fidelity and Guaranty Company	Clark, Edgar B.	8,000	Incompetent person	7 Mar 1907	2	149
4243*	Frideger, Daniel S.	National Surety Company of New York	Frideger, Mary	500	Incompetent and insane person	9 Mar 1907	2	149
4246*	Whitehill, W. W.	American Bonding Company of Baltimore, Maryland	Pepper, Gertrude (aka Pepper, May)	5,000	Minor	19 Apr 1907	2	151
4246*	Whitehill, W. W.	American Bonding Company of Baltimore, Maryland	Pepper, Clarence	5,000	Minor	19 Apr 1907	2	151
4246*	Whitehill, W. W.	American Bonding Company of Baltimore, Maryland	Pepper, John	5,000	Minor	19 Apr 1907	2	152
4247*	Burns, Sadie R.	Burns, Annie J.; O'Sullivan, Daniel	Burns, Elizabeth Frances	700	Minor	9 Mar 1907	2	148
4247*	Burns, Sadie R.	Burns, Annie J.; O'Sullivan, Daniel	Burns, Mary Gertrude	700	Minor	9 Mar 1907	2	148
4248*	Davis, J. M.; Allingham, Adda	American Bonding Company of Baltimore, Maryland	Davis, Mary E.	3,200	Incompetent person	8 Apr 1907	2	150
4253*	Coltrin, Laura L.	Hunt, W. J.; Coltrin, H. C.	Hunt, Hazel Berna	3,800	Minor	[5 Apr 1907]	2	150
4273*	Vaughan, Marvin T.	Hatcher, George J.; Eardley, W. J.	Wade, John D.; Wade, Elizabeth	300	Minors	22 May 1907	2	154
4275*	Shores, Ida F.	The Title Guaranty and Surety Company	Shores, Leander	4,500	Incompetent person	17 May 1907	2	153
4284*	Parent, Hattie M.	McNear, George P.; Pepper, Phebe	Parent, Arthur M. [Parent, Arthur W.]	1,000	Minor	13 Jun 1907	2	155
4287*	Thompson, Rudolph	Maclay, Thomas; Hopkins, S. J.	Tomasini, Waldo A.	7,400	Incompetent person	13 Aug 1907	2	156
4291*	Corria, A. F.	Bush, G. H.; Isola, A.	Robbins, George A.	300	Minor	10 Jun 1907	2	157
4292*	Case, Sarah J.	Case, W. E.; Rea, M. A.	Page, Charles E.	50	Minor	5 Jun 1907	2	154
4318*	Poggetto, Charles Dal	National Surety Company of New York	Sciutti, Antonio	3,600	Incompetent person	21 Aug 1907	2	157

Case #	Principals	Sureties	Bound to	Amount ($)	Type	Date	Book	Page(s)
4321*	Tuttle, E. F.	American Bonding Company of Baltimore, Maryland	Tuttle, Gladys Dexter	1,660	Minor	[12] Aug 1907	2	156
4324*	Barry, William R.	Skiffington, John; Woodley, George	Barry, Julia	29,700	Incompetent person	17 Aug 1907	2	155
4338*	Santos, Antonio	Cabral, John; Silver, Joseph	Paivo, Mariano	1,200	Insane person	16 Sep 1907	2	158
4340*	Blackburn, Frank L.	Edgeworth, W. J.; Collins, F. M.	Rugg, J. T.	1,000	Incompetent person	10 Sep 1907	2	158
4344*	Hauto, Anna F.	National Surety Company of New York	Hauto, Dora	200	Minor	23 Sep 1907	2	159
4344*	Hauto, Anna F.	National Surety Company of New York	Hauto, Elsa	200	Minor	23 Sep 1907	2	159
4344*	Hauto, Anna F.	National Surety Company of New York	Hauto, Edward	200	Minor	23 Sep 1907	2	160
4344*	Hauto, Anna F.	National Surety Company of New York	Hauto, Ernest	200	Minor	23 Sep 1907	2	160
4344*	Hauto, Anna F.	National Surety Company of New York	Hauto, Anna	200	Minor	23 Sep 1907	2	161
4344*	Hauto, Anna F.	National Surety Company of New York	Hauto, Olga	200	Minor	23 Sep 1907	2	161
4344*	Hauto, Anna F.	National Surety Company of New York	Hauto, Marie	200	Minor	23 Sep 1907	2	162
4355*	Drees, Matilda A.	Pometta, D.; Pometta, Deborah	Drees, Grace E.	1,000	Minor	14 Oct 1907	2	162
4355*	Drees, Matilda A.	Pometta, D.; Pometta, Deborah	Drees, Sybil V.	1,000	Minor	14 Oct 1907	2	163
4366*	Voss, Anna K.	Kruse, H. A.; Gibbens, A. S.	State of California; The Superior Court of Sonoma County appointed Anna K. Voss the guardian of the estate of Arthur Edwin Voss, a minor, on [?] Dec 1907 upon her executing this bond.	1,000	Minor	23 Dec 1907	2	165
4373*	Gill, George W.	Weber, H.; Nauert, Frederick A.	Gill, Warren S.	100	Minor	[16] Dec 1907	2	164
4373*	Gill, George W.	Weber, H.; Nauert, Frederick A.	Gill, Leon	100	Minor	[16 Dec] 1907	2	164

180

www.ingramcontent.com/pod-product-compliance
Lightning Source LLC
Chambersburg PA
CBHW080422270326
41929CB00018B/3128